After Critique

OXFORD STUDIES IN AMERICAN LITERARY HISTORY

Gordon Hutner, Series Editor

After Critique

TWENTY-FIRST-CENTURY FICTION
IN A NEOLIBERAL AGE

Mitchum Huehls

OXFORD
UNIVERSITY PRESS

OXFORD
UNIVERSITY PRESS

Oxford University Press is a department of the University of
Oxford. It furthers the University's objective of excellence in research,
scholarship, and education by publishing worldwide.
Oxford is a registered trademark of Oxford University Press
in the UK and in certain other countries.

Published in the United States of America by
Oxford University Press
198 Madison Avenue, New York, NY 10016, United States of America

Library of Congress Cataloging-in-Publication Data
Names: Huehls, Mitchum, 1976–
Title: After critique : twenty-first-century fiction in a neoliberal age / Mitchum Huehls.
Description: New York : Oxford University Press, [2016] | Series: Oxford studies in American
literary history ; 13 | Includes bibliographical references and index.
Identifiers: LCCN 2015025561 | ISBN 978-0-19-045622-1 (cloth) | ISBN 978-0-19-045623-8 (updf)
Subjects: LCSH: American fiction—21st century—History and criticism. |
Politics and literature—United States—History—21st century. |
Literature and society—United States—History—21st century. |
Neoliberalism—United States.
Classification: LCC PS374.P62 H84 2016 | DDC 813/.609355—dc23
LC record available at http://lccn.loc.gov/2015025561

1 3 5 7 9 8 6 4 2
Printed in the United States of America
on acid-free paper

For Gibson and Oscar,
all head and heart

{ CONTENTS }

Just moments before walking out into lower Manhattan to join the zombie hordes that have overwhelmed his final bulwark, Mark Spitz, the protagonist in Colson Whitehead's *Zone One*, realizes the futility of humanity's attempt to triumph over the zombies: "Why they'd tried to fix this island in the first place, he did not see now. Best to let the broken glass be broken glass, let it splinter into smaller pieces and dust and scatter" (257). Accepting that things simply are what they are, that current conditions can't be changed, improved, or imagined otherwise—surely this suggests a depressingly resigned capitulation to the status quo. And yet, there's something faintly encouraging, even resolute, in what might very well be Spitz's final thought as a human: "Fuck it. . . . You have to learn how to swim sometime" (259). Behind Spitz's plucky resolve to dive headfirst into "the sea of the dead" lies a sense that the zombie apocalypse, even as it annihilates our old sense of hope, change, and progress, might also elaborate new conditions of possibility. Thus, even in his dire state, Mark Spitz speculates about the new modes of being the zombie plague might institute: "Let the cracks between things widen until they are no longer cracks but the new places for things. That was where they were now. The world wasn't ending: it had ended and now they were in the new place. They could not recognize it because they had never seen it before" (257–258). Far from capitulation, Spitz's decision to go swimming with the zombies actually signals his concerted willingness to begin mapping this new dispensation.

After Critique contends that we increasingly live life in this "new place." The prime agent of this transformation, our very own zombie plague: neoliberalism, understood here as *the* socio-cultural dominant of our contemporary moment. No longer just a set of free-market economic policies with an attendant ideology (although it is still that too), over the past few decades neoliberalism's entrepreneurial, profit-maximizing, cost-benefit rationalization of contemporary life has massively expanded into domains of human existence previously untouched by such economizing. As neoliberalism's for-profit spirit increasingly infects education, art, the environment, health and fitness, romance, politics, security, public space, recreation, war, and childhood, it becomes not just an entrenched mode of thought but an entirely new mode of being. As in *Zone One*, we can think of that new mode of being as zombification, but only if we also appreciate that the new ways of being in this new place might also afford unique possibilities, new places for new things, that we can't always recognize because we've never seen them before. In that spirit, *After Critique* identifies apparent forms of capitulation to the neoliberal status quo ("best to let broken glass be broken glass") that might actually run counter to the neoliberal status quo ("new places for things"); it locates the possibility, and not just the complicity, in letting things be what they are. Instead of critiquing and resisting, instead of imagining alternatives external to neoliberal totality, *After Critique* joins Mark Spitz in saying, "Fuck it," let's see what happens when we swim with the zombies.

Lest I appear intellectually crass and politically reckless, I'd emphasize that *After Critique* is not alone in voicing these sentiments. As the ensuing chapters will describe, many prominent twenty-first-century fiction writers model a similar approach to politics in our neoliberal age. In addition to Colson Whitehead's work, *After Critique* discusses novels by Uzodinma Iweala, Helena Viramontes, Karen Tei Yamashita, Percival Everett, Mat Johnson, Kim Stanley Robinson, Tom McCarthy, and David Foster Wallace, but I would also describe work from Jennifer Egan, Salvador Plascencia, Ben Lerner, Paul Beatty, Teju Cole, Joshua Ferris, Jenny Offill, and Laird Hunt, among others, in a similar way. In fact, this project began with the rather simple observation that many contemporary authors, despite their overt engagement with various political concerns ranging from the economic to the environmental, seem curiously reluctant to critique the injustice and inequality that they clearly recognize as endemic to twenty-first-century life. Why, I wondered, were so many fiction writers so consistently declining the opportunity to critique the status quo, challenge systemic exploitation, and envision better futures? It seems too easy to read this trend as merely symptomatic of neoliberalism's capacious grasp. Surely contemporary fiction's pervasive aversion to critique signals more than its complicit resignation to existing power formations. These authors seem too careful, and too intelligent, to produce texts that might be so easily reduced to manifestations of their current material conditions. I began to wonder instead what we might see if we read these texts more generously. Rather than identifying the signs and symptoms of neoliberalism tainting these works, what new places might we discover if we tried to inhabit the world the way these texts and their characters do? What if these authors writing after critique are trying to recognize something they've never seen before? What if they're actually identifying, or even making, new places for things?

My hunch, then, is that many contemporary authors who at first glance might appear to be abandoning politics are actually entirely rethinking what politics looks like in our neoliberal age. They recognize that neoliberalism has a firm grasp on contemporary political formations, that most every way a given political question might be represented, framed, described, or debated ultimately reinforces the neoliberal status quo. And this leads them to conclude that representation itself—the use of language and other sign systems to make meaningful, referential claims about the world—might be too compromised for politics. And so, they've begun allowing "the cracks between things [to] widen"; they've begun searching for some "new places for things." In particular, *After Critique* highlights contemporary literature's treatment of four distinct political topics that neoliberalism seems to have thoroughly captured: human rights, the relation between public and private space, racial (in)justice, and the risks posed to and from the environment. I could have chosen others, but these four matters of concern offer a felicitous range of scope and scale (from the individual to the collective, the local to the global) while also intersecting with some of US fiction's most dominant contemporary themes: human rights, the city, race, and ecology. These political issues and themes are of course not unique to the United States, but my focus on US fiction (with the exception of Tom McCarthy, whose reconceptualization of the environment isn't nation-specific) recognizes that the privileged position of individual privacy and liberty in US culture inflects these political themes in distinctly American ways. In fact, as I'll eventually demonstrate, the pronounced emphasis on the autonomous, entrepreneurial individual that pulses through US history and culture resonates with neoliberalism in a way that only exacerbates our current inability to represent, think through, and resolve the impasses and paradoxes that define political discourse around these four issues.

To be sure, some contemporary authors continue to hold fast to the representational language of critique, believing that their descriptions and claims are somehow immune to neoliberal appropriation. More interesting to me, however, are those authors who replace representational forms of meaning-making, which use referential language to depict, reflect, or say something about the world, with more ontological forms of meaning-making, which derive value from the configuration and interrelation of beings, human or otherwise. (If representations are meaningful because of the way language refers to the world, then ontology is meaningful because of the way beings exist in relation to each other and to larger assemblages of beings, which obviously requires a new understanding of what it means to mean.) Ontological forms of value production allow these authors to evade neoliberalism's totalizing capture of contemporary political discourse; in turn, they can engage neoliberalism on its own ontological grounds, as a unique configuration of being rather than as a set of ideological beliefs. Rather than pointing to and revealing what's wrong with neoliberalism (that would be the critical approach that relies on representation to show us the world in a specific way), these authors inhabit the world neoliberalism has produced in an effort to reconfigure the positions, relations, and connections that it establishes among the beings and objects of the world (that would be the ontological approach that still produces value, but only as a function of being and relation, not through representation). There is no single way this occurs, and no text abandons standard representational modes altogether. But in general we will see an array of contemporary works that favor presence over absence, being over meaning, and connection over reference. *After Critique* not only avers that this ontological turn in contemporary US fiction is crucial to thinking about literature after postmodernism, but it also holds that this literature's commitment to ontological value production marks a positive, post-critique response to the representational challenges neoliberalism poses for thinking about politics today.

The chapters are organized to move us from a low to moderate engagement with ontological presence to a much more fully blown investment in literature's ontological production of value. The human rights chapter initiates that trajectory by looking at two child-soldier narratives, Ishmael Beah's *A Long Way Gone* and Uzodinma Iweala's *Beasts of No Nation*. As the simultaneous victim and perpetrator of human rights abuse, the child soldier embodies the representational challenges facing human rights discourse: does the child soldier deserve full human rights by virtue of his humanity alone, or does the fact that he's also a murderer suggest that those rights can only be conferred artificially through the state? Beah, whose memoir stands as a counter-example in the chapter, ignores the duplicities of child soldiering to insist on his status as a deserving subject of human rights. In Iweala's novel, however, the protagonist willingly embodies the ambivalence of his position as both murderer and victim. Because this leaves him unable to predicate his humanity on natural human rights, he instead produces the value of his humanity by linking his present circumstances to meaningful presences from his immediate past. This produces a self defined by a continuity of ontological presence, not by the representation of experience, belief, and value. The result is a notion of the human that stands beyond the core representational paradox of human rights.

The next chapter examines two novels about Los Angeles—Karen Yamashita's *Tropic of Orange* and Helena Viramontes's *Their Dogs Came with Them*—in the context of the vexed relationship between public and private space under neoliberalism. Refusing to critique privatization with the rhetoric of public space, both authors develop new ways to generate meaning and value in and out of the neoliberal city by imagining urban development as a complex mixture of public and private values. With Yamashita's turn to networked maps that shift in time and Viramontes's fixation on an assortment of unassuming objects that suture together the space of the city, this chapter identifies alternative modes of value production that supersede the ideological divide between public and private that drives neoliberalism's treatment of urban space.

Identifying an impasse in neoliberalism's circular treatment of race—specifically, its simultaneous commitment to diversity and colorblindness—the following chapter investigates new forms of racial thinking that refuse to ask what race means, represents, or indexes. I locate one such approach in the novels of Colson Whitehead and Percival Everett, each of whom develops an object-based understanding of race. That is, each imagines race as a thing that variously does or does not connect to and interact with other things in the world. This allows race to be substantial and significant (or not), but only as an object in the world, not as a sign or symbol requiring interpretation. Not only does this approach challenge neoliberalism's tendentiously oscillating deployment of diversity and colorblindness as ideal yet mutually exclusive forms of racial thinking, but it also results in a body of literature that helps us see what might count as African American literature today. In particular, this chapter situates Whitehead's and Everett's work in the context of Kenneth Warren's provocative claims about the end of African American literature, suggesting that Whitehead and Everett chart a new ontological path for twenty-first-century black writers in the United States.

After Critique's concluding chapter extends back out from the racial subject to describe a much broader ecology of ontologically equivalent things in the world, both human and nonhuman. Highlighting neoliberalism's simultaneous capture of environmental sustainability and deep ecology, this chapter looks at recent environmental literature and identifies a strong posthuman ecology that might transform neoliberalism from within. Mat Johnson's *Pym* gets things started with yet another novel reluctant to critique, a novel that instead highlights new forms for engaging neoliberalism's callous exploitation of our environment. In Kim Stanley Robinson's *Antarctica*, that form proves to be science, which Robinson advocates as a way of speaking for the world without imposing human interest, subjectivity, or perspective on it. Finally, Tom McCarthy's *Remainder* shows us that science is not the only way to welcome the world. Literary fiction can too when it opens itself up to nonidentity, to the entire universe of things and the shared oblivion toward which they tend.

This is where *After Critique*'s investigation of contemporary literature's post-critical ontological turn ends—with a literature that refuses ideological critique, prefers ontological rather than representational value production, and views everything in the cosmos with a measured and neutral eye. A brief coda on David Foster Wallace's *The Pale King* explicitly considers the forms of reading most conducive to such literature. In particular, I'll draw on that novel's treatment of accounting to describe a post-symptomatic reading method that shares contemporary literature's more ontological commitments. In other words, the coda asks, if the novels collected here resist critique in the ways I will describe, then what implications might that have for our own modes of critical reading? I offer *After Critique* itself as an answer to that question, as throughout the book I will model forms of attentive reading that I hesitate to describe as either symptomatic or surface readings. Instead, as I argue implicitly throughout and more explicitly in the coda, the current methodological debate about reading has taken place in dangerous isolation from contemporary literature's own reconsideration of how literary meaning and value might be produced. If texts are themselves shunning standard representational forms and instead producing value ontologically, then reading symptomatically does a disservice to the text. In that regard, the turn away from critique that I observe in contemporary fiction goes hand-in-hand with contemporary post-critical, anti-symptomatic forms of reading. But not for any tendentiously ideological reason. It's not that one way of reading is better, or more correct, than another. It's just that different modes of producing meaning require different modes of making sense of meaning. Crucially, we don't need symptomatic *or* surface reading to figure out exactly how a text produces its meaning and value. Unless you're someone who thinks that you produce the text's meaning and value for it, it's easy to appreciate that a text's mode of value production precedes our reading of it. Thus, to read well is simply to read in a way that aligns with a text's approach to value. Which is really just another, more complicated way of saying that it's not fair to treat anti-symptomatic reading symptomatically, to suggest that reading otherwise is just a symptom of one's blindness to a text's symptoms. To do so is to insist that there's only one way for things to mean, which, if you've read any of the novels I discuss in *After Critique*, you know just isn't true.

{ ACKNOWLEDGMENTS }

While writing *After Critique*, I heard many voices inside my head. Thankfully, they belonged to brilliant friends and colleagues whose thoughtful contributions hover behind and course through this book. Countless conversations scattered here and there over many years resound again and again, like a permanent cocktail party—or perhaps hotel bar—of the mind. Always in attendance, Rachel Greenwald Smith has been this work's most valuable and supportive mirror. Drinks are also on the house for Dan Grausam, Andy Hoberek, Mike LeMahieu, Mark Pedretti, and Matt Wilkens. And it wouldn't be a party without Michael Clune, Sam Cohen, Jane Elliott, Jason Gladstone, Matt Hart, Joe Jeon, Katie Muth, Mathias Nilges, and Benj Widiss.

Intramurally, many members of the UCLA community have also proved indispensable to this project's success. First, I thank the UCLA English Department, chaired by the generously supportive Ali Behdad, for the time, space, and funding so necessary for productive research. The UCLA Friends of English have also provided enthusiastic support—both friendly and fiscal—for the book's final execution. I am additionally grateful to the bright and intrepid undergraduates who were the beta testers for much of this material. Their comments and questions, insights and observations, in seminars on the literature of human rights, the post-civil rights era, and the urban geography of Los Angeles, were crucial to this project's earliest gestation. Colleagues participating in the department's Americanist Research Colloquium also read, commented on, and greatly improved two of the book's chapters. I am particularly grateful for the insightful feedback Kate Marshall, Mark McGurl, and Sianne Ngai provided on chapter one, while Joe Dimuro, Chris Looby, and Sarah Mesle all contributed to the shape and scope of chapter three. Special thanks go to the sagacious Michael Cohen who revealed to me precisely what my book was trying to be about even as I was too dense to see it at the time.

Although anonymous reader reports obviously make it hard to know whom to thank, thanks are nevertheless in order for *After Critique*'s anonymous readers whose careful attention and attentive care helped push my thinking to a place it would have never found without them. The same is true of Gordon Hutner, the series editor for Oxford's Studies in American Literary History, who believed in and supported this book through the review process while also providing vital assistance with my revisions. Brendan O'Neill and Maya Bringe have also been similarly generous in dealing with my endless questions and concerns, ushering the project to fruition. I also appreciate readers at *Modern Fiction Studies*, where a very different version of chapter one appeared, and at *Arizona Quarterly*, where a truncated form of chapter two appeared, who helped me refine the arguments that would eventually ground *After Critique*'s largest claims.

Finally, as I relearn most every day when I arrive home from campus, my professional life only works, is only fulfilling, because of the love and support I receive from my family. My sons, Gibson and Oscar, remind me with penetrating clarity what does and doesn't matter. And my wife, Marissa, turns me inside-out, showing me myself in a way that makes my thinking, and my feeling, more stable and secure. (And as an added marital bonus, she'll discuss immanence and the dialectic whenever I want.) I am so very grateful for these three beautiful people whose love, affection, trust, caring, and ridiculous senses of humor make my life better in every way. Thank you.

After Critique

{ Introduction }

We Have Never Been Neoliberal

CRITIQUE'S COMPLICITY, CAPITULATION'S PROMISE

> *There is no term as useful for the construction of the future as
> 'genealogy' is for such a construction of the past. . . . The opera-*
> *tion itself, however, consists in a prodigious effort to change
> the valences on phenomena which so far exist only in our own
> present; and experimentally to declare positive things which
> are clearly negative in our own world, to affirm that dystopia
> is in reality Utopia if examined more closely, to isolate specific
> features in our empirical present so as to read them as compo-
> nents of a different system.*
>
> —FREDRIC JAMESON, *Valences of the Dialectic*

> *The world of meaning and the world of being are one and the same
> world, that of translation, substitution, delegation, passing.*
>
> —BRUNO LATOUR, *We Have Never Been Modern*

Neoliberalism is an amorphous mess of an idea, naming economic,
political, and socio-cultural phenomena. In economic history, for
example, it describes the macroeconomic monetary policies developed by Milton Friedman and other Chicago School Hayekians in
the 1960s; the Nixon Shock of 1971 that floated US currency, effectively dissolving the international economic arrangements of the
Bretton Woods system; the Volcker Shock of the early 1980s that
indirectly raised interest rates to stimulate capital accumulation;
the 1989 articulation of "the Washington consensus," the ten free-
market principles that would define future domestic and international development; the liberalization of trade policies through
international arrangements like NAFTA, CAFTA, and the euro in
the 1990s and 2000s; the 1999 repeal of key provisions of the Glass-
Steagall Act, which effectively dissolved the regulatory boundaries

between commercial banks and securities investment firms; and the World Bank's austerity measures and "structural adjustments" that have reshaped sovereign state economies from Central America to Greece over the past forty years.[1]

In politics, those profit-maximizing, free-market economic policies function ideologically, grounding political positions and movements that have a more oblique relationship to the economy. For example, the ideal of privatization so foundational to the free flow of capital motivated the aggressive union-busting of the 1980s. Even more pernicious, Reagan and Thatcher deftly linked their neoliberal economic policies (lower taxes, deregulation, and private markets) to broader conservative positions against communism, welfare, immigration, and affirmative action, thereby founding the so-called moral majority. In effect, neoliberalism's economic rationality was politicized and marshaled to establish conservative voting coalitions, enact regressive tax legislation, and erode the social safety net. Notions of liberty, individualism, and privatization justified regressive gender, racial, sexual, and class politics, and continue to do so today.[2]

In addition to these economic and political formations, we can also identify neoliberalism's profound influence on society and culture more broadly. Wendy Brown's sense that neoliberalism now casts "all dimensions of human life . . . in terms of a market rationality" captures this more granular expansion of neoliberalism into most every facet of daily existence (Brown, "Neo-liberalism" ¶ 9). There's perhaps no better example of neoliberalism's rampant reduction of life to economy than National Public Radio's *Planet Money*. Initiated in the early days of the Great Recession with a stated mission of "explaining the economy," the show has since gone on to submit most every aspect of contemporary life to market analysis. *Planet Money*'s producers and hosts have economized college degrees, border and immigration policy, climate change, gun control, holiday gift-giving, the public safety that firefighters provide, preschool, pop music, food, your descendants, organ donation, the Super Bowl, winter, public school teachers, gay marriage, death, marijuana, and the Egyptian Revolution, always in an effort to determine the "value," "price," or "cost" of each. Under this new dispensation, data reigns, and individuals are encouraged to subject their thinking about all domains of society and culture to a rigorous economic calculus committed to efficient profit maximization.

In a March 1979 lecture at the College of France, Michel Foucault named this neoliberal individual *homo œconomicus*, observing that "he is the subject or object of *laissez-faire*" (*Birth* 270). Foucault's suggestion that neoliberalism evolves an entirely new species of human nicely captures how the pervasive insinuation of a specific rationality—an epistemology grounded in free-market competition, entrepreneurialism, and profit-maximization—eventually impresses itself ontologically. Neoliberalism as a way of thinking about the world gradually becomes a way of being in the world. In current debates about neoliberalism, a whole lot depends on how you interpret this expansion from a mode of thinking to a mode of being. In particular, a lot depends on whether we view Foucault's *homo œconomicus* as a normative or a post-normative formation. (If something is normative, its value, shape, or condition is predicated on a predetermined and artificially constructed standard or model—that is, on norms. If something is non-normative, or post-normative, it might be natural, or it might ground its value in some entirely different way.) So if neoliberalism is normative, it prescribes a set of beliefs and values, behaviors and practices, that function as a governing norm for *homo œconomicus*. If it's post-normative, it still has influence and power, but not as a collection of legislated norms that directly impinge on, construct, and actively determine *homo œconomicus* as a subject in the world. Instead, as we'll see, post-normative neoliberalism derives influence and power from its hands-off, administrative shaping of lived environments.

Determining whether neoliberalism functions as a primarily normative or post-normative phenomenon is so crucial because each version entails a specific way of thinking about neoliberalism's production of meaning and value. And it's important to decide how you think neoliberalism produces its meaning and value—how it signifies in the world—because that directly affects how you might respond to it politically.[3] Normative neoliberalism signifies representationally. Norms are specific representations of preferred modes of thinking and being; family, the media, technology, teachers, culture, corporations, and political leaders all represent norms to us in various ways. As representations, however, norms implicitly acknowledge that things might be otherwise. In other words, norms' reliance on representation makes them contestable, which in turn determines the nature of our political response to them. In particular, we challenge normative thought and behavior by offering competing representations of the world that critique the normative status quo. If you think that neoliberalism is a normative phenomenon, then your politics will be grounded in representational critiques of neoliberalism.

But if Foucault actually characterizes *homo œconomicus* as a post-normative ontology, as a mode of being untouched by governing norms, then neoliberalism's influence doesn't derive from a specific set of values and practices that it represents as preferable to some other set of values and practices. If neoliberalism doesn't actually impinge on and actively mold our systems of belief and action, then it must be producing its value and influence non-representationally. (I will describe this non-representational value production later in the introduction.) And just as the representational nature of normative neoliberalism entails a politics of critique, the non-representational nature of post-normative neoliberalism entails a different form of politics, a politics that must forgo critique to intervene instead in post-normative neoliberalism's administrative configuration of lived space. In short, normative neoliberalism is representational and encourages a critical politics; post-normative neoliberalism is non-representational and precludes a critical politics. And yet, post-normative neoliberalism still produces forms of meaning and value, just not representationally; and it can still be engaged politically, just not with critique.

Although this will initially sound like a paradoxical thing to say, *After Critique* contends that neoliberalism actually functions normatively and post-normatively at the same time. More precisely, neoliberalism institutes norms, but in doing so it also creates the conditions that render those norms obsolete. On its face, neoliberalism is normative, representational, and thus ostensibly open and susceptible to political critique. And yet, because it has such a totalizing grasp on normative representation that it's become impossible to represent things otherwise, its norms are entirely circular and beside the point. Given this circularity (which I name the neoliberal circle and discuss at length later), neoliberalism effectively becomes post-normative, non-representational, and immune to political critique. Unfortunately, scholars rarely look at these two aspects of neoliberalism simultaneously and instead tend to highlight one or the other depending on their own political predilections.

For example, Wendy Brown's work exemplifies those who would read Foucault as a normative thinker of neoliberalism: "In contrast with an understanding of neoliberalism as a set of state policies, a phase of capitalism, or an ideology that set loose the market to restore profitability for a capitalist class, I join Michel Foucault and others in conceiving neoliberalism as an order of normative reason that, when it becomes ascendant, takes shape as a governing rationality extending a specific formulation of economic values, practices, and metrics to every dimension of human life" (*Undoing* 30).[4] This seems perfectly accurate to me, but I think that Brown draws the wrong political conclusion from this characterization of neoliberalism. Although she acknowledges that Foucault doesn't necessarily share her political vision, she clearly indicates that Foucault's normative take on neoliberalism makes her own "neo-Marxist critique of neoliberal rationality" possible (55). Except, if I'm right about the way neoliberalism functions normatively and post-normatively at the same time, then the post-normative aspect of neoliberalism will make those political critiques circular and impotent. That is, if neoliberalism is really as totalizing as Brown describes, then there really isn't any counter-normative ground from which meaningfully resistant critique might be leveled. If "the normative reign of *homo œconomicus* in every sphere means that there are no motivations, drives, or aspirations apart from economic ones, that there is nothing to being human apart from 'mere life,'" then from what ground can critique be staged (44)? This is, I think, the point at which it stops making sense to think of neoliberalism normatively. In a world where neoliberalism touches everything but the barest of life, you can certainly make critiques, challenge norms, and offer competing representations of the world, but given neoliberalism's omnipresence, the position you hold will be just as neoliberal as the position you're against.

Coming at things from the other direction, Daniel Zamora suggests that Foucault's descriptions of neoliberalism actually emphasize the many ways in which it relinquishes normative control of *homo œconomicus*. By Zamora's account, Foucault viewed neoliberalism as "a form of governmentality that was much less normative and authoritarian than the socialist and communist left, which he saw as totally obsolete. He especially saw in neoliberalism a 'much less bureaucratic' and 'much less disciplinarian' form of politics than that offered by the postwar welfare state" ("Criticize"). In other words, this post-normative aspect of neoliberalism actually leaves *homo œconomicus* alone; it's only concerned with what Foucault describes as the "*conduire de conduits*" (the conduct of conduct), not with the actual content of our beliefs and behaviors (Foucault, *Dits et écrits IV* 237).[5] This seems perfectly accurate to me as well, but as with Brown's normative take on neoliberalism, I think Zamora also draws the wrong political conclusion from Foucault's characterization of post-normative neoliberalism. For Zamora, Foucault's description of post-normative neoliberalism indicates an "indulgent" "attraction" to neoliberalism at the heart of Foucault's work ("Criticize"). Implying that Foucault might very well be a closet neoliberal, Zamora charges that Foucault's thinking, which he describes as perfectly aligned with neoliberal values, "actively contributed to [the] destruction [of the welfare state]" ("Responsibility").[6] Zamora is correct to sense that this post-normative take on neoliberalism feels very comfortable with, maybe even complicit with, neoliberalism, and he's also correct that it undermines the kind of "neo-Marxist" critique that the left wants to make against neoliberalism. But even as neoliberalism's post-normativity might signal the end of a critical leftist politics, it doesn't necessarily signal the end of politics altogether. And it most certainly doesn't make Foucault a right-wing, Milton Friedman–loving conservative. Instead, as Clive Barnett sagely observes, "It seems to me that the affinity that Foucault appears to have displayed [for neoliberalism] might be just as well taken as an occasion to rethink both of those ideas" (i.e., both neoliberalism and the politics that strive to oppose it) ("Bad Foucault").

Such rethinking is precisely the goal of *After Critique*.[7] In particular, that rethinking will reverse Brown's and Zamora's points, demonstrating instead that it's actually the politics of oppositional critique that remains perpetually complicit with neoliberalism, while it's those post-normative ontological forms and modes, which might at first glance look like mere capitulations to neoliberalism, that offer the most possibility for undoing neoliberalism as we know it. Critique capitulates, but apparent capitulation opens potentially new modes of being, and politics. Treating neoliberalism normatively, critique only reinforces its representation of the world. Embracing its post-normativity, however, defuses neoliberalism's potent normative rationality, allowing us to see that what sometimes feels like a soul-sucking, brain-consuming zombie plague is actually just an ad hoc and ever-shifting assemblage of being, a perpetually improvised (re)configuring of the connections and contradictions that define life in the twenty-first century. In this way, we might say

that neoliberalism both does and does not exist. It exists as a normative force that motivates and defines the contemporary production
of meaning and value, but it doesn't exist if we can fully appreciate
its post-normativity.

Purification and Hybridization

Or, to borrow from Bruno Latour, we have never been neoliberal.
Here's what I mean. The relationship between the normative, representational aspect of neoliberalism and the post-normative, non-
representational aspect of neoliberalism bears a notable resemblance
to the relationship between purification and hybridization that
Latour describes in *We Have Never Been Modern*, which makes perfect sense if we think of neoliberalism as one particular form modernity takes in the twenty-first century.

For Latour, a founding act of purification—divvying the world
into subjects and objects, culture and nature, society and science,
human and nonhuman, opinion and fact—defines the advent and
growth of modernity. At the same time, however, Latour suggests
that these acts of purification facilitate a world of hybrids defined
by the blending together of subject and object, culture and nature,
society and science, and so on. In effect, the insistence of purification, the demand that everything be either subject or object, leaves
the door open for the proliferation of subject-objects that our purified thought simply ignores. "By rendering mixtures unthinkable,"
Latour explains, "the moderns allowed the practice of mediation to
recombine all possible monsters without letting them have any effect
on the social fabric, or even any contact with it" (*Modern* 42). "The
less the moderns think they are blended, the more they blend. The
more science is absolutely pure, the more it is intimately bound up
with the fabric of society." Purification thus "accelerates or facilitates" the production of hybrids, "but does not allow their concep-
tualization" (43). Kant provides an apt example with his famous
distinction between things-in-themselves and the knowing subject.
Even as Kant severs the subject from the objective world of things-
in-themselves, purifying each domain, he also introduces many layers of mediation (perception, cognition, the categories) that connect
the knowing subject to the object world. For Latour, those mediations are just as real, just as meaningful, as the subject and object

poles they traverse. We need to acknowledge their blended ontologies as readily as we recognize the purified ontologies of subjects and objects. Of course, if the ontologically hybrid intermediaries were acknowledged, they would undermine the purified distinction between subject and object, which is why purification must ignore the impure hybrids it produces. Granting them equal philosophical heft would undo the work that purification does in organizing knowledge and being (56).

Latour suggests that our commitment to purification has made modernity a victim of its own success. It has produced so many hybrids that the purified distinction between subject and object can no longer be maintained: "When we find ourselves invaded by frozen embryos, expert systems, digital machines, sensor-equipped robots, hybrid corn, data banks, psychotropic drugs, whales outfitted with radar sounding devices, gene synthesizers, audience analyzers, and so on, when our daily newspapers display all these monsters on page after page, and when none of these chimera can be properly on the object side or the subject side, or even in-between, something has to be done" (49–50). Specifically, we have to start thinking about the world as a collection of hybrid subject-objects, some of which might lean more subjective and some of which might lean more objective, but none of which is pure. Doing so will allow a more accurate, and hopefully more just, understanding of the world and our place in it.

So what does Latour's thinking about purification and hybridization have to do with neoliberalism and debates about its normativity? Well, normative neoliberalism's representational production of meaning and value relies entirely on a purified distinction between subject and object, but post-normative neoliberalism's production of meaning and value acknowledges and works with the hybrid subject-objects born of normative neoliberalism's insistent purification. In addition, the purified relationship between subjects and objects that facilitates normative neoliberalism's production of meaning and value also drives the political critiques that oppose normative neoliberalism, but the hybrid subject-objects populating post-normative neoliberalism preclude critique and require new political modes. In what follows, I will explain how normative neoliberalism relies on the purified distinction between subjects and objects, but also how its totalizing grasp on both subject and object positions renders political critique impotent. Then I will explain how post-normative neoliberalism collapses that purified distinction, and how in doing so it begins to produce meaning and value ontologically rather than representationally, which in turn opens up new, post-critical forms of politics. Finally, I will suggest why, when wrestling with specific political issues that neoliberalism makes uniquely undecidable, contemporary fiction writers are increasingly rejecting critique in favor of a post-normative, post-critical politics.

The Neoliberal Circle

A 2012 IBM commercial campaign championing its "smart marketing" technologies ably demonstrates neoliberalism's reliance on the purified distinction between subjects and objects. It also shows, however, the way neoliberalism exploits that purified distinction by oscillating with ease between each position—sometimes figuring people as individuated subjects and other times as homogenized objects—until it captures and controls both sides. One advertisement, for example, depicts a group of identically dressed men gradually turning into a group of distinctly dressed men. The voiceover tells us: "Companies used to view us as demographics because they couldn't see what made people different. Today, retailers from the United States to Japan are using analytics to find insight in social chatter, reviews, and sales transactions, helping some companies increase online revenue up to fifty percent, by offering customers an experience as unique as they are." Another commercial in the same campaign reveals a savvy young woman performing various transactions on her phone and tablet while viewers see her words directed to some hypothetical company: "Do you know me? Not my demographic. Not my type, my segment, or my profile. Me. Because the better you know me, the more ways you'll find to make me happy. And I'm so much more than data. When I'm in your store, do I feel at home? When I'm on your site do I feel expected?" And so on.[8] Even as both advertisements suggest that we are not the sum total of our data, that we are uniquely individuated subjects irreducible to demographics, they also signal to IBM's potential customers in the corporate sector that IBM's best algorithms and computer technologies can deliver ideal neoliberal consumers, measurable and quantifiable cogs in the market machinery. This vacillation between subjective and objective representations of the human defines neoliberal discourse. Depending on the audience, the extension of economic rationality to all domains of human existence formats individuals either as subjects replete with entrepreneurial agency or as systematically aggregated objects, instrumentalized parts of a larger machine.

Crucially, we experience these subject and object positions as mutually exclusive. They never overlap; they are purified of each other. The free neoliberal subject's value derives from its opposition to any potential objectivity ("I'm so much more than data"); and the neoliberal object's value derives from its opposition to any potential subjectivity (the analytical "insight" derived from the mushiness of "social chatter, reviews, and sales transactions"). While we experience these subjective and objective representations of the human as mutually exclusive, however, the advertisements reveal that neoliberalism's potency stems from its simultaneous claim on both, from what I described before as neoliberalism's granular intrusion into all domains of human experience. The neoliberal circle vacillates between subjective and objective representations of the individual, playing each against the other, even as we experience those positions as irreconcilable. But as far as neoliberalism is concerned, both positions buttress its laissez-faire engagement with the world. It wins either way.

Consequently, neoliberalism champions our status as homogenized objects (usually as part of a team, network, or community) just as readily as it flatters our unique individuality. It's that moment in most every Dr. Pepper commercial when the unique individual wearing her "I'm a Pepper" t-shirt is joined by thousands of other unique individuals wearing the same t-shirt. This appeal to our object-status also appears in a recent Prius commercial, "A Prius for Everyone," which depicts a wonderful world in which, as the title suggests, everyone drives a Prius. Notably, this advertisement reverses the trope of so many other car commercials in which the automobile of choice breaks from conformity and returns us to our unique, individual selves. As a recent Infiniti ad insists, for example, "Luxury never felt so liberating."[9] Under neoliberalism, these logics are not incompatible. To be sure, an ad appealing *simultaneously* to our status as subjects and objects would be confusing and ineffective; it would violate our sense that these subjective and objective positions are mutually exclusive and purified, defined in relation to each other. But there's certainly no contradiction between one advertisement that appeals to our desire to be unique subjects (Infiniti) and another that appeals to our desire to be objects in a larger group

(Prius). Each equally reinforces neoliberalism's commitment to market efficiency and profit maximization, and the neoliberal circle just keeps on spinning. Or as Latour notes, it becomes "possible to do everything without being limited by anything" (*Modern* 32).

We can already see in these examples that the neoliberal circle severely circumscribes our production of meaningful, non-complicit representations of the world. Whether we imagine ourselves as free individuals or as components in a larger system, neoliberalism's laissez-faire principles are reiterated. But these are just commercials. It's not particularly surprising that what appear to be contradictory marketing messages are actually perfectly coincident with the larger neoliberal project of efficient profit maximization. What's more disturbing is that even our more critical representations of the world succumb to the same complicity with the neoliberal totality because they too juxtapose their subject-based critiques to object-based ones, and vice versa.

To take just one relatively low-stakes example, consider the debate surrounding college basketball players who forgo their degree to enter the NBA draft early. For those who believe in the sanctity of the game, the value of year-to-year team continuity, or even the importance of a college education, this is a tragedy. For those who enjoy seeing young players succeed, attain their highest dreams, and perhaps achieve an improved standard of living for themselves and their families, this is a triumph. The first argument asks the student-athlete to suppress his subjective self-interest for the benefit of a larger institutional structure. The second argument does the reverse, suggesting that the student-athlete's pursuit of his economic self-interest should take precedence over those larger, objectivizing structures. Each position stands as a critique of the other, and yet they both tacitly endorse a neoliberal worldview. The stay-in-school argument seems earnest and sincere, but as indicated by recent discussions about paying student athletes, it also perpetuates the university's crass economic exploitation of unpaid student athletes—a crucial component of the neoliberal university. Similarly, the take-the-money-and-run argument might be perfectly well intended—an early payday represents a substantive benefit for disadvantaged students raised in poverty—but it also produces entrepreneurial subjects reduced to their human capital. On a rhetorical level, then, neoliberalism is just as comfortable with heterogeneous subjects—those entrepreneurial individuals pursuing their rational self-interest—as it is with homogenous objects—those cogs in the machine of system-atized profit-making. So whether we elevate the individual over the institutional and insist on an athlete's right to self-determination, or if we do the reverse and privilege the objective goals of the larger system (be it the team, the school, or the sport) over the athlete's sub-jective self-interest, we are speaking the language of neoliberalism. What seem like opposing arguments actually fit together to form a circle in which neoliberal values always triumph.

Or to put the point in structuralist terms, neoliberalism collapses the semiotic square, which for Algirdas Greimas defined the condi-tions of possibility for all semantic and narrative signification, so that rather than proliferating logical positions and narrative poten-tialities out of an initial opposition, the neoliberal circle actually precludes the production of meaningfully distinct positions. More precisely, its vacillation between subjective and objective positions permits what *appear* to be distinctly opposed critical claims (student athletes should stay in school/student athletes should go pro if they can) because the difference between them is negligible as far as neo-liberalism is concerned. Thus, if the semiotic square defines mean-ing's conditions of possibility, the neoliberal circle defines meaning's conditions of impossibility—that is, the impossibility of generating any critical representation of the world that doesn't in some way reinforce neoliberalism.[10]

Complicit Critique

This is of course horrible news for the political left, which finds itself unable to speak truth to power because power has incorpo-rated so many of its potential truths. On the one hand, neoliberal rhetoric cynically ventriloquizes leftist idealism, readily portray-ing the systematized neoliberal cog exploited by his university as either a selfless team player or a farsighted student committed to self-improvement through education. On the other hand, neolib-eral rhetoric is quick to idealize leftist cynicism, readily portraying the entrepreneurial subject's big payday as either a win for a worker freed from his exploitative labor relationship with the university or as a moment of economic and social uplift. Neoliberalism speaks the language of the greater communal good as a cover for its systematic exploitation of individual-objects, and it speaks the anti-exploitative language of social justice as a cover for its championing of entre-preneurial individual-subjects. In the name of economic rationality, market logic, and maximized self-interest, neoliberalism makes all of the left's arguments for it.

This was evident, for example, in the 2007 Supreme Court deci-sion in *Parents v. Seattle* and *Meredith v. Jefferson*, which declared that public school districts could not consider students' race when assigning them to schools, even if doing so mitigated racial segrega-tion in the district. The Jefferson County school district in Kentucky was once segregated by law, but various forms of affirmative action and school bussing programs redressed the situation by the end of the twentieth century. Since then, the schools resegregated, but the majority opinion maintained that the school districts could not undo the segregation with race-based school assignments because this more recent round of segregation was merely de facto. As Justice Thomas explained, de facto segregation is not racist; it's merely a side-effect of "any number of innocent private decisions" (3). Laws can be unjust, but demographics cannot. In fact, according to Thomas, the true injustice of the case was the damage that the districts' race-based decision-making did to the neutrality of a demographic real-ity born of free individual choice.

And that's the maddening thing about neoliberalism's rationalized discourse: the opponents of race-based decision-making effectively co-opted the social justice discourse of those in favor of race-based decision-making to ultimately defeat race-based decision-making. The struggle for rights and equality was defeated by the language of rights and equality. Both majority and minority opinions, for example, championed equal rights; both sides pointed to the 14th Amendment's "equal protection" clause to justify their claims. Regrettably, this leaves the left bereft of what has historically been its most potent political discourse, social justice. Now, whenever we speak the language of rights and justice, we run the risk of reinforc-ing the very systems of injustice we attempt to combat. Neoliberals, it turns out, love justice and equality too.

Or, to echo Latour once more, the left's capacity for political and social critique has run out of steam. Those argumentative descrip-tions of the world that aim to defamiliarize, disillusion, and debunk our commonly held beliefs, values, and norms, exposing their ideological or discursive construction, their aporias and contra-dictions, their constitutive blind-spots, their racism or economic self-interest—those representational acts are not as effective as they used to be. According to Latour, this is because critique follows a curiously circular logic, a vacillation between subjective and objective arguments notably homologous to the purified logic of the neoliberal circle described above. On the one hand, Latour observes, critics deploy objective facts to debunk the fuzziness of subjective values (e.g., using science to reveal the absurdity of Creationist belief). On the other hand, critics just as confidently deploy subjective values to debunk objective facts (e.g., decrying the cold heart of science and its inability to truly know the human). Crucially, just as the neoliberal circle needs these positions to appear mutually exclusive even though they are mutually reinforcing, Latour explains that critique also prohibits any and all crossover between objective facts and subjective values. As long as the positions remain distinct, we sense no contradiction between our subjective critique of those claims that strike us as overly positivist and our objective critiques of those that strike us as insufficiently rigorous and analytical. Taken together, critics can dismantle most anything they want, although according to Latour very little is gained from doing so. The only truth that critique consistently produces is the tautologous truth of itself: the critic is always right ("Why" 239). We of course saw the same thing with the neoliberal circle. As long as neoliberalism's subjective and objective representations of the human remain distinct, we feel comfortable and confident inhabiting either role, although little is gained from doing so. The only truth that those representations consistently articulate is the abiding truth of market rationality: neoliberalism is always right. We cannot challenge the economization of everyday life by championing the non-quantifiable humanistic values that neoliberalism threatens to destroy because neoliberalism champions non-quantifiable humanistic values too. Or to ventriloquize Margaret Thatcher, "There really is no alternative."

More precisely, there really is no alternative as long as we insist on a critical politics that challenges one way of looking at the world with a different way of looking at the world. As long as politics relies on representation, on subjects over here describing and debating the world over there, all discursive options redound to neoliberalism's benefit because neoliberalism has purified but then captured both sides of the subject-object relation that grounds representation itself. So while there might not be an alternative within critical discourse, there might be an alternative to representation, an alternative way to

produce meaning and value that doesn't rely on the purified distinction between subjects and objects. *After Critique* explores this possibility, identifying alternative, non-representational forms—different
ways to produce the value and significance of the world—that reject
the representational logic of critique in an attempt to challenge neoliberalism's dominance in new and potentially more effective ways.

Post-Normative Neoliberal Ontology

Which is to say, we only suffer the complicity of critique if we accept
the purified distinction between subject and object that allows neoliberalism to play one normative representation of the world off
another, capturing all available discursive terrain. We only lack alternatives if we accept that *homo œconomicus* is, as Foucault observes,
"the subject *or* object of *laissez-faire*" (*Birth* 270). That "or" signifies neoliberalism's purification of the subject-object relation, but as
the subject-object vacillation of the neoliberal circle suggests, the
world might not be as purified as we think. The mushy fluctuation
of the neoliberal circle indicates, in fact, that the world comprises
people, things, issues, and events that are a muddled mix of both
subject and object. Of course, normative neoliberalism and the critique of normative neoliberalism ignore that muddled mix and insist
on purification—that's why they "hold all the sources of power, all
the critical possibilities" (Latour, *Modern* 39). But the only reason
they can counterpose subjects and objects in this purified way is
because the matter under consideration—whether it be consumers,
basketball players, racial segregation, or anything else—is actually a
hybrid mix of subjective and objective attributes. *Homo œconomicus*
is actually "the subject [*and*] object of *laissez-faire*," a hybrid formation that demands a reconsideration of neoliberalism and the politics that might oppose it.

   As Zamora has already indicated, and despite that purifying "or,"
we can begin to see the outlines of this approach in Foucault, who
identifies a post-normative neoliberal ontology emerging as the
state's active construction of the individual wanes:

> You can see that what appears on the horizon of this kind of analy-
> sis is not at all the ideal or project of an exhaustively disciplinary
> society in which the legal network hemming in individuals is taken

over and extended internally by, let's say, normative mechanisms.
Nor is it a society in which a mechanism of general normalization
and the exclusion of those who cannot be normalized is needed. On
the horizon of this analysis we see instead the image, idea, or theme-
program of a society in which there is an optimization of systems
of difference, in which the field is left open to fluctuating processes,
in which minority individuals and practices are tolerated, in which
action is brought to bear on the rules of the game, rather than on
the players, and finally in which there is an environmental type of
intervention instead of the internal subjugation of individuals. (*Birth*
259–260)

Rather than deploying norms that deterministically mold an individual's subjective interiority, Foucault notes that neoliberal governmentality treats individuals as discrete, autonomous beings pinging
around inside a regulated social sphere committed to efficient profit
maximization. Freed from normative construction, the subject is no
longer subjected to ideological representations, no longer suffers a
conspiracy of manipulation and control. An open field of "fluctuating processes" replaces normativity as *homo œconomicus* becomes
an administrated subject-object within the larger system (270).

Although Foucault's ensuing lectures do not actually pursue "the
horizon of this kind of analysis," more than thirty years later we might
very well be living it.[11] Helpfully, the lectures' editors include some of
Foucault's notes, which schematize the direction of his thought. On
the final page of those notes, for instance, speculating about what
this post-normative society might look like ("not a standardizing,
identificatory, hierarchical individualization, but an environmentalism open to unknowns and transversal phenomena"), Foucault
raises a striking question: "But does this mean that we are dealing
with natural subjects?" (261). That is, if governmental administration
of the individual has replaced sovereign discipline, does that mean
that governmental subjects are actually natural? They may be confined to broader systems of control, but perhaps they are no longer
benighted, manipulated, or normativized by those systems. Within
the confines of the open field, Foucault wonders, might it be accurate to describe them as natural and free? If so, then ontology—the
substance and presence of being—becomes much more determinant
of an individual's value and significance than ideology and norms.
The way we see the world or the way the world is represented to us is

much less important than where and what we are within the system, how we fit into the given configuration. We become, in effect, "individual subject[s] of interest within a totality which eludes [us] and which nevertheless founds the rationality of [our] egoistic choices" (278). We can argue that this self-interest is always tendentiously discursive and ideological; if the totality still "founds the rationality of [our] egoistic choices," then surely there are truths that need revealing, manipulative constructions that require unpacking. But Foucault actually suggests otherwise. If the totality doesn't touch us, as long as it entirely "eludes" us, then we should no longer think of ourselves as discursively normativized constructs of the system. We are instead the free ontology *homo œconomicus*, the simultaneous subject-objects of laissez-faire.

Following Foucault's lead, Eva Cherniavsky suggests that neoliberalism's "erosion of normative culture as such, that is culture oriented to the production of reproducible interiorities" (9), leaves in its wake what she calls "serial culture":

> Unlike normative culture, serial culture does not differentiate among identities (between the normal and the pathological, for example), so much as cultivate a process of differentiation that produces an ever-broader spectrum of identities. Rather than interpellate subjects through processes of compulsory (mis)recognition, serial culture releases them into a minutely regulated environment—regulated not because their positions are prescripted, but rather because their movements and affiliations are tracked (as so much social data), archived, mined, risk assessed, and so (variably) policed, overlooked, or supported. (20–21)

Whereas normative culture constructs its subjects, serial culture maps them. In normative culture, your thoughts and beliefs, the ideologies and discourses to which you commit, determine who you are. In turn, political battles are staged ideologically and representationally because changing the world requires changing the way people see and think about it. While critique's techniques of defamiliarization and disillusionment might be powerful political tools in normative culture, serial culture does "an end-run around the work of ideology" (18). To be sure, ideology still exists and norms can still exert significant pressures on the subject, but their significance wanes in post-disciplinary society. Foucault's "rules of the game" are not interpellated ideological beliefs; they are rationalized parameters and regulated environments. As such, post-normative neoliberalism's commitments are not representational; it's generally indifferent to what we think and believe, to the way we see the world. After all, because the neoliberal circle's vacillation brings both subjective and objective takes on the world into its purview, it can afford to be uninterested in our ways of seeing—it's already captured all the ways of seeing. Instead, neoliberalism wants to know where we go, what we do, which links we click. The words on our Facebook pages are not valuable for the thoughts and ideas they communicate, for the ideological alliances they reveal, but for the relations and connections they forge to certain markets.[12]

A small but increasingly vocal minority of social science and policy scholars has begun redescribing, and in turn analyzing, neoliberalism in precisely this way. Skeptical of those discourses treating neoliberalism as a unified ideological force field saturating every domain of human existence, these thinkers instead emphasize the ontological configuration of neoliberalism rather than its ideological and representational hegemony.[13] Clive Barnett puts the matter succinctly: "It seems just as plausible to suppose that what we have come to recognise as 'hegemonic neoliberalism' is a muddled set of ad hoc, opportunistic accommodations to . . . unstable dynamics of social change as it is to think of it as the outcome of highly coherent political-ideological projects" ("Consolations" 10).[14] What we so typically see as an ideological agenda, according to Barnett, is actually just the ongoing reconfiguration of the world.

A Non-Representational, Ontological Politics

This of course requires that we rethink how we might resist or oppose neoliberalism. If neoliberalism isn't actually a hegemonic ideology pitting otherwise sympathetic individuals against the soul-sucking logic of market commodification and bottom-line efficiency, then there isn't any evil apparatus for us to represent, reveal, and resist. Consequently, rather than approaching neoliberalism as a normative program with representational and ideological stakes, *After Critique* recommends a more ontological strategy. If we accept the shift from normative to serial culture that Foucault, Cherniavsky, and Barnett each describe, then surely our tactical responses to and strategic engagements with neoliberalism must also move from the critical to the ontological. Rather than engaging neoliberalism through the critical discursive terrain that it has already captured, why not develop procedures and techniques that adopt its more serialized and networked formulations of meaning and value? What if we engaged neoliberalism on its own ontological terms, if we allowed for the simultaneity (rather than the mutual exclusivity) of subject and object? How would change occur, and how might we measure success?

Initial steps might include altering the given configuration of specific social, economic, and cultural formations; rearranging the established distribution of bodies; and reshaping geographies of inclusion and exclusion. These actions would aim to identify new modes of being that might promote alternative uses and functions within the existing environment. Establishing innovative alliances and commitments among the hybrid subject-objects of a given assemblage, new ontological configurations that counter neoliberalism's profit motive might emerge. We might understand this approach as a scaled-up version of what Foucault describes as "arts of existence"—practices and actions that reconfigure one's "singular being," not one's thinking. It's an approach that analyzes "not behaviors or ideas, nor societies and their 'ideologies,' but the *problematizations* through which being offers itself to be, necessarily, thought—and the *practices* on the basis of which these problematizations are formed" (*Use* 11). In other words, change requires an intervention in ontology's conditions of possibility, its configuration and arrangement, not in its already existing features and characteristics. For example, provocatively arguing that the potential value of the neoliberal condition has thus far been "underestimated," Michel Feher suggests that in lieu of the left's typical displays of critical resistance, we might instead "embrace the neoliberal condition . . . and allow it to express aspirations and demands that its neoliberal promoters had neither intended nor foreseen" (25). Similarly, channeling Foucault, James Ferguson advocates a shift from a leftist politics that fights exploitation and injustice to one that actively experiments with the "arts of government" operating in our neoliberal age (167). According to these approaches, politics would involve repositioning oneself in the social configuration and forging new alliances within a set of rationalized parameters, absent neoliberalism's insistence on efficient profit.

This might initially seem a bit perverse. After all, as Foucault, Cherniavsky, and others suggest, neoliberalism is directly responsible for the production of this subject-object ontology, for establishing this curious mode of being that is simultaneously autonomous and systematized. But as I've discussed above, neoliberalism ignores that hybrid ontology only to capitalize on it, playing the subjective off the objective (and vice versa), always representing either individual or systematic interests, but never both concurrently. Thus, I'm suggesting that inhabiting the hybrid ontology that neoliberalism has produced for us—rejecting its purified, mutually exclusive treatment of subject and object and emphasizing instead that we are, in fact, always both concurrently—might actually go some distance toward diffusing neoliberalism's ostensible omnipotence. Rather than acceding to neoliberalism's vacillation between subjective and objective takes on the human, what if we fully inhabited its subjective and objective modes simultaneously? What if we engaged neoliberalism on its own ontological terms rather than critiquing its ideological red herrings? What if we swam with the zombies? Admittedly, the post-normative result looks disturbingly similar to neoliberalism. (This was Zamora's point.) The ontological equivalence of hybrid subject-objects, for example, eerily echoes the "system of equivalence" by which capitalism reduces culture and history to rationalized market values (Fisher 4). Nevertheless, my wager is that becoming neoliberal—embracing our doubled subject-object ontology—might go some distance toward demonstrating that we've never actually been neoliberal.

Of course, given that politics today continues to be organized around the represented interests of specific subject positions—immigrants, the working poor, NASCAR dads, Wall Street bankers, etc.—we'd be justified in wondering exactly what this subject-object politics looks like. How might value be produced, significance achieved, if not through a subject's representational relation to the world? Here, once again, I find Bruno Latour's work instructive. First, it's worth noting that such a subjectless politics is not a peopleless politics. People matter, but they don't occupy a privileged subject position distinct from everything else in the world. Instead, for Latour, the world comprises actants—that is, anything human or nonhuman that has an effect on anything else—and these actants forge networks and alliances that produce significance and value.[15] To be sure, from one perspective, a politics of agglomerated actants doesn't look like politics at all. It's just a bunch of stuff moving around, linking up, and then unlinking from a bunch of other stuff. In place of belief, ideology, visionary possibility, and utopian thinking, we find only configuration, modulation, and fluctuation as actants arrange and rearrange themselves in new assemblages and networks. Looked at differently, however, this opens up a new kind of politics. If knowledge, power, influence, and value are produced through interactive translations between and among actants, then everything requires constant negotiation—a negotiation that is nothing less than politics in perpetual motion.

This is why Latour suggests that reformist politicians, always ready to compromise, negotiate, and reconfigure, as opposed to revolutionaries, armed with their righteous critiques and utopian dreams, embody the ideal form of politics, even of existence itself. Rather than scorning their hypocrisy and hollow rhetoric, Latour encourages us to "admit that we will never do better than a politician" (*Irreductions* sec. 3.6.3). "Those who believe that they can do better than a badly translated compromise between poorly connected forces always do worse," he warns (sec. 3.6.4). This politics of the "badly translated compromise" replaces politics' typically proleptic investment in the way the world could and should be with a focus on the way the world is. To be sure, change still happens: alliances and networks are always decomposing and recomposing anew. And yet, because humans do not have unique and exclusive control over that process, the most relevant political question always involves the way reality is now. Politics in this scenario involves accurately describing and then slightly shifting the given configuration of a particular system, not imagining futures yet unthought. The critics and the revolutionaries, those who divide the world into the unfortunate way it is and the more ideal way they know it can be, fail to recognize that those two worlds are the same world in which ontologies are pushed and pulled, morphed and melded, into constantly varying arrangements and configurations.[16]

There is a certain amount of immanence to this scenario, but it differs markedly from both Deleuze's "plane of immanence" and the immanence of dialectical critique. To be sure, Latour's networks of ontologically equivalent subject-objects lack any transcendent elevation external to their given configuration. In this way, they complicate standard forms of representation because there's no perspectival remove from which to paint their picture or write their description.

And yet, it's crucial to appreciate that Latourian networks are not just undifferentiated vitalist blurs; this is not the immanence of pure flow purged of significant difference. In fact, quite the opposite is the case: there is radical heterogeneity and proliferating difference among a vast array of discrete, hybrid subject-objects. Graham Harman describes the specific nature of this immanent difference when he explains why Latour is not a Deleuzian:

> [T]here is a major family quarrel underway ... over a highly clas-
> sical problem: the isolation and interbleeding of individual things.
> On one side are figures like Bergson and Deleuze, for whom a gen-
> eralized becoming precedes any crystallization into specific entities.
> On the other side we find authors such as [Alfred North] Whitehead
> and Latour, for whom entities are so highly definite that they vanish
> instantly with the slightest change in their properties. (*Prince* 6)

For Latour, ontologies constantly change and things become new things, but they don't flow or merge into each other. This is not an ongoing process of becoming but a shifting network of intercon- nected beings. *After Critique* is similarly committed to a non-vitalist mode of ontological value production that maintains just such meaningful difference in immanence. In this way, *After Critique* distinguishes itself from theorists of virtuality and becoming, and also from theories of affect which tend to have rather fuzzy accounts of value production because of their focus on the immanence of pre- cognition. In short, I don't think that vitalist theories of immanence (e.g., those found in the work of Henri Bergson, Elizabeth Grosz, Gilles Deleuze, Jane Bennett, and William Connolly) have much impact on the impasses of the neoliberal circle.[17]

Additionally, the differential spaces between discrete ontologies in the Latourian network are not potential sites for immanent critique to animate a process of dialectical change. Like the Latourian world- view, immanent critique precludes a transcendental perspective, locating instead a "formal negativity" at the core of a given configu- ration and "boring from within" to advance the cause of justice and right (Harvey, "Introduction" 5). But even such founding negativity, to the extent that it remains motivated by the critical impulse, runs counter to the principle of ontological equivalence grounding the Latourian system. That critical impulse behind immanent dialecti- cal critique still requires an epistemologically grounded difference between subject and object that Latour's ontological difference between actants avoids.[18] That is, when dialectical thinking identifies a subject-object duality immanent to being, it's still severing subject from object, positioning each as the oppositional foil of the other. That constitutive dialectical tension fuels immanent critique, but to the extent that it's still grounded in the mutual exclusivity of reflexive thought, it doesn't actually maintain the subject-object simultaneity that ontological equivalence requires.[19]

So if this world of "badly translated compromise[s] between poorly connected forces" doesn't reduce to a Deleuzian plane of immanence and shows little truck for even the most immanent of dialectical critique, how exactly does it produce knowledge, value, and significance? What counts as a viable mode of ontological value production anyway? What does meaning look like if, in place of subjects over here using words to make representational sense of the object world over there, we find instead the interconnection of a vast population of hybrid subject-objects? What if even representation itself becomes just another subject-object? How can meaning be made if word and world subsist on the same plane of ontologically equivalent being?[20]

Meaning Ontologically

Under such conditions, we require a new understanding of what it means to mean. It seems inevitable, for instance, that if word and world are truly ontological equivalents, then standard forms of representation—speech, writing, photography, film, etc.—would have to operate a bit differently. The representational arts would not be obsolete, but they would presumably have to produce meaning and value in some other, less representational way. Or, their representational significance would not be primarily grounded in their referential capabilities—that is, in the way they speak of and point to the world. The notion that the representational arts make meaningful claims about the world, that subjects acquire their knowledge of the world through acts of representation: these ideas would have to be reconsidered, or at least tweaked.[21]

So where might value come from when representation is treated ontologically, particularly when its ontology is not afforded any privileged status as representation? Literary scholars have begun answering this question in at least three different ways. First, there has been a renewed interest in exploring the influence of objects on the world, particularly in the cultural sphere. Content to examine objects internal to literary representation, however, this object-oriented approach to literature—frequently operating under the rubric of "material cultures"—tends to neglect the ontology of literature itself. A second approach, proffered by Harman, radically jettisons the representational properties of literature altogether, preferring instead to approach texts as a philosopher might consider any other object in the world: by discerning and differentiating its primary and secondary properties. From this perspective, understanding a text entails separating those features that are essential to its existence from those that are not. Thus Harman proposes modifying texts to discover their core properties: "Instead of just writing about *Moby-Dick*, why not try shortening it to various degrees in order to discover the point at which it ceases to sound like *Moby-Dick*?" ("Well-Wrought" 202). To be frank, this strikes me as rather bizarre—a task that perhaps only a philosopher could love. Moreover, in his effort to undo the ontologically privileged status of literary representation, Harman unnecessarily abandons the question of literary significance and value altogether. A third approach to thinking literary ontology, however, understands that literature still produces value even after it abandons a strictly representational logic. Maintaining the core values of the literary arts (i.e., establishing connection, producing sympathy, triggering change, and affecting the world), this line of thought suggests that literature achieves those ends not by showing and revealing the world to us, but by being in the world with us. In this scenario, the text is treated primarily as a single ontological unit, and its movement through the world meaningfully affects other objects in the world, us included.[22] While this work remains committed to literary value—locating it in a text's networked relations with the world rather than in its capacity for reference—I worry that this approach still sells literature a bit short. In particular, it unnecessarily seals off texts, treating them like stones thrown into a river. How, then, might an ontological approach to literature account for a text's more literary features? Can it tell us anything about literature's language, figures, and forms?

As this is one of *After Critique*'s grounding questions, the ensuing chapters will introduce an array of examples that detail the ontological production of literary value. To lay some foundation for those forthcoming discussions, however, I'd like to dwell for a moment on one of Harman's more useful insights about literary ontology: "The literal and the nonliteral cannot be apportioned between separate zones of reality, but are two distinct sides of every point in the cosmos" ("Well-Wrought" 190). Here Harman indicates that a defining feature of ontologically equivalent subject-objects is their ability to be both what they are and other than they are. Words neither reduce to nor stand apart from the world. Representation is not ontologically distinct from the world it describes; instead, everything in the world, words included, shares the characteristics of word and world simultaneously. If this is true, then standard notions of reference—the possibility that language points to the world without joining it—must be reconsidered.

According to Scott Lash, the ontological heft that Harman's formulation ascribes to representation is more than just idle philosophical speculation. Rather, Lash identifies a specific historical and material explanation—the digitalization of communicative forms in a globalized age—for the increasing obsolescence of standard representational forms that distinguish between word and world. Contending that "late-modern global forms of culture break with the logic of representation," Lash suggests that those representational forms that mediate the world have given way to transmissions which move, change, and reconfigure the world. As Lash explains:

> [L]ate-modern culture, quite rightly understood in terms of "the media," can never represent without sending, without transmitting or communicating. Indeed, contemporary "economies of signs and space," especially in their capacity as information, have a lot more to do with transmission than with representation. That is, in contemporary culture the primacy of transmission has displaced the primacy of representation. Contemporary culture is thus a culture of movement. A culture of moving (quasi-) objects. (276)

Echoing Cherniavsky's serial culture of "movements and affiliations," Lash's description helps us understand that even as neoliberalism's ontologized culture is one of rapid movement and interconnection, it's also not a culture of immanent flow. Knowledge, value, and meaning are still produced, but not in the old representational ways. The most relevant feature of a transmission is not its referent but the connections it makes when it expands outward into the world. I again think here of Facebook and other social media sites where the meaning and value of one's words have little to do with their representational content and everything to do with who sees them, where they go, and how algorithms transform them into marketing data. Or as Lash puts it, "The sending weaves a net, helps to construct a network" (275).

Latour actually still sees this as a referential process, just not in the conventional sense in which signs mediate the meaning of the world to us. Instead, Latour introduces the notion of "circulating reference," a process made possible by a world of subject-objects that have the characteristics of both signs and things (or to use Harman's language, nonliteral and literal). That is, rather than treating representations as ontologically distinct from the world of things they name and describe, Latour sees a sign-thing duality at the core of all entities. Things behave as signs to link themselves forward to other things in the world, which might in turn link themselves forward by functioning as signs as well. Thus, in lieu of poststructuralism's chain of signifiers born from the unbridgeable abyss between signs and things, Latour sees a series of translations (Lash's transmissions) producing a chain of things connected by each link's double nature as thing and sign. This requires treating the same object first as a concrete piece of matter (a thing), next as an abstract form (a sign), and then once again as concrete matter:

> [A]t every stage, each element belongs to matter by its origin and to form by its destination; it is abstracted from a too-concrete domain before it becomes, at the next stage, too concrete again. We never detect the rupture between things and signs, and we never face the imposition of arbitrary and discrete signs on shapeless and continuous matter. We see only an unbroken series of well-nested elements, each of which plays the role of sign for the previous one and of thing for the succeeding one. (*Pandora's* 56)

Just as we replaced a world of purified subjects and objects with hybrid subject-objects, here Latour takes the mutual exclusivity of sign and thing which has historically structured the referential function of representation and replaces it with interconnected sign-things. This account of circulating reference is of course only possible if one also accepts the hybrid subject-object form of post-normative neoliberal ontology. After all, it's that hybrid ontology that allows each link in a chain of circulating reference to connect to its preceding and succeeding links even as it does not require those links to resemble each other representationally. Instead, the succeeding link in the chain lends its own ontological heft, its own position in the social configuration, to the preceding link. New contexts and alliances are established as the initial link connects forward to the ensuing one. Some of the things that were unclear or underdeveloped in the original thing are given shape and voice in the new thing. Ideas, concepts, and values previously excluded from the world find themselves increasingly included. Value becomes a function of position and place, connection and transmission.

A brief detour back into Whitehead's *Zone One* will offer an apt example of what this might look like. Throughout the novel, Whitehead indicates that the zombie plague makes standard representational forms meaningless, just as we've seen with the neoliberal circle: when all the "stories [are] the same," when "every last person on Earth [thinks] they [are] the last person on Earth," the stories become mere "templates" and representational value cancels out (86–87). One character, however, a woman nicknamed Quiet Storm who leads a cleanup crew that Mark Spitz works with prior to his time in Manhattan, invents an alternative mode of meaning-making that thinks past this collapse of representational form. Outfitted with wreckers, tow trucks, and other hauling equipment, Quiet Storm and her team clear freeways of the many cars whose owners succumbed to the plague mid-escape. But instead of just moving the cars off the road, Quiet Storm precisely instructs her team in the proper placement of each vehicle. Mark Spitz doesn't know why, only that she "favored patterns divisible by five, and grouped them by general size and occasionally by color, sometimes even towing a car for miles to fulfill her conception" (142). It's only when Mark Spitz hovers above the cars in a helicopter headed to Manhattan that he sees the suggestion of a meaningful transmission in the car configurations Quiet Storm has ordered. He suspects that a "grammar lurked in the numbers and colors, the meaning encoded in the spaces between the vehicular syllables, half a mile, quarter mile. Five jeeps lined up south by southwest on a north-south stretch of highway" (232). But the script remains illegible, her readership non-existent. As Mark Spitz explains, "We don't know how to read it yet. All we can do right now is pay witness" (233). More than mere representation, Quiet Storm's text is a transmission that alters the landscape rather than just referring to it. Like the zombies whose "inhuman scroll" argues loudly for their presence, for their inclusion in the city, the non-referential language of this auto text speaks the fact of its own existence, translating Quiet Storm forward and linking her to the things her text comprises as well as to those who encounter it. Readers of such transmissions need not discern the world to which they refer or the meanings they represent. Such transmissions make little pretense to representation or reference. Instead, readers must aver the fact of their existence and avow the truth of these petitions for inclusion in the world. In effect, such texts accept the neoliberal condition but also embrace the potential implicit in the attendant shift toward more ontological modes of value production.

Writing in this way wagers that we gain more from risking post-normative, even post-ideological thought than we do from maintaining the representational logic of critique. Neoliberalism owns critique, but it has not achieved an exhaustively totalizing grasp on all possible forms of post-normative value production. To be clear, this is a tactical wager. The question is not, Which view of things—the normative or the post-normative—is actually *true*? As I explained above, they are both true at the same time, but our predilection for critique, for the purified relation between subject and object, has led us to ignore the post-normative features of neoliberalism. A better question is, Which approach will be most helpful given the impasse in critical representation that the neoliberal circle exploits and exacerbates? And I think recent contemporary fiction, with its turn away from critique, has been asking the same question and similarly concluding that we can no longer afford to approach neoliberalism as a representational problem, as an ideological vision of the world requiring our critical engagement. Instead, *After Critique* sees its contemporary literary archive introducing a productive wrinkle into neoliberal totality by considering, not the Marxist alternative to capitalism, but ontology's alternative to standard representational forms.

Exomodernism

If literature were to abandon the strict divide between subjects and objects, if it were to collapse the barricade between signs and things, what might happen? What would literature look like and how might neoliberalism have to adjust? To be sure, a literary rethinking of representational form is not going to bring neoliberalism to its knees. (*After Critique* is not a book about the revolutionary power of literature.) I do think, however, that literature can show us something that we might not otherwise be able to see—namely, potentially productive ways to reconfigure and produce significant value from the subject-object doubleness of our hybrid neoliberal ontology. Nonfictional forms (this book included) can talk about, describe, and represent the idea of ontologically produced value, of meaning freed from critique, but they struggle to produce such value themselves.[23] Literature, however, can afford to mean differently; it can experiment with alternative, post-critical forms of value production and continue to thrive as a significant cultural endeavor. In short, the flexibility of literary form demonstrates new ways of thinking through the impasses of neoliberalism.

The texts I investigate here do not explicitly set out to signify ontologically. And their shared reluctance to critique certainly doesn't lead them all to embrace more ontological forms in the same way. There's no singular example of a text signifying entirely through circulating reference, for instance. Rather, I'd suggest that the ontological turn that I identify in contemporary fiction has developed a bit more organically. If you are writing about the nature of certain political themes in a neoliberal age, and if you have the formal flexibility that literature affords, then neoliberalism's co-opting of critique, its corner on subjective *and* objective representations of the world, might inevitably lead you to more ontological literary forms comfortable with subject-object doubleness. That is, the process of identifying new ways to produce literary value in a neoliberal context prompts a more ontological orientation in contemporary fiction. *After Critique* thus suggests that we should understand the ontological turn in recent twenty-first-century fiction as a response to the representational impasses that both neoliberalism and critique have produced, to the circularity and ensuing hollowness of representational acts that maintain and frequently manipulate the purified divide between subject and object, word and world. This is literature made possible by neoliberalism even as it has not necessarily capitulated to neoliberalism. The ontological forms I identify are not inherently resistant, but it would also be incorrect to view them merely as complicit symptoms of the neoliberal cultural dominant. They frequently look like capitulation, but I think they hold out some promise.

In fact, I'm tempted to designate this discrete body of literature "neoliberal fiction," but Walter Benn Michaels has already deployed that term in a strictly negative sense, using it to name a contemporary archive that for Michaels is only ever complicit with a loathsome neoliberal project.[24] Thus, I second Mark McGurl's introduction of the term "exomodernism," which he describes as "a projection of posthumanist thinking into the cultural realm," an approach to cultural production that "positions itself strategically outside of rather than after the modern and postmodern" ("Cultural Geology" 381). McGurl carefully acknowledges that traces of the exomodern are woven throughout modernism and postmodernism, and he also observes that exomodernism is more of a nebulous sensitivity to human insignificance than it is a discrete aesthetic mode or historical period. Nevertheless, he also grants it the power "to crack open the carapace of human self-concern, exposing it to the idea, and maybe even the fact, of its external ontological preconditions, its ground" (380). For McGurl, this occurs primarily through the human's confrontation with a "new cultural geology" that positions the human relative to billions of years of geologic time and space. *After Critique* suggests that humans might learn the ontological lessons of exomodernism not just from geology, but also from neoliberalism. The conceptual impasses that the neoliberal circle introduces to the politics of human rights, private and public property, race, and the environment also "crack open the carapace of human self-concern," short-circuiting critique's representational forms and ultimately demanding a heightened attentiveness to our shared ontological ground.

Before arriving at exomodernism, however, postmodern literary production struggled to deal adequately with the impasses neoliberalism provoked. In fact, the two competing strands of literary postmodernism—experimentalism and multiculturalism— effectively inscribed the neoliberal circle at the heart of late twentieth-century literary production itself. The experimentalists championed the slippery, subjective play of language while the multiculturalists grounded their meaningful politics in the objective world. This is the first half of the circle, completed when the positions reversed: multiculturalists emphasized subjective identity while the experimentalists highlighted opaque textuality as material object. With both multiculturalism and experimentalism able to serve as either the subjective or objective foil to the other, it's little surprise that critique

was ascendant during the postmodern era. Exploiting the irredeem-
able gap between word and world, postmodern experimentalists and
multiculturalists turned on each other, highlighting everything the
other didn't see. Free to pick and choose their relative privileging of
subjective and objective truth, critical texts revealed hidden truths
about the world and critical readers revealed the hidden truths of
texts; everyone was right, and everyone was wrong, all at the same
time. Framing its debates in this way—in terms of the representational relationship between subject and object, word and world—late
twentieth-century literature was condemned to spin its wheels and
perpetuate the neoliberal status quo.[25] The apparent antagonisms
between these two competing veins had to be resolved,[26] and critique had to be challenged, before literary culture could properly
address the neoliberal age.[27]

Literary culture was fully aware of its conceptual impasses by
the end of the 1980s (they are quite exaggeratedly dramatized, for
example, in Trey Ellis's *Platitudes* from 1988), but it took a while
before a coherent set of tactics and techniques would emerge that
might warrant the articulation of an entirely new literary movement
beyond postmodernism.[28] One attempt—represented for instance,
in texts like Pynchon's *Mason & Dixon*, Morrison's *Paradise*, Roth's
American Pastoral, and DeLillo's *Underworld*—pursues a historical
turn that Sam Cohen reads as a reaction against and a correction to
Francis Fukuyama's contention that history ends with the Cold War's
demise. This post-Cold War return of historical thinking shares the
stage with a second attempt to supersede postmodernism's impasses,
the post-ironic fiction best represented by the likes of David Foster
Wallace, Dave Eggers, Benjamin Kunkel, Jeffrey Eugenides, Jonathan
Safran Foer, and Jonathan Franzen. Like the turn to history, the New
Sincerity's earnest commitment to affect, angst, and human connection can be seen as a response to neoliberalism's gradual expansion
into the personal and the social throughout the 1990s. In a world
where even the years are subsidized by multinational corporations,
Wallace's post-irony represents a last ditch effort to eke out a space
immune to neoliberalism's reach.

I think these initial attempts to outrun postmodern impasse
deserve the moniker post-postmodern, and I think they are notably
distinct from the exomodernism I describe above and throughout
After Critique. In particular, exomodernism abandons the word-
world model of reference that so bedeviled postmodernism in a

way that post-postmodernism's double turn to history and sincerity never fully does.[29] To be sure, post-postmodernism is definitely up to something new, but what's new about it might just be that white men have finally come around to writing affecting texts that make sincere attempts to connect with the world.[30] Of course, when multicultural authors were doing this in the 1970s and 1980s, they were deemed naïve by the more experimental strand of postmodern authors and the scholars who adored them. Now, that divide between the multicultural and the experimental that defined postmodernism has been transformed into the divide between the neo-realist and the experimental. It's essentially the same debate, (which is why post-postmodernism doesn't actually move beyond the word-world model of reference at the heart of postmodern representation), but now it's a debate staged almost entirely among white men—the identity at issue now is Franzen's Midwestern white guy.[31] Thus, instead of the schism in postmodern literature between the likes of Gloria Anzaldúa, Alice Walker, and Leslie Marmon Silko on the one hand, and William Gaddis, Thomas Pynchon, and Robert Coover on the other, we now have a seemingly endless debate between Jonathan Franzen, on the side of affecting readability, and Ben Marcus, defending formal innovation and experiment.[32] Meanwhile, authors like Chris Abani, Uzodinma Iweala, Helena Viramontes, Uwem Akpan, Colson Whitehead, Percival Everett, Karen Yamashita, Paul Beatty, Salvador Plascencia, Teju Cole, Helon Habila, Jennifer Egan, Ben Lerner, Rivka Galchen, and Mat Johnson are producing some very crucial fiction. You might even call it a new American canon.[33]

More so than the post-postmodernists, these exomodern authors represent a decisive break from postmodernism precisely to the extent that they avoid the division between realism and experimentalism altogether. Or as Ramón Saldívar's and Caren Irr's respective studies suggest, because this "postracial" and "newly nomadic" literature is marked thematically by the economic supersession of the cultural, a deep suspicion of ideologies of all stripes, a commitment to presence, and an increased prominence given to things, it is in turn devoted to literary forms that are neither reflexive nor recursive, that favor networks over oppositions, and that successfully produce meaning without conventional forms of reference. Current theorizations of post-postmodern literature do not and cannot account for the body of exomodern literature that constitutes the primary focus of *After Critique*. Such literature emerges out of the neoliberal era, runs the risk of complicity with neoliberalism, but also develops techniques allowing it to intervene in or move beyond neoliberalism without capitulating to it. In short, exomodernism's ontological turn toward a subject-object doubleness allows it to engage neoliberalism in ways that neither postmodernism nor post-postmodernism ever could. Now, let's go see what it looks like . . .

Turning to Presence

THE CONTINGENT PERSONS
OF HUMAN RIGHTS LITERATURE

*Human rights must be dealt with as an enigma, and new ways
of representing it must be found.*
—NICK MANSFIELD, *"Human Rights as Violence and Enigma"*

As neoliberalism worms its way around the globe, grounding governmental policy and foreign affairs in a bottom-line, economic rationality, human rights has emerged as a popular discourse for exposing and redressing injustice.[1] The non-quantifiable humanity of the human makes an enticing foil to the calculated efficiencies of neoliberalism and the many wrongs perpetrated in its spirit. Human rights discourse has recently appeared, for example, in the challenge to Russia's stance on homosexuality and its related imprisonment of several members of the feminist punk band Pussy Riot; in the American Studies Association's controversial academic boycott of Israel; in the media attention to working conditions and elevated suicide rates at Qualcomm factories in China; in the criticism directed at international retailers linked to the fatal garment factory fire in Dhaka, Bangladesh; and in the perpetual debate over US intervention in whatever violent international conflict has captured our attention at the moment.

When human rights discourse engages these social, political, and economic concerns, it implicitly speaks the language of normative critique. Human dignity has been violated; individuals have been instrumentalized; wrongs require righting; and international human rights standards provide the normative ground—part legal and part moral—for making the requisite corrections.[2] The subject who claims human rights, whether for herself or for another, critiques present conditions while indicating a preferred course of action more closely hewn to the principled values and norms of established human rights doctrine. And yet, even as human rights discourse offers an irrefutably desirable humanistic vision—as Gayatri Spivak acknowledges, human rights delineate a world that we "cannot not want to inhabit"—I will argue here that its reliance on normative critique condemns human rights discourse to easy appropriation by a neoliberal project ultimately at odds with human rights goals (*Outside* 236).

Of course, observing human rights' potential complicities and contradictions is not a particularly new argument, but the attempt to abandon their normative ground and attendant critical potency is. As I will show, the neoliberal circle's doubled claim on both subjective and objective formulations of human rights makes it difficult for normative thought to escape neoliberal complicity. In turn, the potential effectiveness of human rights discourse is gravely compromised. But my interest in abandoning the language of normative critique doesn't stem from some utopian pursuit of an ideologically pure human rights project. My point is not that human rights besmirched by neoliberalism are too tainted, but rather that the human in human rights doesn't accurately describe the nature of the human in our neoliberal age. Human rights treats humans as either purified subjects or objects, but this neglects the ways in which humans are also hybrid subject-objects. As I suggested in the introduction, the neoliberal circle exploits the purified distinction between subjects and objects but has much less purchase in the realm of hybrid subject-objects.

The goal here, then, is not to save the human from neoliberalism, but to re-present the human as a hybrid subject-object in the context of neoliberalism. Indeed, because neoliberalism equally co-opts human rights subjects and human rights objects, it poses a profound representational challenge for human rights: how to conceive and articulate a notion of the human that remains non-complicit with the neoliberal status quo? In an effort to think through this representational challenge, this chapter examines two different portrayals of child soldiers. As the simultaneous subject *and* object of grave violence, the child soldier complicates human rights representation, potentially foiling the neoliberal circle's easy appropriation of human rights discourse. While one text, Ishmael Beah's *A Long Way Gone*, ignores those complications and struggles to squeeze the child-soldier narrative into the conventional representational forms of human rights address easily co-opted by neoliberalism, the other text, Uzodinma Iweala's *Beasts of No Nation*, grounds the protagonist's humanity in the presence of given contingencies, thereby pursuing a non-normative, post-critical formulation of the human that resists the neoliberal circle's capture.

Human Rights Representation and Paradox

The human rights project relies on acts of compelling and convincing representation. The victim of human rights abuse must represent herself to those institutions that might redress her suffered injustice. Human rights organizations must represent human suffering to those national and international groups powerful enough to alter the conditions—war, racism, famine, poverty, displacement—that cause human rights violations. Even the rights themselves must be represented to those who lack them as desirable ends worth pursuing. The underlying premise of such representational acts is that language bridges the gap between those without rights and those with them, but also that some forms of language do so better than others. Thus, Lynn Hunt connects the eighteenth-century emergence of rights discourse to the contemporaneous ascendance of the novel, which, according to Hunt, enhanced the affective and empathic powers of readers, teaching them "nothing less than a new psychology" and laying "the foundations for a new social and political order" (39). In current human rights work, narrative storytelling establishes the interest and sympathy required for action. Or as James Dawes explains, "Many of the most recognizable organizations that intervene in humanitarian crises do so in large part by using language instead of food, medicine, or weapons" (*World* 1–2). Echoing these observations, Joseph Slaughter avows that "what literature does clearly has some influence on human rights" ("Foreword" xii), and Sophia McClennen claims that "cultural representation . . . is a battleground through which communities define themselves and their relationship to others" (3).[3] In all of these ways and more, human rights representations ask us to recognize and understand each other, and ourselves, as fully human.

This is the founding insight of Joseph Slaughter's excellent *Human Rights, Inc.*, which details how the *Bildungsroman* promulgates the recognition of an individualized, rights-based humanity. Describing the *Bildungsroman* as the "novelistic wing of human rights," Slaughter thoroughly explains how this particular narrative form naturalizes the "common sense" of human rights and "disseminates its norms" (25). Slaughter's analysis is helpful not only for its careful consideration of literary form's participation in normative human rights thinking, but also because it illuminates a representational crisis at the heart of the human rights project—a crisis that the *Bildungsroman* resolves narratively. This crisis stems from the oft-remarked paradox between the natural and political grounds of human rights: even though we all have natural rights simply because we are human, those rights only acquire substantive value when political institutions legitimate, guarantee, and ratify them. Basically, even though we are born with the rights of man, they don't count for much until they are rendered congruent to the rights of citizen. Framing this paradox representationally, Slaughter argues that this "gap between natural and positive law . . . is largely a cultural gap—a gap that is ordinarily bridged not by the coercive force of law but by the 'consensual' work of culture" (55). The success of human rights requires that man and citizen recognize each other and realize that they are one and the same. The *Bildungsroman* excels at this. Its unique tautological-teleological structure—the way it narrates the process by which an individual eventually becomes the subject that he's turned out always to be—represents the possible concord between the natural and political predicates of human rights. Or as Slaughter explains, "The *Bildungsroman* generally makes legible this esoteric, impossible plot structure of human rights subjectivation" ("Enabling" 1415).

Representations that bridge the paradox between the natural and political foundations of human rights meet new challenges, however, when power discrepancies accrue to the natural-political divide. The representational act that asks a rights-granting political state to recognize the humanity of the voiceless subaltern condemned to bare human existence is much more complicated than the *Bildung* narrative that cultivates an individual's recognition of the tautological humanity he's always already had. As Wendy Hesford relates, for example, problematic structural imbalances always intrude whenever human rights victims require others to articulate the rights they don't have. Such imbalance introduces the possibility that "hierarchies of recognition and the cultural narratives and structures that

support them" might actually "undermine the pursuit of social
equality and justice" (38). In short, the suspicion and mistrust born of
colonial history, economic exploitation, and geopolitical self-interest
erode the legibility of representations aiming to convince the powerful to recognize rights and the disempowered to accept them. Despite
literature's ability to "sustain ambiguity and complexity," to make
"contradictions commonsensical," the defining disequilibrium of
the natural-political rights paradox makes it exceedingly difficult for
representations to bridge the gap of recognition between human and
citizen (44).[4]

Where the demand for recognition runs up against this power
disequilibrium, human rights representation finds the difficult
divide between subject and object. Spivak puts the matter plainly,
noting that subaltern populations struggling to become "the subject
of Human rights as part of a collectivity" will more likely "remain,
forever, its object of benevolence" ("Use" 172). To make the parallel
clear, then, human rights discourse figures the individual without
rights, the human mired in "bare life," as an object. Once the state
or other rights-granting institution recognizes that individual's full
humanity, she becomes a subject. Thus, human rights representations devise acts of recognition that will transform the individual
from object to subject, but the power discrepancy between human
rights objects and subjects makes successful transformation difficult. In addition to these structural imbalances that erode human
rights representations from within, we might also wonder if the
mutually exclusive logic defining the subject-object relationship
of human rights discourse adequately captures the configuration
of humanity in a neoliberal age. What if we don't actually live in a
world that clearly distinguishes between human rights objects and
subjects? Worse, what if the divide between subject and object at the
heart of human rights thinking actually fuels the powerful spinning
of the neoliberal circle?

Reiterating Olympe de Gouges's centuries-old observation that
rights regimes have "only paradoxes to offer," Costas Douzinas has
noted that human rights discourse "can be adopted by the right
and the left, the north and the south, the state and the pulpit, the
minister and the rebel" (1, quoted in McClennen and Slaughter).
Most contemporary theorizations of human rights representation
acknowledge these duplicities and contradictions, but they rarely
escape them. Some scholars, in the face of pervasive and frequently

unsavory appropriations of human rights discourse, reclaim para-dox as constitutive of human rights;[5] for others, contradictions can be critiqued, arbitrated, and meaningful human rights work can be achieved;[6] some retreat into pragmatism;[7] and still others inhabit the aporia at the heart of human rights paradox, grounding universality in negativity itself.[8]

While all of these tactics smartly consider the representational paradoxes that accrue whenever "we" try to turn "them" into "us," or whenever "they" petition to be included with "us," I contend that human rights can no longer afford to make the best of a paradoxical situation. This paradoxical structure at the core of human rights—the split between already subjectivized individuals with rights and objectivized individuals without them—leaves human rights dis-course ripe for neoliberal exploitation. And once neoliberalism intrudes into the human rights project, the contradictions can no longer be critiqued and arbitrated. This is because, as I'll describe below, neoliberalism doesn't just occupy one side of the paradox between subject and object; rather, the neoliberal circle absorbs the entire paradox—the paradox's constitutive aporia *and* both of its sides. In other words, neoliberalism's appropriation of human rights is categorically different from those of the right or the left, the north or the south, the state or the pulpit, because neoliberalism appropri-ates the entire left-right relationship, the entire north-south relation-ship, the entire state-pulpit relationship, and so on. Thus, we will need to look beyond critique, and beyond the constitutive, aporetic negation, for other truths that neoliberalism's capture of human rights discourse prevents us from uttering.

Neoliberalism and Human Rights

To get there, we need to abandon the notion that human rights and global capital are oppositional antagonists.[9] In fact, to the extent that the normativity of human rights has been thoroughly "contami-nated" by global capitalism, the two are perfectly amenable collab-orators (Cheah 146). For example, "[w]hen aligned with neoliberal arguments about the power of globalization to unify us into a com-mon humanity," Cheah explains, "the moral universalism of human rights discourse can, paradoxically, be used to justify economic glo-balization as a form of postcolonial civilizing mission" (145). Again, this is not to lament that their contamination renders human rights obsolete, or to defend human rights against contamination, but to observe the reciprocal relationship that human rights and global capitalism enjoy. Rather than bemoaning reciprocal complicity, I'm interested in how that complicity helps us better understand the nature of contemporary humanity in an age of neoliberalism.

This mutual reinforcement emerged in the late 1970s and early 1980s as discourses of corporate social responsibility and personhood increasingly aligned the interests of global capitalism and various rights regimes.[10] Not surprisingly, then, "the UN, which throughout the 1970s had worked vigorously to publicize abusive practices of [transnational corporations], reversed its position in the 1980s and began encouraging cooperative partnerships between corporations, UN agencies, and NGOs" (DeChaine 81).[11] I think it's important to appreciate here that this is not just human rights providing an alibi for the expansion of neoliberal economic policies across the globe. It goes the other way too. That is, neoliberalism also provides an alibi for the form of humanity that human rights has always worked to produce: a liberal individual free to autonomously exercise agency, liberty, and choice. Indeed, the concord between capitalism and human rights gradually defined the very foundation of social justice politics, as "[c]onsumer culture provided the modalities through which national and international belongings could be imagined, and resistant identities recognized" (Grewal 17). This reciprocity between the social construction of markets and the market-based construction of society produces significant shifts in the logic of international development, which moved from an emphasis on structural adjustment and privatization in the 1980s and 1990s to a renewed attention to good governance practices that include the recognition of human rights in the late 1990s and early 2000s.[12] Alongside these developments in development, the Clinton administration powerfully yoked together neoliberalism and human rights throughout the 1990s: human rights justified the expansion of free global markets while the expansion of free global markets predicated human rights. In the following decade the Bush administration, operating in the context of its "global war on terror," endorsed, expanded, and more thoroughly militarized Clinton's approach, but human rights were still, at least rhetorically, absolutely foundational.[13]

This growing confluence between neoliberalism and human rights renders the structuring paradox at the core of human rights increasingly irrelevant. Whether you are the victim of human rights abuses or the guarantor and legislator of human rights relief, you are part of the neoliberal project. Or as Paul Bové puts it, "neoliberal state regimes [are] enabling and working in concert with the very forces of globalization inducing the abuses against which rights discourse often is invoked" (174). Because neoliberalism both produces human rights victims and redresses their plight—because it lays equal claim to human rights objects and subjects—bridging the gap of recognition between the righted and the wronged no longer works as a rebuke to the exploits of global capital. Neoliberalism's capacious grasp has eroded the ground of normative critique, leaving us instead with what DeChaine describes as "a globalized world in which the lines between humanitarian conscience and corporate power are becoming ever more blurred and interimplicated" (93). Aihwa Ong describes this post-normative configuration as a "global assemblage," a "site for new political mobilizations and claims" where "[s]pecific problematizations and resolutions to diverse regimes of living cannot be predetermined in advance" (500). Rather than a legible social sphere in which "all citizens [enjoy] a unified bundle of citizenship rights, we have a shifting political landscape" that renders the paradoxes of human rights—specifically, "[b]inary oppositions between citizenship and statelessness"—no longer germane to the representational value of the global assemblage (500, 499). In other words, the given social, political, and economic configuration exceeds the capacity of conventional human rights discourse to distinguish meaningfully between human rights subjects and objects.

Except, even as human rights discourse functions in these descriptions as a post-normative component of neoliberal governmentality, the neoliberal circle actually *deploys* human rights in a way that reinscribes the purified paradox between citizenship and statelessness, subject and object. As Grewal explains, speaking here of the move to refigure women's rights as human rights, "the power of human rights discourse was to represent women as a population ... and also as sovereign autonomous subjects. 'Women' outside the West, in human rights discourses, were represented as *objects* of charity and care by the West but could become *subjects* who could participate in the global economy and become global citizens" (130, my emphasis). Although neoliberalism makes this seem like a teleological project (human rights under neoliberalism transforms female objects into female subjects, with the two categories being mutually exclusive), it's actually a circular one because neoliberalism readily produces both categories of womanhood. Neoliberalism doesn't just produce women as subjects, it also produces them as objects. It implicitly suggests that women are only ever one or the other, positioning each as the other's mutually exclusive foil, but under neoliberalism they are always both, ready to be deployed as either one or the other depending on the needs and interests of neoliberal capital.[14] (As I explained in the introduction, neoliberalism produces a doubled subject-object ontology, but it only *represents* individuals as purified subjects or objects, never both simultaneously.) My thought is that if we extricate human rights discourse from the mutually exclusive logic of subject and object, then we will gain a picture of humanity more in line with the complex, post-normative contingencies of the "global assemblage." And even though neoliberalism is largely responsible for the form of that assemblage, it's better to define the human in its context than it is to carry on with failed notions of humanity that are unintentionally, yet inevitably, complicit with it.

Representing Contingent Humans

Simply put, there is no stable human to represent, no true human for representation to recognize.[15] There are not natural, stateless, victimized objects on the one hand, and politicized, institutionally recognized citizen-subjects on the other. Instead, there are what Upendra Baxi has called "contingent persons," individuals whose being resists recognition-based acts of representation (149).[16] These are, according to Ong, "[d]iverse actors [who] invoke not territorialized notions of citizenship, but new claims—postnational, flexible, technological, cyber-based, and biological—as grounds for resources, entitlements, and protection"; these are individuals who understand that "entities such as corporations and NGOs have become practitioners of humanity, defining and representing varied categories of human beings according to degrees of economic, biopolitical, and moral worthiness"; these are people who experience "the contingent nature of what is at stake in being human today" (504).

To address and represent a contingent humanity, we must figure out how to think post-normatively without slipping into a flimsy relativism.[17] How might we represent forms of contingent personhood when, by definition, the subjecthood and/or objecthood of the contingent person is unavailable for recognition? This is, I think, where literature can be of some assistance. But if the conventional thinking about the relationship between literature and human rights presumes "the urgent need to grasp the characteristics that constitute the bearer of rights and how she is recognizable (to herself and others) discursively, philosophically, corporeally, ethically, and politically," then what might literature that has lost faith in the possibility and utility of such recognitions—while nevertheless remaining committed to an ethos of human rights—look like (Goldberg and Moore 10)? We need a literary form that drastically rethinks subjectivity—not by negating it, ungrounding it, or deconstructing it, as poststructuralism once taught—but by complicating it. We still need to know and understand contingent persons, but we can't do so by recognizing the truths they represent. Instead, we have to describe the relations and connections that make them human in the context of Ong's "milieus of globalized contingency" (499).

One tactic I'll pursue here: comparativism. Sophia McClennen's work takes an initial step in this direction, arguing against the centrality of the subject in human rights discourse and replacing it instead with comparison. She recommends, for example, "displacing the construction of the subject and the ontological categories associated with it, such as nationality, gender, ethnicity, and so on—, as the pivotal concepts that structure the work of both humanists and human rights advocates" (8). This seems indispensable going forward, but McClennen doesn't really push human rights discourse as far away from the truth of subjectivity as she might. Instead, comparativism for McClennen simply puts the subject in dialectical relationship with otherness while acknowledging the necessary imperfections and incompleteness that accrues to any attempt to translate the self to the other, and vice versa. Because comparativism for McClennen "depends on a vision of the self and its other that is meaningfully relational, intertwined in conflict and tension as well as in collaboration and mutual representation" (12), she still emphasizes "recognition as a central feature of ethical comparison" (13). This doesn't adequately move us beyond representational critique; it just makes it dialectical.

Domna Stanton, on the other hand, abandons this preoccupation with ethical recognition altogether, advocating a version of comparison that she names "generalizability." As Stanton explains, in a passage that notably echoes Latour's notion of circulating reference (not to mention the scientific method), she borrows the idea from John Dewey:

> In the pragmatic terms that John Dewey spells out for achieving "the general," in what he calls the continuum of judgment, a proposition proceeds from singulars to other singulars and is proved ... by a sufficient number of particular cases; but all the while, singulars demonstrably refer back to those singulars; then ... propositions proceed from observed to unobserved cases by "a generalizing propensity," which may turn out to be unwarranted and thus would need to be rejected. This movement involves "processes of comparison which extract elements that are *common* to many cases and drop out those that differ," in an effort to control over-extensive inference.

To connect these very abstract processes to human rights, Stanton describes "generalizabilization" as a "contingent process, in which unwarranted generalizations, based on inferences, will need to be rejected," an "open-ended" process that "can produce provisional universalizing statements, propositions that must, of course, be subject to constant re-examination and revision over time to forge and to sustain intersubjective agreements." The goal here is "to find a transactional way to make ever widening connections," to establish what Charles Peirce describes as "a cable whose fibers may be ever so slender, provided they are sufficiently numerous and intimately connected" (77–78, quoted in Stanton).

This form of comparativism differs significantly from that described by McClennen. For McClennen, subjects imperfectly recognize objects, selves make the best sense they can of others, all in an attempt to forge meaningful connections that standardize human rights. Stanton's comparativism, however, is much more networked. Subjects are not at the center, trying to make representational sense of their jumbled milieu. Rather, everything is being compared to everything else, and instead of looking for the truths of those things, this process of comparison only searches for points of common overlap—enough overlap to establish a link between one singularity and another, to align a constellation of allied interests, that might form the basis of human rights action. In this way, the ground of human rights remains non-normative. Connecting singularity to singularity, there is no overarching standard governing these generalizations; the "common elements" comparativism extracts are affiliations, not norms. There are links and connections, but only ever to what's there, to those other presences ready to hand. Moreover, this generalized constellation of allied interests is always subject to revision; it must be constantly interrogated to ensure that the observed commonalities still obtain, are still functional, meaningful, and productive. The individuals participating in such ongoing assemblages can only be contingent persons.

For the remainder of this chapter, I will examine how two literary texts, one nonfiction and the other fiction, address the subjectivity of two contingent persons embroiled in human rights conflicts. Crucially, these contingent persons are child soldiers, both victims and perpetrators, objects and subjects, of human rights atrocities. For my purposes here, the muddled humanity of child soldiers—their doubled subject-object ontology—provides a necessary complication for human rights representation, effectively pushing representation beyond the goal of mere recognition.[18] Because of the child soldier's simultaneous innocence and guilt, in other words, recognizing the truth of his humanity might not be entirely helpful. It might not even be possible. Such representational complications can be fruitful, however, as they help us consider new ways of conceiving the value and significance of contingent persons living in the "global assemblage." Tacitly suggesting that we are all part victim and part perpetrator, the child soldier stands as an extreme example of humanity's core, constitutive duplicity. As such, representations of child soldiers must find new ways to ground humanity beyond the paradox of rights, since, as both subject and object of human rights abuse, their value resides beyond the binary terms of that dichotomy.

Of the two texts that I examine—Ishmael Beah's *A Long Way Gone* and Uzodinma Iweala's *Beasts of No Nation*—Iweala's does a better job innovating new forms that configure the contingent human beyond the paradox of human rights. Beah's text will stand as an example of a representation that forces the subject-object ambiguities of the child soldier into conventional human categories defined by the distinction between those without rights and those with them. Ultimately aiming for a representation that will promote recognition, Beah sensibly chooses memoir as an ideal genre for such a project committed to the tautological-teleological reconciliation between the human-object without rights and the citizen-subject with rights. But as I'll argue, the ambiguous contingency of Beah's child-soldier status is too much for the genre to bear; Beah and his humanity remain unrecognizable. In *Beasts of No Nation*, on the other hand, Iweala embraces a comparative approach to subjectivity that stands here as one possible way to think the human beyond the purified subject/object divide so readily exploited by neoliberalism. Rather than pursuing recognition, Iweala's novel only hopes to achieve overlap. Consequently, *Beasts* prolifically deploys simile to establish the primacy of comparative, networked connections among singularities—an approach that takes Stanton's "generalizability" as a more productive alternative to the paradoxical pitfalls attending any rigid distinction between human rights subjects and objects.

The Truth of the Embedded Self

"My high school friends have begun to suspect I haven't told them the full story of my life," Ishmael Beah writes at the opening of *A Long Way Gone*. The memoir that ensues fills in that story, disabusing his friends of the notion that it must have been "cool" to grow up in Sierra Leone where Beah saw "people running around with guns and shooting each other" (3). More shockingly, the memoir asks us to recognize that Beah didn't just witness such terror, he caused it: "My face, my hands, my shirt and gun were covered with blood. I raised my gun and pulled the trigger, and I killed a man. . . . I angrily pointed my gun into the swamp and killed more people. I shot everything that moved" (119). The ebullient subject that Beah's friends know and love, it turns out, was once an object, a stateless, lawless individual operating beyond the logic of human rights. Highlighting his objecthood, for instance, Beah reports that after these executions, "I only drank water and felt nothing. As I walked back to my tent, I stumbled into a cement wall. My knee bled, but I didn't feel a thing. . . . Nothing happened in my head. It was a void" (120). Having been objectified into a killing machine, Beah's story recounts the arduous path back to the fully human subject of human rights who walks amongst us today, delivering readings at Starbucks, speaking at the United Nations, and bantering with Jon Stewart on *The Daily Show*.

What moral, legal, and rhetorical gymnastics are required for us to make room for this person in our world? How can a lawless killer also be a UNICEF advocate for Children Affected by War? How is it possible that these two people are one and the same, and what representational forms can best establish their coincidence? Beah obviously has some exculpatory evidence working in his favor: he was only thirteen when he became a child soldier; he was forcibly recruited into the army; he was fed massive amounts of drugs; he had no other choice. But also, he's charismatic and quite handsome; he's an eloquent writer and compelling speaker; he has a great smile and a story that sells. More to the point, Beah benefits from the fact that human rights discourse—and the media spectacle promoting it—treats its subjects and objects with mutual exclusivity. Sure, Beah did some horrible things, but when he killed all those people he was an object of human rights atrocity, not a subject of human rights privilege. The testimonial truth of his memoir establishes this, freeing him from responsibility for whatever wrongs he committed as an object and grounding his transformation into a human rights subject.

Beah establishes the mutual exclusivity of his subjecthood and objecthood while discussing certain images that he sees in the moon. As a six-year-old, Beah recounts, he was "fascinated with the different shapes that [he] saw inside the moon." Establishing continuity with that six-year-old self, the post-child-soldier Beah reports, "Whenever I get a chance to observe the moon now, I still see those same images I saw when I was six, and it pleases me to know that part of my childhood is still embedded in me" (17). Here, Beah's core humanity, a subjecthood linked to the capacity for transformative, figurative vision, brackets his dehumanized years as a child soldier, assuring us that his foray into violence and mayhem was an anomaly distinct from his true self, a self that remains permanently "embedded" within him. Nevertheless, Beah knows that we can't just ignore the atrocities that he committed as a child soldier in the Sierra Leone military. To align the six-year-old version of his humanity with that of the post-atrocity voice of the memoir, Beah must accurately represent the events that transpired while he was a child soldier. The long path back from objecthood, the process by which we can recognize that the child soldier and the UNICEF advocate are one and the same, requires a story that captures the literal truth of Beah's violent past. After all, without an accurate accounting, how can we be sure that Beah's subjecthood and objecthood really are mutually exclusive? With recognition as his goal, Beah's decision to write a memoir—a testimonial which, along the way, explicitly reminds us that "whenever a story is told, it is worth listening to"—makes perfect representational sense (74).

However, despite its commitment to the inherent value of stories and its need to tell a true one, Beah's memoir also highlights a persistent failure to recognize the truth of stories. Once Beah becomes a refugee traveling from village to village, for example, those not yet touched by the war "refuse to accept" the information that he shares (5). Acknowledging his own failure to recognize a story's truth, Beah is conscripted into the military shortly after informing us that "night has a way of speaking to us, but we almost never listen" (81). And once he begins fighting, Beah snorts a potent mixture of gunpowder and cocaine that leaves him sleepless for days, forcing him to begin many of his wartime stories with a disclaimer about the uncertainty of his memory. Thus, despite the explicit assertion that we should listen to his story, and despite the imperative that he tell a true one, Beah also implies that the contingencies of child soldiering will make it difficult for us to believe him, that the path from object to subject is representationally dicey.

The memoir resolves this apparent contradiction through the figure of Laura Simms, a storyteller Beah meets at a United Nations conference where he learns "how to tell [his] stories in a more compelling way" (196). When a storyteller traumatized by drugs and violence tells stories so horrific that his audience responds skeptically, perhaps craft can intervene to forge a more reliable connection between speaker and audience. To do so, of course, one must abandon the idea that the resulting story will be true in any literal way. Instead, the story will presumably speak to broader truths that supersede the contingent details so easily lost in the fog of war, effectively bridging the divide between Beah's particular experiences and their universal resonance. This is the kind of story Beah tells, for example, when he speaks at the United Nations "about the lives of children in Sierra Leone and what can be done about it"—a story designed to convince those who lack any firsthand experience of the terrible conditions in his native country (185). Such stories do not require literal truth to be effective. When belief and understanding are your goals, then crafting a compelling story is more important than pinpoint precision, which is precisely what Beah discovers when, after challenging the details of his friend's story, he is promptly rebuffed: "I am telling the story, so I can tell *my* version" (74).

Curiously, however, Beah does not apply these lessons to the auto-biographical representation he offers in *A Long Way Gone*. He certainly tells a compelling story, but he steadfastly refuses to admit that crafting an engaging story that articulates larger, more resonant truths might require sacrificing the literal truth of his contingent experiences as a child soldier. Despite the disbelief and forgetfulness that plague his account, for instance, he still insists, "To this day, I have an excellent photographic memory that enables me to remember details of the day-to-day moments of my life, indelibly" (51). And yet, shortly after the book's release, journalists at *The Weekend Australian* published rather convincing evidence that Beah's account misses the mark on many fronts: he claims to have joined the Sierra Leone army at thirteen, but they argued he was fifteen; he reports fighting for two years, but they said two months; he details a fight at a UNICEF facility that left six boys dead, but UNICEF found no record of the event. Many have come to Beah's defense by pointing to the larger truths of his narrative. Laura Simms, for instance, rebuffed the paper's questions by asking, "If you were a kid in war, would you have a calendar with you after you had lost everything and were running through the bush?" (Hogan). And although they could not verify Beah's account, UNICEF graciously released a statement asserting, "It is our view that even one day as a child soldier is one day too many" (Appleyard). But Beah chooses not to accept the cover that Simms and UNICEF offer; he doesn't insist on his right to tell *his* version of his story. Instead, he stubbornly asserts the literal truth of his memoir: "I was right about my family. I am right about my story. This is not something one gets wrong. . . . Sad to say, my story is all true" (Appleyard).

Why does Beah refuse recourse to the subjective rights of the storyteller and insist instead on the testimonial truth of his memoir? His decision, I would suggest, is a function of his memoir's goals. If Beah wanted his audience to recognize the horrible truths of child soldiering, then detailed veracity would take a backseat to a presumably larger truth, as Simms and UNICEF suggest it should. But Beah's representation has a different goal, a goal that does not aim outward to a broad universal message, but inward to the particular truth of his own individual humanity. His representation doesn't ask readers to recognize the grave injustices of child soldiering; instead, the memoir asks us to recognize that Beah's pre-atrocity self remains embedded in his post-atrocity self, and to in turn recognize that his years as a child soldier are a mutually exclusive anomaly. This goal becomes clear once Beah is removed from the war and begins his rehabilitation at a UNICEF repatriation center for child soldiers, where he meets periodically with a woman named Esther. In what amounts to a series of impromptu therapy sessions, Beah "delve[s] into [his] recent past" (155), "tell[s] her some of [his] dreams" (160), and "talk[s] about the lives [he] had lived before and during the war" (165). The point of these stories, of course, has nothing to do with Esther's understanding of Beah's experiences; instead, the goal is to help Beah find the embedded self that lies buried beneath "the fastened mantle of [his] war memories" (145). To find the predicate of his true humanity again, Beah must repopulate his mind with memories of his past selves, a process that involves telling Esther stories about his recent and distant past, categorizing them according to the purified, mutually exclusive divide between human rights subject and object.

This is, in effect, a truth-and-reconciliation model of human rights redress. Assuming that most perpetrators are also, in one way or another, victims, the truth and reconciliation model prefers storytelling to punishment, with the crucial condition that everyone's stories are accurate and true.[19] In the memoir, UNICEF staff introduce this idea to Beah as they repeatedly avow that he bears no blame or responsibility for the human rights violations that he perpetrated or suffered. But to be blameless, to once again coincide with his embedded humanity, his stories must tell the literal truth of his actions. A generalized truth about the horrors of war is not sufficient to obtain the reconciliation the memoir aims to achieve. Consequently, all evidence to the contrary, Beah insists that his memoir is absolute fact. If the goal were merely to testify, fiction would suffice; but when that testimony must also redress and repair human rights violations, the stories must be true. To no longer be defined by the indiscriminate killing he perpetrated as a child soldier, he must accurately testify to his indiscriminate killing. Thus, when the Australian journalists point out the many falsehoods of Beah's memoir, they threaten Beah's self-reconciliation and implicitly suggest that the memoir fails as a representational act of human rights recognition.

In effect, Beah's memoir and the controversy surrounding it demonstrate just how difficult it is for representation to access the embedded self of contingent persons. Beah believes that his stories provide such access, but in practice they only prove their own inability to maintain the fidelity to the facts of history necessary for a full return to that self. To be clear, the mistake is not Beah's belief in stories. The mistake is believing that stories can draw a straight line from object to subject, that they can accurately fill in the chronology of events that would return the full privileges of human rights subjectivity to the previously objectified child soldier. Or perhaps the mistake is believing that an obvious and representable difference exists between human rights subjects and objects in the first place, that the subjectivizing power of human rights can be disentangled from the muddled contingencies and subject-object doubleness of child soldiering. To be sure, stories can play a vital role in figuring humanity, but only if we abandon the idea that we already know what the human is and should be.

Bad Beasts, Good Beasts

Equally crucial, however, is to appreciate that our inability to know the human in advance does not necessarily entail that the human is nothing, a blank slate just waiting to be inscribed with meaning and value. Abandoning the positivism of Beah's embedded humanity does not require a full retreat to the negated ground of poststructuralism's constitutive absence. Instead, rather than being what it always already was or what it can never be, what if the human were simply what it is at any given moment? Rather than being predetermined, or even normatively determined, such a human would be contingently determined by the relevant presences inhabiting her past and present. Defined by sites of overlap and connection with other presences in the world, this contingent person remains too enmeshed in the given configuration to be exclusively subject or object. In turn, neoliberalism cannot easily appropriate the contingent person since neoliberalism requires individuals who can be easily figured as either subjects or objects, not as a muddled mess of both. As I suggested earlier, literary form is particularly well-suited for exploring and representing the subject-object doubleness of neoliberal ontology. In *A Long Way Gone*, we saw the testimonial truth of memoir struggle to reclaim Beah's unique human subjectivity from the subject-object doubleness of his child soldiering. But in Iweala's *Beasts of No Nation*, we will see the logic of simile establish subject-object doubleness as the defining feature of humanity. This will in turn refute the apparent mutual exclusivity of subject and object that leaves the human so easily co-opted by neoliberalism.

Before war came to his unnamed West African village, Agu, the first-person narrator and protagonist of *Beasts*, shared Beah's belief that language can help us recognize the world. "Pointing to each word and asking what is that what is that," for example, the words of his mother's Bible stories directly correspond to images in his head: "Each time she is reading this story I would be thinking in my head that I am standing here looking at how all the army is shining with gold and bronze in the sun" (25). Once war comes to his village, however, Agu quickly learns that its realities do not correspond to his mother's stories. After his mother and sister flee and his father is murdered, Agu is left alone, and the Commandant, the unnamed leader of the soldiers who have just perpetrated these atrocities, easily convinces the traumatized Agu that joining their ranks will allow him to avenge the horror that "the enemy" has wreaked. Rather than referring literally, then, the Commandant's words acquire meaning solely from his capricious decree. The enemy is the enemy because he says so.

Or in literary terms, the Commandant replaces Agu's literal mode of reference with a catachrestic one that violently transforms children into soldiers, friends into enemies, and murder into justice. In rhetoric, catachresis denotes the misuse of language, but I use it here as Gayatri Spivak does, to name a universalizing "master word" that claims to describe a specific group—in Spivak's case, "woman," "worker," and "proletariat," and in the Commandant's case, "soldier," "spy," and "enemy"—even though there are no true examples of that group (*Post-Colonial* 104). Whereas literalism purports to refer truly and particularly, catachresis, which radically severs words from their referents, only sees blank spaces—beasts of no nation—waiting to be filled in with groundless meaning. As Beah's text has shown, literalism is the representational mode of the hopeful human rights subject who relies on its supposed transparency to make his humanity recognizable and knowable. Catachresis, on the other hand, is the representational mode suffered by the beleaguered human rights object. Erasing difference and ignoring the given configuration, catachresis makes indiscriminate killing easy. Or as Agu says, "I am killing everybody, mother, father, grandmother, grandfather, soldier. It is all the same. It is not mattering who it is, just that they are dying" (135).

But as Agu's experiences suggest, neither of these representational forms adequately captures his humanity, which is always more than literal but never wholly catachrestic. Agu is not what he always already is, but he's also not a negation waiting to be filled. Agu senses as much when, despite the Commandant's universalizing catachreses, one particularizing distinction continues to nag at him: the difference between being a "bad boy" and being a "soldier." He repeatedly tries to convince himself that being a "soldier" precludes him from being a "bad boy"—"soldier is not bad if he is killing"—but "it is never working because I am always feeling like bad boy" (23–24). Agu wishes the distinction between soldiers and bad boys were mutually exclusive, but here he realizes that it's quite blurry. Even as the catachreses of child soldiering insist that he can't be bad because he's just following orders, a residual moral compass suggests some lingering value, some present particularity to Agu's humanity that the Commandant's catachreses cannot universalize away. However, because we do not simply know bad boys when we see them, that value is more than merely literal. Instead, Agu's humanity will have to be figured. To understand the true nature of his humanity at any given moment, Agu must link the few contingent singularities of his present to the residual particularities of his past. Which is to say, Agu is not looking for the enduring and incorruptible truth of his embedded self, some kind of inherent humanity that he will recognize as such once he finds it. Rather, he's searching for a version of humanity that is neither wholly subject nor wholly object but is instead a contingent configuration comprising both. As the first-person narrator of his own child-soldiering story, he's also looking for the representational mode—somewhere between the literal and the catachrestic—that will allow him to articulate it.

The creation myth of Agu's village gives us an idea of what this representational mode might look like. In the myth, a great warrior and a river goddess have twin boys born with the ability to transform themselves into animals. Sometimes they are monkeys climbing trees for fruit; at other times they are birds enjoying the view. One day, one of the sons drinks from the river as an ox while the other hunts as a leopard. The leopard returns empty-pawed and attacks the unsuspecting ox. In the ensuing brawl, they become human and recognize their mistake just before dying. When the mother finds her fallen sons, she moves away to a land that becomes Agu's village (49–50). Thus, a founding absence—the death of two sons—predicates the creation of Agu's village, suggesting, as does the novel's beastly titular metaphor, the danger of reducing humans to animals, of treating subjects as objects. And yet, the creation myth's monkeys and birds also raise the interesting possibility that turning into a beast might not always be bad. Some figurative forms are productive; others are deadly. The issue seems to involve determining how those transformations, those figurations, can be controlled. How can we become other and more than ourselves without falling off the catachrestic cliff?

The answer lies in the transformation's temporal form. Wartime in the novel is marked by an undifferentiated present conducive to catachrestic transformations that reduce subjects to mere absence, ignoring whatever present and prior value those subjects might embody. For example, as Agu is "chopping and chopping and chopping" an innocent mother and daughter to pieces in the continuous present (51), he catachrestically transforms them into his enemies: "This woman is my enemy. She is killing my family and burning my house and stealing my food and making my family to scatter" (50). As the repetitive present participles and the insistently present tense of the passage indicate, such transformations are only possible when time is timeless, when history collapses into the present, erasing all temporal distinction. Or as Agu explains, "It is night. It is day. It is light. It is dark. It is too hot. It is too cold. It is raining. It is too much sunshine. It is too dry. It is too wet. But all the time we are fighting. No matter what, we are always fighting. All the time bullet is just eating everything" (117). The novel captures this all-the-time time with hundreds of present participles that operate sometimes as infinitives—"Commandant is starting to sweating"— and sometimes as adjectives—"I am sadding" (13). Most notably, the present participles appear even if the recounted events occurred in the past, as when Agu refers to "the boy who is finding me," even though Agu has already been found (5). Collapsing all temporal distinctions into a permanent present, the participles aptly capture the perpetuity of war's violence. For example, Agu describes being raped by the Commandant the previous evening as "what he is doing to me last night" (91). Just as the Commandant's wartime catachreses fail to distinguish among different categories of people, capriciously figuring soldiers as spies, innocents as enemies, so too does the war's perpetual present preclude the differentiation necessary for Agu to know how to be human. He laments at one point, for example,

"Time is passing. Time is not passing. Day is changing to night. Night is changing to day. How can I know what is happening? . . . How can I know what is happening to me? How can I know?" (52). In effect, war robs the human of any potentially grounding presence that might allow it to constitute a self.[20]

These skewed perceptions of time and their devastating effects suggest that Agu's humanity will be returned to him, that he will cease being a beast susceptible to the Commandant's catachrestic decrees, once he identifies a representational mode that permits temporal distinction and differentiation, once he finds a grounding greater than absence. And this is precisely what he finds in the ritual that, prior to the war, transformed the boys of Agu's village into men. Based on the village creation myth that describes both successful and unsuccessful transformations of humans into beasts (remember, the boys thrive as monkeys and birds but kill each other as ox and leopard), Agu's description of the ritual accentuates the distinct temporal markers that define the parameters of the boys' transformation into men. For instance, before the ceremony, everyone mingles and chats until "KPWOM! The first drum is beating and AYIIIEEE! Then first dancer is shouting out to be telling everyone to shutup and just be watching" (54). Other temporal markers—drums, meals, and dances—punctuate the day's events until the setting sun initiates the culminating Dance of the Ox and Leopard. After the dance, the entire village walks to the river where the head boy sacrifices an ox with a machete: "Blood is flying all over his body and he is wiping it from his mask with his hand. Then he is putting his hand where he is cutting and collecting the blood to be rubbing on his body. When he is finishing, all the other is doing the same until everyone is covering in so much blood." A concluding drum then halts the ritualized blood bath, signals the participants to remove their masks, and declares the boys men (56).

This sacrificial ox blood echoes the blood that flows from the murdered mother and daughter: Agu tells us, "I am liking the sound of knife chopping KPWUDA KPWUDA on her head and how the blood is just splashing on my hand and my face and my feets" (51). And yet, although Agu's violent sacrifice of the mother and daughter ensure that he "cannot be going back to doing child thing" (93), it also doesn't make him a man in the same way that the village ritual would have: "I am thinking, if war is not coming, then I would be man by now" (56). Agu's childhood has been stolen from him, and the war's perpetual present deprives him of the objects, rituals, and temporal differentiation that might meaningfully ground his nascent manhood. As with the successful and unsuccessful transformations detailed in the village creation myth, Agu also intuits that achieving one's manhood through war is much riskier than achieving it through ritual reenactment. There's something about being transformed into a beast by village ritual that is categorically different form being transformed into a beast by a maniacal war commander. The ritual allows the boys to be more than they are, more than literal, but its modulated temporality also controls what would otherwise be a rampantly catachrestic transformation. Instead of a manhood catachrestically produced as a name covering a foundational absence, the ritualized production of manhood succeeds because it grants humanity a prior referent besides absence. That is, the ritual does not catachrestically write over a founding absence but instead refigures an already existing story. The difference is between signifiers that only cover emptiness and signifiers that refigure and reinterpret prior formations of value and meaning, even if they aren't literally true. The former sees the human as nothing more than an object or founding absence while the latter treats the human as the ongoing process of negotiating and translating its subject-object doubleness. Because this process is not just covering over a core absence but is instead building on an already given configuration, it requires tropes other than catachresis to articulate a newly configured human.

As is apparent from the novel's very first page, Agu's trope of choice for this project is simile: "I am feeling itch like insect is crawling on my skin"; "I am hearing . . . the sound of truck grumbling like one kind of animal, and then the sound of somebody shouting . . . in voice that is just touching my body like knife"; "there is light all around me . . . crossing like net above my body"; "I am feeling my body crunched up like one small mouse"; "my shirt is so wet it is almost like another skin"; and "my muscle is paining me like fire ant is just biting me all over my body" (1). Just like the temporalized village ritual that grants the young men a productive beastliness, simile establishes an object's referential value in relation to a prior configuration of value and understanding, to a presence that already exists. It compares and draws generalizations from the common and overlapping properties of two singularities, relating the contingent person in the present to experiences and knowledge that he carries with him from the past. For instance, when Agu finds himself surrounded by unfamiliar trees, he names them according to simile's analogic: "There are tree with leaf that are having five point, so I am calling them the star-leaf tree because it is like their leaf is becoming the star in the sky when they are falling. . . . And there is some smaller tree with vine that is strangling them. I am calling these tree the slave tree because they are slave to the vine that is using them to climb up to the sun" (41–42). Here, the value of the simile does not derive from an embedded truth or even from a normative standard but simply from the correlation of two observed, singular truths that in turn permit comparative generalization.

Simile's strategic importance for Agu becomes clear at the novel's conclusion when he finds himself in a rehabilitation center telling a white woman named Amy about his experiences. The parallels to Beah's meetings with Esther are striking, but whereas Beah is anxious to set the record straight and recover the subjective truth of his embedded self, Agu is reluctant to talk about his past because, as he tells Amy, "it will be making you to think that I am some sort of beast or devil" (142). With simile, however, Agu can acknowledge that he was in fact *like* a beast without having to actually *be* a beast. Or perhaps more precisely, the simile articulates the truth of Agu's humanity because it allows him to represent himself as both beast and human, object and subject, simultaneously. His beastliness is not anomalous or mutually exclusive to his humanity; it's constitutive of it. The simile makes representational room for the human's subject-object doubleness while literalism only sees subjects and catachresis only sees objects.

Consequently, Agu's simile-laden story walks back the Commandant's catachrestic transformations without resorting to Beah's project of total self-reconciliation. Agu's victims might "go to toilet like sheep or goat or dog" (20); and Agu might be "like cow and belonging to one owner which is gun" (128); but as long as they are only "like" these things, they are also always something else as well. There are certainly points of general overlap, but there are also crucial differences. Both are true. Or as Agu finally admits to Amy, "[F]ine. I am all of this thing. I am all of this thing, but I am also having mother once, and she is loving me" (142). Whereas Beah brackets his years of child soldiering, figuring himself during that time as an object of human rights that will eventually be transformed into a subject of human rights through the representational power of memoir,

Agu accepts the complexities of child soldiering and acknowledges, through simile, that they are always with him. Just as the boys participating in the village ritual must become beasts to become men, Agu uses simile to portray a version of humanity that is always simultaneously self and other, subject and object, human and beast. In *Beasts*, therefore, the human turns out to comprise generalized comparisons between current and past configurations of one's contingent personhood.

Without any normative grounding, however, this version of humanity could very well have to relinquish human rights discourse altogether. What lies beyond the paradox of human rights might very well be the absence of human rights. And yet, that absence is not an emptiness; it's not a timeless nothing that can be catachrestically overwritten by the powerful interests of neoliberal capital. There is still something there; namely, that which came before. What's more, comparison allows the contingent present to establish a valuable continuity with that which precedes it. By identifying points of common overlap and generalizing outward from them, the human acquires substantial, if not exactly inherent or permanent, meaning and value.[21] Crucially, this also returns presence to the human, albeit in a rather complicated and increasingly networked form. It's a presence that can't be reduced or exclusively categorized as subject or object precisely because it's also a presence defined by the alliances and affiliations it achieves with other subject-objects.

As such, I'd suggest that this version of humanity actually stands some chance of success within the neoliberal dominant. By virtue of its ever-shifting complexity, however, its success will not stem from critique or opposition; this is not a version of humanity that can counter and dismantle neoliberalism. But it's also not particularly appropriable by neoliberalism either. In fact, it more or less mirrors it, at least up to a point. It accepts the subject-object doubleness that defines the ontology of neoliberalism's *homo œconomicus*, but it refuses to be deployed in a way that might ever render subject and object as mutually exclusive formations. Or, it refuses the purification that fuels the neoliberal circle. When Beah describes himself as a human rights subject in juxtaposition to the human rights object that he was as a child soldier, he makes it too easy for neoliberalism to capitalize on his story. And when Agu succumbs to the Commandant's catachrestic objectification, he participates in the lawless conditions that justify future neoliberal intervention in the form of NGO's, economic development, and other humanitarian aid. But when Agu tells Amy that he is both "doing more terrible thing than twenty thousand men" *and* that he is his mother's son, that he is both murderer, rapist, devil *and* that he is loved, he articulates a complicated, muddled humanity that brings the neoliberal circle to a halt.

Embracing Objects

PUBLIC AND PRIVATE SPACE IN LITERARY LOS ANGELES

*We run into many things and these contacts, even if fleeting,
are of profound consequence. In dealing with, respecting, being
stopped by, creating, judging, buying, altering, placing, using
and disposing of goods, people are simultaneously manipulating and deploying the make-up of their own selves.*
—HARVEY MOLOTCH, *"Objects and the City"*

In its 2005 ruling in *Susette Kelo v. City of New London*, the Supreme
Court upheld contemporary eminent domain law, affirming local
government's right to take private property for future public use.
Predicated on the takings clause of the Fifth Amendment—"nor
shall private property be taken for public use, without just compensation"—eminent domain provides us parks, roads, libraries, light
rail transit, community centers, airports, and public utilities. With
the neoliberalization of urban planning and city governance over
the past several decades, it has also delivered business improvement
districts, gentrified waterfronts, revitalized city centers, pedestrian
malls, upgraded health care infrastructure, and other forms of public-private development that define the neoliberal city.[1] Facilitating
such public-private partnerships through eminent domain law is
legal because of an important court decision from 1954—*Berman
v. Parker*—that redefined public use as public purpose, a broader
standard that private development meets just as easily as public.
This expanded interpretation of the takings clause allows the state to
invoke eminent domain for any project furthering the public interest, even those that are privately owned and without substantial public access.

When Susette Kelo sued New London, Connecticut, to dispute its eminent domain seizure of her privately owned home, she was specifically challenging the indiscriminate breadth of public purpose. Rather than transferring Kelo's property to the state, the city intended to give her property to the privately controlled New London Development Corporation—not to build playgrounds and swimming pools, of course, but to attract multinational corporate investment in the region. In fact, the development company had already lined up Pfizer Pharmaceuticals as the anchoring tenant of a project promising 1,400 new jobs, a revitalized waterfront, and millions in new tax revenues—all benefits that the city believed were in the public interest.[2] By a five-to-four margin, the court agreed, ruling that the intended benefits of the city's redevelopment plan met the public use requirement in the takings clause.[3] While the public expressed near universal outrage[4] and bemoaned the end of individual private property rights,[5] legal scholars were entirely unsurprised[6] since *Berman*, and another case from 1984 (*Hawaii Housing Authority v. Midkiff*), had firmly established the broader notion of public purpose as legal precedent.[7]

Kelo's five-to-four decision broke along the court's ideological divide—Kennedy's swing vote supported the left-leaning majority of Stevens, Ginsburg, Breyer, and Souter while O'Connor's swing vote joined the right-leaning minority of Rehnquist, Scalia, and Thomas—but the majority and minority opinions muddle that divide in provocative ways.[8] By loosening private property rights so that government can intervene in projects that promote the greater public good, Stevens's majority opinion resonates with the left's general championing of the public over the private, the collective over the individual. And yet, the idea that public good flows from private corporate investment—the tendentious premise of the right's reflexive compulsion to downsize and privatize—would give many progressives pause. The majority opinion written by the court's left-leaning judges is also classically conservative to the extent that it upholds "a federalist vision of local democratic decision-making, judicial restraint, and due deference to elected officials," all values that the right frequently finds lacking in the left's supposedly "activist judges" (Gostin 11). On the other hand, the minority opinions from the conservative dissenters read like bleeding-heart pleas for the downtrodden.[9] In *Kelo*, the conservative justices are the activists, going so far as to invent new property rights (e.g., "Susette Kelo's 'right' to be free from the exercise of eminent domain") that do not actually exist in the Constitution (Mihaly 55). And yet, the minority opinion is also conventionally conservative to the extent that it treats private property as a natural and inviolable right.[10]

The *Kelo* decision is so interesting, then, because it takes two standard left-right narratives and renders them chiasmatic rather than parallel. In the first narrative, the left is socialist and communitarian while the right is libertarian and individualistic. *Kelo* reinforces this narrative as the left-leaning judges ruled in favor of government intervention at the expense of individual privacy. The second narrative holds that the left cares more about the marginalized, impoverished, and dispossessed while the right, preferring bootstraps to big government, supports free markets, private enterprise, and corporate investment. *Kelo* flips this narrative: the left ignores the plight of the little guy while the right decries corporate privatization.[11]

Andrew Stark has written an entire book about this disembedding of public and private values from conventional left-right political categories. He describes, for example, private gated communities that incorporate as cities to provide public services for their residents—services such as trash collection, building inspection, and security—even as those same gated communities keep out the riff-raff by privatizing those spaces and events that in most cities belong to the public (e.g., roads, parks, civic buildings, parades, and festivals). On the flip side, of course, cities struggling to finance basic public services turn to private enterprise; business improvement districts allow private companies to clean, landscape, and secure large chunks of the city's public space; and impoverished neighborhoods demand barricades and gates to secure their communities against drugs and crime (9–12). Stark identifies similar inconsistencies in the recent recession: "a bipartisan consensus supported the use of a private sphere mechanism, the mortgage market, to pursue public sphere goals of wealth transfer, and then a public sphere mechanism, redistribution by the state [i.e., the bank bailouts], to accomplish private market goals of risk transfer" (193). Rather than a clear and politically consistent divide between public and private values, then, Stark describes policy "clashes in which each side relies coequally on public and private values. It is just that both sets of values are capable of jointly supporting—depending on which side is applying them—the same two contrary policy courses" (192). As in *Kelo*, a case in which homeowners, corporations, and cities all embody both public and private interests depending on who's making what argument, Stark explains that these situations emerge because "[a]ny given unit—individual, family, market, civil society, or state—can lay claim, often at one and the same time, to both a more public and a more private character than any other" (199).

For Stark, all of this circularly inconsistent logic should give us good cheer; it's a sign of the productive overlap between otherwise polarized views on public and private space. "[B]ecause the two sides divide over the application of values that each side accepts," Stark explains, "we might be able to find in those mutually accepted values a path to principled compromise" (4). (Susette Kelo and Pfizer Pharmaceuticals both love private property. Maybe they can work it out!) Personally, I'm much less sanguine. What I see in these examples is the neoliberal circle's totalizing capture of the public-private rhetorical terrain. In the *Kelo* case, for instance, the majority's "greater good" decision furthers the ambitions of unbridled capital and reinforces local government's entrepreneurial function. Similarly, the minority's defense of individual property rights can be dressed up in the language of social justice, but it ultimately sanctions a market-friendly worldview. Eminent domain's collective land grab reduces individuals to parcels of land for the taking (neoliberalism's objectivizing mode); the fight against eminent domain champions individuals' free-market rights and liberties (neoliberalism's subjectivizing mode); and neoliberal principles triumph either way.

This is precisely how the neoliberal circle operates. On the one hand, the everyday workings of the neoliberal city blur and undermine any meaningful distinction between public and private space: the true nature of neoliberal space is its hybrid, public-private doubleness. On the other hand, neoliberalism encourages and deploys concepts, rhetoric, and discourse that represent public and private as purified, mutually exclusive domains. By capturing the entire public-private relationship, neoliberalism ensures that arguments favoring the public over the private *and* those favoring the private over the public will ultimately reinforce its core values. We see this quite clearly in *Kelo*: the law speaks as if a meaningful distinction exists between public and private property despite all evidence to the contrary.

In other words, it's telling that the majority opinion in *Kelo* does not complicate or challenge the distinction between public and private but instead simply affirms that *private* development meets the legal standard of *public* use. No one is changing the language of the Fifth Amendment to declare that private property shall not be taken "for public-private use, without just compensation." It's still public use (at least rhetorically and under the law), and the nearly universal outrage at the decision indicates that the general populace also shares the court's purified understanding of public and private space. Those who oppose *Kelo* from the left, for instance, see a state abdicating its public responsibilities and selling out to private corporations: Pfizer is not public; parks are public. Those who oppose it from the right, however, see a state flagrantly trouncing individual private property rights in the name of some socialistic public good: there is nothing potentially public about Susette Kelo's privately owned land.

But neoliberalism is not really committed to the private over and against the public, or vice versa. As David Harvey explains, neoliberalism is not merely a return to laissez-faire liberalism but is instead defined by the massive public intervention—in the form of "military, defence, police, and legal structures"—required "to guarantee ... the quality and integrity of money ... [and] the proper functioning of markets" (*Brief History* 2). Neoliberalism has not just united left and right "as partners in a quest for national economic growth," it has also united public and private in that same pursuit (Prasad 3). Consequently, neoliberalism's true commitment is to a blurry and indeterminate relationship between public and private space even as it plays each off the other to achieve its bottom-line goals. In other words, neoliberalism is more than happy to let the mutually exclusive debate between public and private values fester because both sides of that debate reinforce its broader public-private worldview.

Such circularity makes it quite difficult to critique our way out of these impasses. Whether we champion the public over the private, the private over the public, or the public-private itself, we're furthering neoliberal goals and values. As in the previous chapter, I hope to demonstrate here that the flexibility of literary form can innovate modes of value production that might help us think beyond the limitations imposed by this public-private iteration of the neoliberal circle. Thus, after more thoroughly exploring how the neoliberalization of the city created these complications, I will turn to two literary texts—Karen Yamashita's *Tropic of Orange* and Helena Viramontes's *Their Dogs Came with Them*—that in many ways give themselves over to neoliberalism's blurry treatment of the relationship between public and private space. Refusing to critique privatization by privileging the public, each looks to objects and the spatial relations they configure to imagine forms of social arrangement that supersede the mutual exclusivity of public and private. Without that purified logic, the neoliberal circle cannot spin, and we are left instead with assemblages of objects (humans included) that derive value from the unique set of connections and alliances they constellate at a given moment. Even as these assemblages are neither private nor public, they do still manage to be collective, social, political, and valuable. Agu's similes in *Beasts of No Nation*, which produced value out of the overlap of a given contingency, initiated this movement toward the object world, and here we'll see Yamashita and Viramontes articulate a thicker notion of object-based, constellated value.

Neoliberalized Cities

A fair number of scholars still view the neoliberalization of urban space as an inherently privatizing force that must be countered by a rejuvenated commitment to public space and communal ownership. Arguing that "public life is undermined by the growing phenomenon of private government," for example, such analyses of neoliberalism commit themselves to a generally stable, oppositional relationship between public and private domains (Kohn 2).[12] From this perspective, neoliberalism's tendency to muddle the public-private relation—through, for example, the promotion of public-private partnerships, business improvement districts, and development corporations—stands as a direct threat to a sanctified public domain: "by blurring the distinctions between private property and public space, [corporate producers of space] create a public that is narrowly prescribed" (Mitchell 141). Unsurprisingly, this dichotomous approach inevitably views neoliberalism's public-private partnerships as mere privatization, as "Trojan horses" of urban development that deliver free-market economics to unsuspecting communities and cities (Miraftab).[13] Thus, even as Hackworth acknowledges that public-private partnerships "operate in a murky economic context," he contends that scholarship must focus on their "role as an agent of capitalism" (76).

In adopting this mutually exclusive approach to the relation between public and private space, however, Hackworth runs up against the powerful neoliberal circle, which never met an oppositional stance it didn't love. As he readily acknowledges, leftist opposition to neoliberal privatization tends to "paradoxically produce a confusing set of commonalities with the neoliberal right" (195). When advocates for public space argue for a more decentralized state or individual social rights, for example, they echo neoliberalism's own commitments (194). Margit Mayer provides a whole laundry list of paradoxes that foil the earnest defender of public space: neoliberalism easily adopts the language of "civic engagement" that motivates many forms of resistance; organizing acts of resistance might actually manufacture consent; championing workers' rights might accidentally legitimize exploitative labor relationships; and saving buildings from demolition might prompt new forms of development and gentrification (109). Add to that already dispiriting list Arlene Dávila's thorough examination of gentrification in Spanish Harlem, which describes the limited power of cultural forms of resistance to neoliberalism. While deeply sympathetic to the power of cultural identity, Dávila ultimately concludes that "ethnic pride and Puerto Rican and Latino claims to El Barrio were many times at the heart of people's embracing neoliberal logics favoring the privatization and purchasing of place" (209).

Given these ambivalences, complexities, and contradictions, perhaps it would help to think about neoliberalism as a deeply ambivalent, complex, and contradictory process. Hackworth wants to portray a "murky economic context" as an explicit "agent of capitalism," but I say, why not more murk? In other words, maybe neoliberalism isn't just a privatizing force. Perhaps public-private partnerships aren't simply privatization in disguise and are instead complicated formations that exceed the descriptive capacity of those terms.[14] What if the rhetorical and discursive circularity of neoliberalism isn't a problem as much as it's just a logical extension of its complicated growth and development on the ground? Would the circularity disappear if our rhetoric more closely matched the reality? Perhaps neoliberalism's greatest strength is its ideological *in*consistency, its pragmatic ability to be whatever it needs to be in a given situation. Peck and Tickell certainly suggest as much when they explain:

> To a greater extent than many would have predicted, including ourselves, neoliberalism has demonstrated an ability to absorb or displace crisis tendencies, to ride—and capitalize upon—the very economic cycles and localized policy failures that it was complicit

in creating, and to erode the foundations upon which generalized or extralocal resistance might be constructed. The transformative potential—and consequent political durability—of neoliberalism has been repeatedly underestimated, and reports of its death correspondingly exaggerated. (400)

According to Leitner, Peck, and Sheppard, this remarkable adaptability extends even to those who oppose and resist neoliberalism. Not only have "contestations shaped the emergence, forms taken by, and hybridity of really existing neoliberalism," but "emergent neoliberalisms [also] coexist with contestations, each shaping while also being shaped by its others" (313). In these formulations, then, neoliberalism is hybrid, contingent, and fungible; it reinvents itself, compromises, and adapts. Its failures are its greatest successes, its weakness its greatest strength. Its "bipolar disorder" guarantees its "institutional promiscuity and ideological sprawl" (Peck 30).[15]

There is, of course, a risk in articulating "the ontology of neoliberalism" as "an evolving web of relays, routines, and relations" (34). For one, our perspective on neoliberalism might become so particular and localized, so caught up in the complex and constantly shifting spatial arrangements and alliances, that neoliberalism as a unified concept might slip away into the ever-changing flow of the urban landscape. This "empirical approach" to "actually existing neoliberalism" corrects the "ideological approach" to neoliberalism—which, "on the basis of theoretical faith," waits for neoliberalism's internal contradictions to produce its demise—but it also "run[s] the risk of underestimating the very same fiscal, institutional, and ideological 'constraints' that political economists may be prone to exaggerate" (Leitner, Peck, and Sheppard 317). In short, if neoliberalism is so diffuse that it's everything everywhere, then it stops functioning as a productive analytic category.

This is precisely the kind of criticism that some have leveled against a recent trend in urban studies that reimagines cities as assemblages.[16] Inspired by Deleuze and Guattari's thinking about territory as well as Latour's work on actor-networks, assemblage theorists tend to view urban spaces as so ongoingly contingent that they can only be understood as configurations of "practices and politics," not as deployments of ideology and power (McCann and Ward, xvi). Consequently, Brenner, Madden, and Wachsmuth worry that assemblage theory's "highly ambiguous" understanding of "political economy" and "the concept of capitalism itself" "amounts to a retreat from precisely those political positions and analytic vantage points that enable urban theory to engage in the project of critique" (123–124). Committed to a version of urban studies that "continue[s] to explore the prospects for the critique of capitalism that are immanent within contemporary sociospatial relations across places, territories, and scales," these critics do not want to see "the intellectual project of urban political economy" displaced by ontologically equivalent actants (133 and 125).

This strikes me as a reasonable concern. As I discuss in the introduction, too much vital immanence can certainly undermine analysis. At the same time, however, I'd also suggest that assemblage theory's greatest contribution to thinking the city might just be its reluctance to critique, immanently or otherwise. After all, avoiding critique is not tantamount to the abdication of political economy.[17] (Latour, for example, is very clear that ontologically equivalent actants should still be understood as strong or weak, powerful or impotent, just or unjust, and so on.) We can presumably still think and talk about the commodification of urban space, economic and cultural power discrepancies, displacement and gentrification, without committing ourselves to the dream that the proper analysis and critique of the system's core contradictions will eventually lead to its downfall. An analysis that starts with ontology, that embraces objects, does not necessarily accept the status quo, nor does it preclude claims about inequality and injustice. It simply prevents us from presuming the answers beforehand. And as long as we can still generate claims about inequality, power, and justice, then I think that the intellectual space we gain by abandoning critique in favor of a more thorough investigation of our ontological ground is well worth whatever "analytic vantage point" we might have to abandon. To give increased attention to objects, to the way objects constitute space and configure quasi-publics, is not to ignore political economy but to refocus our attention on an overlooked feature of it. The human is not precluded; it just loses its centrality and is instead more thoroughly integrated into and affected by the physical environment.[18]

Such is the message of Harvey Molotch, who notes that objects "call forth a particular behavioral repertoire that becomes intrinsic to worlds of sociality and production" (68). Suggesting that this attention to objects in no way undermines political analysis, Ash Amin wants to replace the urban humanist belief that good cities are born from increased interaction between strangers in public space with a form of civic responsibility produced by our ongoing imbrication with the materiality of space itself:

> [T]he situation [of being in space] itself—characterized by many bodies and things placed in close juxtaposition, many temporalities, fixities and flows tangled together, many rhythms and repetitions of use, many visible and hidden patterns of ordering, many domestications of time, orientation, and flow, many framings of architecture, infrastructure, and landscape—profoundly shapes human conduct, including the balance between civic and noncivic behavior and belief. Accordingly, practices of recognition of the commons, curiosity for others, or civic responsibility may have more to do with the disciplines of presence and regulations in a plural space and with the everyday negotiation of ordered multiplicity (human and non-human) than has been hitherto recognized (635–636).

True, this might not be the politics that will defeat neoliberal capitalism, but there is a politics here, and, most importantly for our purposes at the moment, it's a spatial politics that precedes the purified distinction between public and private space that is so integral to the spinning of the neoliberal circle and the broader spread of neoliberal capital. It's a politics that refuses to privilege the public over the private, or vice versa, and that instead articulates specific configurations of interaction and value out of the unique gravities that different objects bring to specific spaces.

Thus, rather than an ownership notion of space—that is, an approach that reinforces a rigid divide between public and private—we might try to think space *prior to* its designation as public or private. This is what Nicholas Blomley attempts in *Unsettling the City*: an approach to urban space that questions "the ways in which property's ontological and political diversity has been rendered invisible" by a notion of space that only operates according to the public-private divide. For Blomley (moving us now toward this chapter's literary treatment of these concerns), property and space are intimately connected to narrative and its world-shaping capacity (50–51). The ownership model, of course, tells an overdetermined narrative in which "the contingent politics of social relations disappear" (51). (We might think of this as the urban studies version of the tautological-teleological power Slaughter ascribes to the *Bildungsroman* in the context of human rights law.) But the

increasingly convoluted relationship between public and private
has prompted several legal scholars to tell a different story, to think
about property and the space it comprises as an ongoing interpretive process rather than as an object of exclusively public or private ownership. Laura Underkuffler, for example, concludes that
we must "envision change *as a part of* the idea of property," arguing that property does not automatically confer ownership rights
(48). Instead, property "simply describes, or mediates, the tensions
between individual interests and collective goals, which are resolved
and re-resolved as circumstances warrant" (54). Carol Rose takes
this idea even further when she theorizes property as "persuasion,"
as an ongoing cultural narrative that we construct and interpret to
configure and justify the relations, rules, and conditions that a given
property regime institutes. Or as Blomley puts it, property and its
spaces are cultural because they are "not a static, pregiven entity, but
depend on a continual, active 'doing'" (*Unsettling* xvi).

In what follows, I will examine how Yamashita's and Viramontes's
texts reimagine the social production of space, thinking beyond the
mutually exclusive divide between public and private to ultimately
foil the neoliberal circle. Both novels do so in the context of the Los
Angeles freeway system, an interlocking maze of public infrastructure built for both public and private good, at both public and private expense. It's precisely in those muddled spaces produced by the
urban freeway that both novelists manage to think space differently.
Demonstrating a general reluctance to critique, *Tropic of Orange*, in
both content and form, teaches us how to read the global networks of
neoliberal capital outside the purified divide between public and private space. *Their Dogs Came with Them* is also highly networked, but
it ultimately emphasizes the ontology of specific, concrete objects
that similarly escape the mutual exclusivity of public-private thinking. For Viramontes, the novel itself is one such object, and so *Dogs*
actually uses narrative form as the foundation for rethinking property and the spaces it configures. Taken together, both novels achieve
a public-private simultaneity that might, on the surface, echo a kind
of neoliberal, public-private partnership. The difference, however, is
that the novels never allow public and private to stand in mutual
opposition to each other, which, as I explained above, is key to the
functioning of the neoliberal circle. They both, in effect, think space
prior to its division into public and private, thereby escaping the
neoliberal circle's tendentious purification of that relation.

As in the previous chapter on human rights, the unique episte-mologies made possible by specific literary forms make this shared project possible. In *Tropic of Orange*, I will focus on the orange itself as a trope that never turns, and in *Dogs* I will highlight a narra-tive structure configured through concrete objects internal to the text. While these novels make compelling arguments about the muddled value of public and private space in a neoliberal age, I also hope that my attention to their formal innovations will further distinguish these works from their postmodern forebears. In their common embrace of objects, *Tropic* and *Dogs* extend early twenty-first-century literature's investment in non-human presence. While the previous chapter highlighted the contingent presence of the prior configuration—which simile exploited to produce the human's subject-object doubleness—here the physicality of actually existing objects establishes a public-private doubleness resistant to critique, and to neoliberal capture as well.

Rhythm and Networks

Tropic of Orange begins in the Mexican vacation home of Gabriel Balboa, an East Los Angeles Chicano with a successful career as a journalist. Gabriel views his private property romantically, as an opportunity to own a little part of his *patria*, the country where his grandfather supposedly fought alongside Pancho Villa. His owner-ship impulse extends beyond land and culture, however, to include the Tropic of Cancer itself, which happens to run directly across his property "like a good metaphor" (5). To complement the walls demarcating his private plot of land, Gabriel plants two orange trees on either side of his property to highlight the segment of the Tropic that belongs to him as well.

As the narrator makes clear, however, these trees, imported from an orange grove in Riverside, California, which was itself imported from Brazil in 1873, do not belong in Mexico any more than Gabriel does (11). Unsurprisingly, one of the trees quickly dies, and Gabriel's orchard of non-native species soon becomes a fetid botanical waste-land. Animals breach the walls of his house nightly, his cows over-turn their fences, and the roses abandon their lattice in favor of a banana tree. Unlike his neighbor Doña Maria, whose apparently authentic connection to the land yields acres of thick, lush corn,

Gabriel imposes artificial notions of property and possession that the natural orders of the earth will not abide. Mexico clearly does not care for Gabriel's lines, walls, fences, or lattice.

And yet, *Tropic of Orange* is not a story about nature's inevitable recrudescence in the face of private property's arbitrary and artificial demarcations. Refusing to reinforce the mutually exclusive relationship between public and private by using nature to critique private property, Yamashita instead turns her attention to the unique forms property takes in an era of neoliberal globalization, in a world where ownership and possession are as fluid as the identities of the individuals populating it.[19] Put differently, the novel is called *Tropic of Orange*, not *Tropic of Cancer*, for a reason, and it's not just because Henry Miller got there first. The natural boundary marked by the sun's relation to the earth's axial tilt might supersede whatever private property rights Gabriel claims through the laws of real estate, but the Tropic of Cancer's natural laws are themselves trumped by a different boundary line—the tropic of orange—which ultimately governs the novel's content and shapes its form.

Initially, the tropic of orange maps perfectly onto the Tropic of Cancer. It's formed when an orange on one of Gabriel's trees releases a thin filament extending "in both directions . . . east across the highway and west toward the ocean and beyond" (12). The orange itself is a product of globalization: global warming prompts an early blossom that some over-industrious African bees pollinate to yield the "small growing globe" that slowly ripens into an orange. Given its anomalous origins, Rafaela, the housekeeper living in the vacation house while Gabriel works in Los Angeles, views the fruit as "an aberrant orange," "an orange that should not have been" (11). Already we can see, then, that Gabriel's normatively constructed sense of private property is not being overthrown by the natural order of things. Rather, unsettling the boundaries of both nature and private property, the tropic of orange's aberrance overthrows the very distinction between the natural and the normative. As soon as the orange falls from the tree and rolls "just beyond the frontiers of Gabriel's property to a neutral place between ownership and the highway," it's clear that the tropic of orange marks a new boundary, a new production of space (neither wholly public nor wholly private) in an age of globalization (13). Defining a spatial arrangement "beyond . . . property," the tropic of orange demarcates a "neutral place" beyond natural and normative boundaries, beyond the mutually exclusive relationship between public and private space.

This neutral space moves and shifts across the region once Arcangel, a mythical character who travels from Mexico to Los Angeles over the course of the novel, plucks the orange off the ground, puts it in his suitcase, and starts walking. As flexible and transitory as global capital itself (the orange crosses the border on "waves of floating paper money ... a graceful movement of free capital ... carried across by hidden and cheap labor"), the orange's motion through space radically warps and reconfigures the landscape of Mexico and southern California (200). The walls and fences on Gabriel's property are stretched and bent (70 and 142); his neighbor's house is farther away than it used to be (119); "curved space" in South Central LA allows a young gang member to dodge a bullet (86); a sushi bar appears "to tilt and sag with an indescribable elasticity" (129); and the Harbor Freeway stretches into the surrounding environs of Los Angeles (189–190). As some very proprietary gang members realize, the orange's skewing of the urban grid threatens everyone's territorial claims. "How come a little crew with a bit-time two-block piece of the action now's got a three-mile fiefdom," they complain (188). The Crips and Bloods consult the Thomas Guide and hire a lawyer to draw up a contract all "corporate-like," but the tropic of orange won't behave (187). As Buzzworm, a self-appointed community organizer who prides himself on the close contact he maintains with the *gente*, observes, the accelerated warping of space and usurping of private property is "beyond our control" (188). Not because a nefarious neoliberal puppet-master manipulates space and property according to his dastardly whim, but because a strange street performer thousands of miles away found an orange and put it in his suitcase. *Tropic of Orange*, in other words, doesn't identify conspiracies of capital as much as it does contingencies of capital, suggesting that such contingencies are activated by unassuming objects like oranges.[20]

The novel not only emphasizes the spaces those contingencies reconfigure, but it also highlights the affiliations and assemblies they produce. On the bus journey north, for example, the orange demarcates a safe space for travelers, protecting them from a villainous organ smuggler. The orange prevents the smuggler from approaching the passengers, but when Rafaela "skid[s] perilously south," the man attacks. Once on the bus, however, the tropic of

orange "reassert[s] itself" (185–186). As the orange's journey continues, it attracts a "great multitude," ultimately delivering hordes of
immigrants into the heart of Los Angeles (211). The global south
"crush[es] itself into every pocket and crevice, filling a northern
vacuum with its cultural conflicts, political disruption, romantic
language, with its one hundred years of solitude and its tropical
sadness" (170–171).

But the orange constitutes only one of the novel's object-oriented
assemblages. Concurrent to the orange's northward journey, a homologous neutral space emerges in Los Angeles when the driver of a red
Porsche passes out and swerves into a propane truck that promptly
jackknifes and explodes, backing up traffic on the Harbor Freeway.
At the end of the traffic jam a second propane truck explodes when a
semi-truck crashes into it, creating "[a]n entire mile of cars trapped
between two dead semis, not to mention two craters, fires, and the
debris from the blasts" (112). Like the tropic of orange, this space is a
product of globalization: the driver of the Porsche passes out when
he bites into another aberrant orange, this one belonging to a drug
syndicate that packs oranges with cocaine to move across the border; and the space itself is bracketed by one of globalization's most
powerful engines—semi-trucks and the containers they carry. Also
like the tropic of orange, this is a space beyond property that produces new assemblies of people: as the owners abandon their cars,
homeless people flood out of a roadside encampment which, like the
orange's "place between ownership and the highway," is sandwiched
between a retaining wall and the interstate; next, standard notions
of value disappear as "Porsches, Corvettes, Jaguars, and Miatas [are]
suddenly relegated to the status of sitting or powder rooms" while
spacious vehicles like vans, camper trailers, and Volvos become
more valuable; finally, the contents of these revalued vehicles are lib-
erated and redistributed among the new occupants of the mile-long
space between.

Most notably, and again as we saw with the tropic of orange, these
events are contingent and their value is neutral: the narrator neither
champions nor condemns the homeless occupation of the freeway.
Thus, when one character romantically wonders "if the storming of
the Bastille could not be compared to the storming of this mile-long
abandoned car lot," the narrator promptly squelches such politicized
speculation with a terse, "Perhaps not" (122). This is not a radical
revolution or a violent overthrowing of the established order; the

homeless do not erect a communitarian utopia or viciously critique private property. Instead, just as the orange-oriented immigrants are "filling a northern vacuum," the car-oriented homeless are simply "life fill[ing] a vacuum, reorganizing itself in predictable and unpredictable ways" (121).[21] To be sure, the assemblage is political: it alters the occupation of space, redefines the value of commodities, and shifts the power dynamics of the urban landscape. But its political value doesn't fit any predetermined ideological categories; it can't be compared to the storming of the Bastille. Instead, like water spreading over an uneven space, the motion of the homeless is determined by the objects that they do or do not run into.

The orange, the abandoned cars, and the life that accretes around them pose an interpretive dilemma. What value—political or otherwise should we ascribe to such neutrally contingent events? How can we integrate these assemblages into our understanding of the world without overdetermining their significance? How exactly should we read the orange, and by extension, how should we read *Tropic of Orange*? The character in the novel who best answers these questions is Manzanar Murakami, a Japanese American named for the Manzanar Concentration Camp in southern California where he was born during World War II. Manzanar was once an esteemed surgeon, but he intentionally walked away from that life, choosing instead to live among the homeless and spend his days atop a freeway overpass "conducting" the traffic. Fascinated by the "complexity of human adventure over lines of transit" (56), Manzanar sees the totality of the land's spatio-temporal configurations simultaneously:

> On the surface, the complexity of layers should drown an ordinary person, but ordinary persons never bother to notice, never bother to notice the prehistoric grid of plant and fauna and human behavior, nor the historic grid of land usage and property, the great overlays of transport—sidewalks, bicycle paths, roads, freeways, systems of transit both ground and air, a thousand natural and man-made divisions, variations both dynamic and stagnant, patterns and connections by every conceivable definition from the distribution of wealth to race, from patterns of climate to the curious blueprint of the skies.

From this "great theory of maps . . . spread in visible and audible layers," Manzanar chooses, "sometimes purposefully, sometimes at whim, to create the great mind of music" (57).

Manzanar thus takes the neoliberal city's contradictions and differences—the immigrants from the global south, the homeless population of Los Angeles, the urban renewal that destroys private residences, the freeways that fracture urban space—and shapes them into a symphonic composition that articulates the city's constant spatial production. As the narrator observes, "[S]tanding there, he bore and raised each note, joined them, united families, created a community, a great society, an entire civilization of sound" (35). As with the contingent contradictions that he reads, his symphonic compositions comprise objects and events indiscriminately. Thus, when the semi-trucks explode on the freeway, he conducts his way through it, incorporating "the metallic crash," "the snap of delicate necks, the squish of flesh and blood" into his score (55). And later, when the homeless flood the freeway, he rhythmically integrates dozens of car alarms into "the thudder of helicopters, the sirens of fire trucks, the commentary of newscasters, the opening and slamming of car doors, hoods, trunks, and glove compartments, and the general chatter of festive shopping and looting" (122).[22]

Like the container trucks "moving here and there, back and forth," rendering "[n]othing ... more or less important," the value of Manzanar's composition has little to do with its content. There is content, but its value is constellated, not represented. Snapped necks and squishy blood are equivalent to semi-truck wheels, a motorcycle's exhaust, the footsteps of a pedestrian, the homeless, cocaine-laced oranges, etc. For Manzanar all these objects are just the assorted components of the ever-expanding layers of the world: "there are maps and there are maps and there are maps," and he can "see all of them at once" (56). Manzanar's maps, in other words, are not reductive, manageable representations of space; they aren't substitutive metaphors. Rather, because "[e]verything [has] its own sound," they incorporate the stuff of the world into the ongoing production of space. In turn, Manzanar's rhythms render property, whether private or public, an entirely protean phenomenon. Notions of private and public have no inherent value beyond the differential role they play in the ongoing score of spatial production. In this formulation, what Henri Lefebvre might call "rhythm's right to difference" replaces the right to both public and private space (384 and 396). And it's in this right to difference, this right to assemble the world and constellate meaning, that something like politics can occur. Even as this approach precludes the application of predetermined political value and ideological belief (that's why it rejects metaphor), it still allows us to assemble constellations that can enact specific change in the world. In the novel, for instance, Buzzworm commits to the long-term process of "gente-fication," in part by encouraging his community to connect with their neighborhood trees (83). Similarly, Arcangel uses the orange to form a coalition that will support him in his wrestling match against SUPERNAFTA. Their battle has obvious political implications, but it's premised on Arcangel's neutral observation that "[t]here is only changing" (258).

Manzanar's refusal to ideologically value content beforehand, along with his insistence on the ontological equivalence of his symphony's components, give Yamashita the jump on neoliberalism. Of course, there's also something quite risky about modeling one's production of value on the neutral "here and there, back and forth" of container trucks. In doing so, Yamashita must embrace the destructive power of neoliberalism—its obliteration of the distinction between public and private, for example—as the ground for her own reconfiguration of spatial value. Because she takes the value-neutral contingencies of neoliberalism seriously *and* refuses the bait of a mutually exclusive approach to public and private space, however, Yamashita reduces neoliberalism itself to just another ontologically equivalent chunk of Manzanar's score. It's precisely because she refuses to predetermine the politics of the neoliberal city that she might intervene significantly in it.

But Yamashita still has work to do. A world in which "nothing is more or less important" still requires a theory of meaning and value, and Yamashita finds it in the form of the network. In particular, she finds it in Manzanar's score, in his networked configuration of the spatio-temporal differences among discrete objects. If Manzanar achieves this through his conducting, Yamashita does so through the figure of the orange. In a sense, the orange is a figure that refuses figuration, a tropic that never tropes.[23] The Tropic of Cancer might run through Gabriel's property "like a good metaphor," but the tropic of orange supplants the Tropic of Cancer's metaphorical logic, replacing it with a trope that refuses to turn.[24] In place of metaphor's representational logic that turns the figure toward the world, Yamashita's orange forges connections and accrues affiliations. It's a magnet moving through space and time. Because its value is a function of its interconnections, however, it's also not an allegory. It doesn't maintain a consistent meaning as it moves across the continent, and it lacks representational value. The orange's relevant feature is not its symbolic meaning but its connectivity. And that connectivity, emptied of metaphorical value, frees the orange to serve as a nodal point in a broader network of constellated and inevitably political value. Thus, over the course of the novel the orange links Mexican immigrants, the Los Angeles homeless, the entire global south, transnational trade, colonialism, and drug trafficking, along with Brazil, O. J. Simpson, California, Tropicana, and so on. The value of the orange cannot be reduced to metaphor, and it cannot be absorbed into flow. Its value is simply the accumulating and shifting totality of its affiliations, alliances, and associations, and that's precisely what makes it politically valuable. Unsurprisingly for a novel published in 1997, Yamashita links this mode of constellated value production to the Internet. A place in which "everything could be inferred from everything" (245), the net is also a picture that gets "larger and larger," a story that we can follow or abandon, but never stop (249). In this formulation, we see the ongoing motion of rhythm (we can't ever stop) tempered by the presence of a story, a story much like *Tropic of Orange*, comprising increasingly interconnected objects, events, and populations, the values of which derive from the new forms of agency, power, and force born of connectedness itself.

As Doreen Massey observes, property and the space it occupies are "constructed out of the multiplicity of social relations across all spatial scales, from the global reach of finance and telecommunications, through the geography of the tentacles of national political power, to the social relations within the town, the settlement, the household and the workplace" (4). Such complexity, the novel suggests, requires a quicker, more agile literary mode, a more nimble, rhythmic rendering of spatial value that can think beyond the purified distinction between public and private. Recognizing that "*for better or worse*, populations in one part of the world are inevitably affected by events in another," this is precisely what *Tropic of Orange* offers (Adams 268, my emphasis). Most importantly, the novel's reluctance to critique, along with its openness to the contingencies of the object world and the assemblages they produce, allow the novel to get the better of global neoliberalism, effectively reducing it to just another formation or configuration to be incorporated into the networked score. It's the difference between, on the one hand, feeling compelled to dismantle the rhythms of neoliberalism, and on the other, incorporating neoliberalism into the larger rhythm of spatial production.

Stories and Objects

Interconnection also emerges as a dominant theme in Helena Viramontes's *Their Dogs Came with Them*, a novel that separately traces the lives of three young Angeleno women over the course of two days in 1970. Tranquilina, the thirty-three-year-old daughter of Mama and Papa Tomás, ministers to the downtrodden of East Los Angeles in her family's storefront church. Turtle, an eighteen-year-old AWOL from her neighborhood gang, drifts around town while her brother Luis and the rest of the McBride Street Boys search for her. The youngest, Ermila, a fifteen-year-old living with her strict grandparents, is still in high school and a bit out of her depth dating Alfonso, an older member of the McBride Street Boys gang, while beating back advances from her cousin Nacho visiting from Mexico. Most of the novel's action takes place in 1970 under the shadow of the fictional Quarantine Authority which has implemented checkpoints and curfews for the residents of East LA, claiming that a rabies outbreak necessitates a heightened level of containment. The narrative also includes frequent flashbacks to 1960, when the freeways were run through East Los Angeles communities, and to other chronologically indistinct moments in the characters' pasts as well. Setting and other context clues help readers determine the chronology of events specific to each of the three women, but there is not enough context to ascertain the chronological relation of events across the three separate plot strands. Even in the 1970 present of the novel, the characters cross paths, but readers don't necessarily know it at the time. (For example, when Turtle appears in a chapter focalized through Tranquilina, Turtle is described as a male "cholo," and we only see her silhouette [83].) Like East LA itself—a neighborhood bulldozed by the Dodgers in the 1950s, fractured by highways in the 1960s, and quarantined by police in 1970—the characters are isolated from each other, severed from a communal public sphere.[25]

Clearly, the novel's narrative construction dramatizes the problem of connection, requiring the committed reader to resolve its narrative fractures and fragments by identifying the links among Tranquilina, Turtle, and Ermila. In foregrounding the challenge of interconnection in this way, Viramontes implicitly critiques the injustices that various state and corporate powers have inflicted on East Los Angeles residents. But I also think that Viramontes's project is bigger than mere critique. (As I will highlight, many portions of the novel are quite skeptical about the potency of a critical Chicano politics.) For Viramontes, the question of whether and how things connect to each other opens onto much broader questions about the nature of property and the relationship between public and private space. After all, specific formulations of public and private property ground the conditions of possibility for human connection, community formation, and even, I will suggest, reading literature.

My discussion of the novel will highlight three notable contributions Viramontes makes to current thinking about the relationship between public and private space. First, Viramontes does not hesitate to defend the value of private property, a defense that counters a reflexive privileging of public collectivity that is common to much Chicano literary and cultural production. The marginalized and downtrodden need more private property, Viramontes contends, and dreams of a precolonial past, border-transcending connections to the earth, or ethnic community don't provide that. Second, despite that defense of private property, Viramontes also highlights its contingency and artifice, in turn reformulating the private as deeply imbricated with the public. Finally, by associating the mutually constitutive production of public and private space with storytelling, Viramontes deploys the novel itself as a model for new social forms and spaces irreducible to the merely public or the merely private. Whereas *Tropic of Orange* articulated those new forms and spaces through the network, Viramontes moves more concertedly toward the ontology of objects themselves, taking the mutually *constitutive* relationship between public and private as the defining feature of things in the world. For Viramontes, understanding this dual nature of an object's ontology is precisely what makes politics—in the form of human, communal, and narrative connection—possible.

First, let's look at Viramontes's defense of private property, which pivots on a crucial distinction that emerges early in the novel between earthquakes and earthmovers. The novel begins in the kitchen of a house on First Street in East Los Angeles, where the owner, an elderly Mexican woman named Chavela, reluctantly prepares to move. Chavela is relocating against her will, forced to make way for the freeway slowly branching its way across Los Angeles in the middle of the century. The year is 1960, and as she packs, Chavela chats with her five-year-old neighbor, Ermila, telling her about a previous displacement she suffered seventy-seven years earlier when an earthquake in Mexico "cracked my tierra firme, mi país" and made everyone "crazy from having the earth pulled out right from under them."[26] Instructing Ermila on "how it feels to have no solid tierra under you," Chavela explains that the earthquake made her a "coiled earthworm without the earth" no longer able to live like the "bursting red hibiscus bushes that bloom lush and rich as only ancient deep-rooted hibiscus shrubs can do" (7). As the bulldozers rip up roots both literal and figurative to make way for the freeway, Chavela firmly impresses the inevitable truth of displacement—whether by "earthquakes or earthmovers"—upon Ermila (8).

Ten years later in 1970, after the freeways have "amputated the streets into stumped dead ends" and severed neighbors and neighborhoods from each other, Chavela's prediction comes true: Ermila stands in her living room, "the epicenter beneath her," "waiting for the quaking to cease" (77). But this shaking is not from an earthquake, and it's not from bulldozers. It's from the Quarantine Authority's helicopters which are circling over Ermila's house, shooting stray dogs in their fight against rabies. These parallel acts separated by a decade—the initial displacement and land grab that undermines private property rights and the ensuing containment that violates community connection and public space—are clearly related: the quarantine is a metaphor of containment that articulates the long-term effects of the freeway construction's forced displacements. The initial loss of private property to the state reorganizes public and private space in a way that reinforces state control over already marginalized populations.[27] But even though Viramontes figures the Quarantine Authority's helicopted intrusions as an earthquake, and even though Chavela sees "earthquakes or earthmovers" as equivalent causes of displacement, it's also worth noting that no actual earthquakes occur in the novel's historical present. Instead, distinguishing between "earthquakes and earthmovers" is crucial for disentangling the novel's arguments about public and private space. If you suffer an earthquake, you blame God. But if you lose your house to eminent domain, or if you are required to stay indoors after a certain hour each night, you blame the state. Chavela claims that the earthquake "just wasn't right," the identical phrase that Ermila uses when remembering how Turtle's brother Luis once pulled a lizard from "a mound of bulldozed earth" and snipped off its tail: "It's not right, she knew, even if they witnessed a miracle" (6). But an earthquake isn't right in a very different way than de-tailing lizards, or taking someone's private property, isn't right.

Much in *Dogs* suggests that Viramontes is trying to shift the discourse of Chicano politics away from the injustice of earthquakes
and toward the injustice of earthmovers. In emphasizing the threat
that the state poses to private property and possession, *Dogs* dis-
tances itself from three major leitmotifs of Chicano politics, each
of which privileges public community over private ownership: faith,
the land, and *El Movimiento*. Rejecting her parents' spiritual commitments, Tranquilina most clearly articulates the novel's spurning
of a faith-based worldview. Tranquilina used to share Mama's belief
in boundary-transcending miracles—including the family mythol-
ogy that Papa, invested with ancient Aztec powers, can fly—but after
a harrowing rape, Tranquilina actively doubts her mother's stories
(46). Additionally, she increasingly feels that Mama's singular focus
on spiritual salvation ignores the more material injustices of the here
and now. Believing that "everything happened here on these sidewalks or muddy swamps of vacant lots or in deep back alleys, not up
in the heavens of God," "Tranquilina could no longer make that leap
of faith" (34). Rather than wasting her time on the spiritual lives of
the dispossessed, Tranquilina focuses on their immediate worldly
needs, as we see when she drives around town searching for Ben, one
of her mentally disturbed parishioners. This worldly search is conspicuously juxtaposed to Mama's spiritual project when Tranquilina
passes Mama preaching on a street corner in the driving rain, believing that "the drenching downpour was her consecration, the hail
itself a swell of zealous applause" (216). In fact, Mama so fervently
believes that "the divine and the real [are] one and the same" (216),
that she and her family "[do] not belong to this world" (203), that
when Papa eventually dies in the 1970-present of the novel, Mama
doesn't even seem to notice (98).

Prior to her rape, Tranquilina shared her parents' belief in
miracles, but she grounded that belief in the land, not in the sky.
Nevertheless, because this aspect of Tranquilina's worldliness
evinces the same naïveté that defines Mama's more heavenly orientation, the novel remains equally skeptical. Like Chavela's earthworms
and hibiscus bushes, Tranquilina grows up with a deep affinity for
the land: "Barely six, she had escaped under houses where tempera-
tures dropped ten degrees less and where the earth, for some reason,
had the consistency of gold talc. . . . Her fidelity to earth, or better,
her understanding of miracles came . . . from spent silence in the
dankness and dampness of unvisited spaces." Modeling a collective

logic that erases all spatial and social distinction, the earth grounds Tranquilina's belief that "boundaries didn't exist between her life" and the lives of those to whom she ministers (93). This of course makes her an exemplary evangelical, but her rape proves that this borderless communal logic grounded in the soil is too broad. In Texas the same earth that connects her in Christian communion is forever tainted by her assailant who, smelling of "fermented earth" (213), pushes her down "face first, her mouth grit-full of soil" (31), rapes her, and then flees, making "deep prints on the earth as he ran" (215). Just like the lizard that loses its earth only to lose its tail, Tranquilina not only loses her connection to the earth, but she also loses a piece of herself.[28] The earth, of course, does not cause the rape, but it clearly betrays her and reveals the limited utility of her fidelity to it. After all, the rapist does not believe in boundaries between people either, and neither does Luis, torturer of lizards. Thus, the rapist's attack on her individual sovereignty, on the private property of her self, is just the darker flip side of Tranquilina's own desire to erase individual boundaries in the name of a transcendent spiritual collectivity.

As the language of borders and boundaries throughout these scenes suggests, Mama's faith, Chavela's "tierra firme," and Tranquilina's earth resonate not only spiritually, but also politically. Not surprisingly, then, *Dogs* is similarly suspicious of a tendency in Chicano politics—specifically, the *Movimiento* politics of the 1960s—to assert a historical continuity between past and present that supersedes the colonial and imperial privatization of space that has occurred in the interim. Such a belief in the history-transcending continuity of earth clearly aligns with Chicano nationalism's commitment to a more public organization of space and more collective forms of belonging and possession. But if Tranquilina's "fidelity to earth" fails for a lack of distinction and differentiation, so too do such expansive political goals. Indeed, even though the past and its peoples are present throughout the novel, their salutary effects are consistently undermined. In the novel's opening scene, for instance, Ermila stacks "large, empty Ohio Blue Tip matchboxes . . . into a pyramid on the kitchen table" (6). Working with only right angles, this pyramid surely evokes an Aztec past, which is why we might be surprised that Chavela's ensuing search for a match to light her cigarette leaves the pyramid scattered across the table (6). But the novel consistently dismantles such classic conceits of Chicano culture and politics. As a teenager, for instance, Ermila and her friends attend Garfield High and participate in the blowouts, but only "for the fun of it" and definitely not "to demand a better education [or] declare Chicano power" (50). Ben, the mentally disturbed parishioner Tranquilina searches for in the rain, scurries past the MEChA table at USC because "he resist[s] being lifted up into a gathering mass of swirling political storms" (118); and he only wears a brown beret because a cute co-ed gave it to him, not because of his "Chicano alma and corazón" (117). The narrator even mocks a mural of "La Virgen de Guadalupe floating above the great pyramids" because the Chicano storeowner who requested the mural "seemed prouder of being Mexican than the Mexicans" (71). As with Mama's belief in miracles and Tranquilina's belief in the earth, Chicano politics' commitment to an imagined past free of divisive difference and distinction is impotent in the face of real-life material dispossession. The residents of East Los Angeles do not require spiritual, rhetorical, or historical salvation; they need property, not earth.

And yet, a great deal of skepticism also surrounds those characters who take up the capitalist mantle of hard work, personal responsibility, and private property. Although the narrator clearly respects and honors these characters, the successful outcome of their private enterprise is far from certain. After all, Ermila's ennobling survey of workers walking to catch the early bus—women "carr[ying] with them the weight of a family or two or three," wearing "the poker face of their responsibility"; laborers with a "profound belief in hard work," a "determination as blinding as the California sun," and a "sense of commitment" grounded in the "belie[f] [that] they held the world together with the glue of their endless sweat . . . carry[ing] everything needed to assist them in holding up the operations of commerce"—bathetically ends with the pessimistic conclusion: "We're fucked" (176–177). Which is perhaps simply to say, just as Mama's otherworldly approach to material dispossession only gets her wet, an exclusively private approach to material dispossession will only get you on an early commuter bus to the garment district.

Splitting the difference between Mama's miraculous approach to loss and these workers' materialist approach, *Dogs* introduces the notion of story as a form of private property. The connection is made in a scene from 1970 when Ermila and her teenybopper friends, each of whom has suffered some form of loss, hang out after school and engage in what the narrator calls "talkstory": Mousie, whose brother returned in pieces from Vietnam, "cross-stitch[es] him together" with daily personal anecdotes (61); Ermila, deserted by her parents when she was still a baby, conjures stories about a personal history she can't actually remember; Rini, whose father abandoned her, gossips about the letters and gifts he sends her in the mail; and Lollie, whose family has been shamed by a relative's poor business decisions, imagines a glamorous life in which she is married to Peter Tork, the guitarist from the Monkees. Describing these stories as "[t]he only things they cherished, their only private property," the narrator explains how the girls, through story, "design escape routes, rehearse their breakout and hurl their futures over the roadblocks of their marooned existence" (61–62). To be sure, Viramontes is not naïvely suggesting that stories can somehow redress actual material loss. As the narrator says of Turtle's condition, for example, "[I]f-onlys were just as empty as her pockets" (220). What Viramontes is doing, however, is drawing on the form of stories to develop a notion of property that is stronger than Mama's miracles but weaker and more contingent than strict material ownership.

For Viramontes, stories are somewhere in between; they are simultaneously material and immaterial, private and public. Ben, the mentally disturbed parishioner Tranquilina searches for in the rain, is one of the few characters who clearly understands this feature of stories. In a telling flashback to his childhood, for instance, Ben's sister Ana joins him on the roof of their apartment and tries to convince him that the stars are God's eyes watching over him. But Ana's faith-based discourse strikes Ben as ridiculous. For Ben, the roof is his "one private space," not a site of heavenly transcendence (273). Ben thus requires a more tangible discourse than Ana's rhetoric can provide: "Nothing but the wrong words came out of her lips in explanation. . . . She didn't know how to convert the mysteries into something solid or organize the Scrabble-game alphabet into make-sense words. Faith couldn't be sculptured for Ben" (274). Although Ana doesn't make the connection, when she observes moments later that "wind need[s] resistance to make its invisibility felt," we receive the explanation for the failure of Ana's story: her wholly spiritual language lacks the materiality required to substantiate the invisibility of belief.

Other stories in the novel, however, do have enough material presence to make the invisible visible but not so much material presence that they become overdetermined and static. Such stories are, as the novel repeatedly suggests, like dust. In fact, several stories in the novel are quite literally born of dust: "out of the pulverizing dust of heaved-up dirt and cement," for example, Turtle conjures an image of Chavela making ice-cold lemonade on the front porch of her now vacant house (27); and Mousie's stories about her brother are prompted by his cremation—his reduction to dust—which she fears has left his soul too immaterial for admission to heaven. Like the material resistance that makes the wind's invisibility felt, the dust in such stories—the residual trace of things lost—provides the physical material for creating new stories.

This is in contrast to other textual formations—specifically the graffiti tags that the McBride Street Boys paint on the blank slates of freeway on-ramps and overpasses—which display a false confidence in their enduring materiality: "Tonight the McBride Homeboys would . . . record their names, solidify their bond, to proclaim eternal allegiance to one another so that in twenty, thirty years from tonight, their dried cemented names would harden like sentimental fossils of a former time" (163–164). Of course, the opposite happens and such overdetermined assertions of property value are eventually reduced to dust: "the tags would crack from the earthquakes, the weight of vehicles, the force of muscular tree roots, from the trampling of passersby, become as faded as ancient engravings, as old as the concrete itself, as cold and clammy as a morgue table. . . . Not even concrete engravings would guarantee immortality" (164). Just as Ana's story about God's eyes lacks sufficient visible material to give it value and meaning for Ben, the gang fails to appreciate the inevitable erosion of value and meaning that time's invisibility will wreak on their tags.

Consistent with this notion of story, the novel highlights the inevitable contingency of many of the stories it contains: the details of Mama's stories "change with every telling" (38) and Tranquilina cannot reconstruct them (47); the "bits and pieces" of story that Lollie's parents tell about their sordid family history "refuse to come together" (185); and Ben, the novel's only writer, becomes angry at "the uncertainty of it all," at the fact that "[s]tories, like life, had no logical conclusion" (123). Not surprisingly, the contingency of story is echoed in the novel by the contingency of property: Ermila's boyfriend's mother requires "a two-year layaway plan" to buy a new couch (301); and when Turtle is offered a job at a corner convenience store, it's on the condition that she arrive promptly at seven the following morning. Like a story with "no logical conclusion," however, Turtle's layaway period proves disastrous. After accepting a ride from Santos, a fellow gang member, she is chased by police helicopters, smokes a joint laced with PCP, stabs Ermila's cousin Nacho with a screwdriver, and dies from police fire, all before she can get to work the next morning. Clearly, the inevitable fact of contingency, the intrusion of the invisible into the visible, requires a different form of possession and ownership that balances the known and the unknown, the owned and the unowned.

Two concluding scenes give us a sense of what this new form of possession might look like. First, when one of the McBride Street Boys mumbles something in Ermila's window about the gang's plans to kill her cousin Nacho in revenge for his assault on Ermila's boyfriend Alfonso, Ermila is left with a host of unanswerable questions but quickly concludes that there is "[n]o time to deliberate cause and effect because she had to get to the bus depot as soon as possible to warn Nacho" (316). Instead of logic, plans, and causality, "[t]he only plan she had was to run, run her sneakers like she did in gym class while reciting the Hail Mary, for the rhythm of it, the chant consuming her instead of the agony" (317). This qualification, "for the rhythm of it," is crucial (and it should also remind us of Manzanar's rhythmic productions of value in *Tropic*). Inhabiting the living sliver of time between past and future, known and unknown, Ermila relies neither on rigid plans nor immaterial belief, but instead on the material properties of text—on the cadence of words fueling the motion of her body, not on the representational content of those words.

Second, after Turtle kills Nacho and the police kill Turtle, another moment of heightened uncertainty arises in the text. The police, unsure of "who the victims were, who the perpetrators were," turn their guns on Tranquilina and order her not to move. But Tranquilina refuses and instead hurls her concluding words— "*We'rrrre not doggggs!*"—at the police. Tranquilina's words "crash into one another" like "a speeding blur of raging language," and like Ermila's Hail Marys, she takes possession of language, mobilizing herself forward into a future that remains contingent and unknown (324). Consequently, the novel ends with Tranquilina "summon[ing] the stories of Papa and Mama's miraculous escape," "fill[ing] up with the embrace of ancestral spirits," and "riding the currents of the wilding wind . . . beyond the borders, past the cesarean scars of the earth, out to limitless space where everything was possible

if she believed" (325). Tranquilina's belief differs significantly from
Mama's mystical belief in miracles, however, because Tranquilina
here believes in the simultaneous materiality and open-ended
contingency—"the limitless space where everything was possible"—
of language and story.[29] Tranquilina replaces miracles with stories.

Here, then, is Viramontes's story-based reconception of private
property. In both cases, Ermila's and Tranquilina's possession of language models a form of ownership that is neither exclusively private
nor exclusively public but is instead a complicated mixture of the
two. You own the story that you have written—its value primarily
a function of its physical presence rather than its representational
content. But you are also always open to the contingent possibilities
beyond the already written story, and in this way you never truly
achieve full private possession of the story. This is a model that sees
stories and property as a blend of stability and contingency, known
and unknown. Property in the novel is not a discretely bound object
that either is or is not owned but is instead a dusty materiality hovering at the interface of past and future. Thus, it can't be reduced
to the mutually exclusive logic of public and private. The orange
functioned similarly in *Tropic*, but here it's language and story that
mediates that line between the knowable past that we can privately
possess and the unknowable future that belongs publicly to all. And
to have possession of *that*, to think of property rights as the right to
the interface between past and future, private and public, known
and unknown, is to adopt an understanding of property that simultaneously values the affective attachment we feel toward the private
and admits that the line between private and public is always dusty.

This is where the question of narrative interconnection comes
back into play. The novel's disparate plot strands and perforated
chronology are not just formal embodiments of its characters' displacements and containments, but they also transform the novel
itself into an object of contingent ownership for its readers. That is,
the uncertainty that Viramontes builds into *Dogs* requires that readers too inhabit that interface between known and unknown, owned
and unowned, as they make their way through the text. Scattered
like dust across the novel, a collection of unassuming objects—a
white package, a dog's teats, a brown beret, a paperback novel, and
an empty apricot crate—draw readers into that interface, provisionally assisting them in unifying the three plots unfolding over two
days in 1970.

For example, Turtle, penniless on a Friday morning, prowls the neighborhood looking for food when she sees two unnamed women cross the street at "Hastings and First" (27), "cradling a package wrapped in white paper" (28). Readers have no way of knowing that these women are Tranquilina and Mama until, in the following chapter, the pair retrieves some meat, "wrapped tightly in white butcher paper," that they will serve after that evening's church service. We readers first meet Ben at this same church service, carrying "a paperback novel clamped under his arm" (88) and "dressed in dirty blue jeans and brown beret" (89), but it is not the first time we have seen him. The same morning that Turtle crosses paths with Tranquilina and Mama, she also sees "a Che Guevara wannabe" reading "a brick of a paperback" and wearing "a brown beret flopped on his head" (17). Without these overlaps, sutured together with white butcher paper, a paperback novel, and a brown beret, Turtle's and Tranquilina's plots would remain hopelessly isolated from each other.

Similarly, Turtle's and Ermila's plots come together through the teats of a dead dog and an apricot crate. Shortly after she passes Tranquilina and Mama, Turtle sees "a bloodied dog's carcass" with "purple droopy teats," a victim of the previous night's rabies crackdown (29). Later in the novel, Ermila witnesses this same dog's death from her living-room window: "Above the woven arteries of freeways, a copter's searchlight swept over the roadblocks to catch a lone stray running out of the edge of light. The bitch zigzagged across the pavement of First Street, its underbelly droopy with nursing nipples" (77). This information helps us connect Ermila's and Turtle's plots: Ermila witnesses the dog's bloody execution and Turtle discovers the remains the next morning. That same morning, as Ermila readies herself in the bathroom, Nacho sneaks outside and pushes an empty apricot crate beneath the bathroom window to spy on his cousin (183). Later that night, as Turtle hops from cemetery to cemetery looking for a place to sleep, she walks past Ermila's house and offhandedly notes "a wooden fruit crate leaning under the bathroom window for no apparent reason" (221). Later that night, this is the same crate that Ermila finds conveniently placed, "as if someone had anticipated her escape," as she sneaks out of the house in her attempt to save Nacho from the McBride Street Boys' violence (317). Readers are thus only able to correlate Ermila's and Turtle's actions with the help of the dog and the crate.

Such objects inhabit that fine line where the known and unknown, the owned and the unowned, of the story meet—that constantly moving domain from which story simultaneously establishes a past that can be possessed and reaches forward into the unknown beyond of "limitless possibility." As such, these objects embody a unique form of private-public ownership that connects the individual to the collective, the private to the public, in a way that allows each to coexist without compromising the other. Characters own these objects or make them their own, but they also come out of nowhere and exist for "no apparent reason," language that clearly highlights their contingent and story-like aspect as well. Readers also take possession of these objects, but only to put them to a similarly mixed private-public use. We use them to produce our own knowledge and understanding of the novel; but we also use them to assemble connections and communities that would otherwise not exist because of the novel's tendency to isolate its characters in their own private worlds. The act of reading, in effect, produces a narrative commons that nevertheless depends on the more limited and private ownership of specific material objects. These objects and the use to which readers put them reconfigure the kind of community that the intrusive freeways and the Quarantine Authority have destroyed in East Los Angeles. In effect, these objects embody and inhabit space prior to its purified division into public and private, and in that way, they also foil the logic of the neoliberal circle.

But that's not all. These objects don't just connect otherwise isolated plot strands; they do so from an ambiguous place within the novel's own narrative temporality. Specifically, when all of the plot threads are laid atop one another, it appears that either Ermila's plot is missing a day, or Turtle's plot has an extra day. This discrepancy effectively makes the novel itself ontologically homologous to the apricot crate, the dog's droopy teats, and all the other objects that remain simultaneously stable and contingent, known and unknown, throughout the text.

It takes some explaining, but here's how the novel either adds or subtracts a day from itself: We know that Thursday afternoon, Ermila and her friends hang out after school eating onion rings and drinking RC (55). Ermila arrives home late, has an awkward sexual encounter with her cousin Nacho, and witnesses the helicopter chasing the dog with an "underbelly droopy with nursing nipples" (77). On Friday morning she wakes up, receives Rini's phone call, meets with her friends to plot the vandalism of Jan's car, performs said vandalism, takes a bus to the beach to meet Alfonso, encounters Nacho instead, takes a bus back home, waits in line at a Quarantine Authority checkpoint, and goes to bed. At 1:42 a.m. she learns of Nacho's impending death, runs to the bus stop to warn him, but arrives too late. Ermila's plot thus consists of two days, Thursday and Friday. Nacho's plot, which is wrapped up in Ermila's, corroborates this. On Friday morning, he wakes up from his Thursday night encounter with Ermila, spies on her in the bathroom, finds her ID in her jeans pocket while folding the laundry and realizes she will need it to get past the Quarantine Authority later that night. So that evening he drives his van to the beach to accost Ermila, but Alfonso, Ermila's boyfriend, is already there waiting for her. Nacho beats up Alfonso, drives home, and makes his way to the bus station because he knows that the McBride Street Boys will seek prompt retribution for his assault on one of their own. In Ermila's and Nacho's plots, therefore, Nacho dies on Friday night. (Figure 1)

The temporal incongruity emerges when we lay Turtle's and Tranquilina's plots on top of Ermila's and Nacho's. If Turtle sees the dead dog the morning after Ermila sees it killed—the same morning Turtle crosses paths with Tranquilina and Mama—then their plots must begin on Friday morning because Ermila witnesses the dog's death on Thursday night. Thus, on Friday morning, Tranquilina and Mama go to their church and spend all day preparing food for that evening's service and meal. Meanwhile, we witness a passing encounter between a homeless woman and a gang member (83). That homeless woman eventually stumbles upon the church service, goes inside, eats dinner, and is saved by Mama even as Papa Tomás dies. Later, we realize that the gang member the homeless woman encountered was Turtle (217), and after their paths cross we follow Turtle as she spends the night jumping from cemetery to cemetery looking for a place to sleep. On the Friday night that Nacho is killed in the Ermila-Nacho plot, therefore, Tranquilina is taking care of her dead father at the church and Turtle is sleeping in cemeteries. But Turtle is supposed to be stabbing Nacho and Tranquilina is supposed to be coming to his aid.

In Turtle's and Tranquilina's plots, however, those events don't occur until Saturday night. After Papa Tomás dies on Friday night, the homeless woman returns to the church the next day, Saturday, and cooks with Tranquilina who is waiting for Ana to arrive so they

Thursday		Friday				
Ermila and friends hang out after school	Ermila returns home late and sees helicopters shoot droopy-teated dog	Nacho spies on Ermila before she leaves the house	Ermila skips school to meet with friends	Ermila and friends vandalize Jan's car	Ermila goes to beach to meet boyfriend Alfonso but finds Nacho waiting for her instead	Ermila returns home, is alerted at 1:42 a.m. of the threat to Nacho's life, and arrives at the bus station too late to save him

FIGURE 1 *Ermila's and Nacho's Timeline*

can go out searching for her brother Ben. It is during this Saturday night search that Tranquilina coincidentally runs into Nacho at the bus station just before he is killed. This Saturday night is then also the same night that Turtle receives her job offer, is chased by a helicopter while driving with Santos, and then eventually tracks down and kills Nacho.[30] (Figure 2)

Depending on how you look at it, then, either a day is missing from Ermila's plot or an extra day intrudes into Turtle's and Tranquilina's plots. So when I claimed that the droopy-teated dog establishes a coincidence between Ermila's and Turtle's plots, it both does and does not do that. Because Nacho's death occurs Friday night in one plot and Saturday night in another, the dead dog both does and does not get shot Thursday night and lie dead on the street Friday morning. At first, it's an object that aligns Ermila's and Turtle's Friday mornings, but then as more of the plot unfolds, that alignment jumps the tracks. To the extent that such objects both do and do not belong to a specifically grounded time and place, they are, in their very ontological constitution, simultaneously available and unavailable to us as readers. The objects, like the novel itself, inhabit that dusty interface between what we know and what we don't know, between what we can own and that which can never be owned.[31]

Identifying this public-private doubleness as the constitutive core of objects, including the novel itself, Viramontes imagines an ontological dimension—perhaps the dimension of story—that exceeds the mutually exclusive treatment of public and private that drives this particular neoliberal circle. It's a dimension in which, as in the novel itself, there are "no logical conclusion[s]" (123); "actions no longer need motives" (263); and all the component parts "refuse to come together" (185). Yamashita envisions a similar dimension—that neutral space "between ownership and the freeway"—where networks grow and ultimately replace outmoded notions of public and private. Viramontes pushes even further, however, when she suggests that objects themselves embody a public-private ambivalence that in turn facilitates connection between people, and between people and the world. In this scenario, the relevant feature of an object in the world is not its ideological value, its incarnation of either private or public principles. Instead, objects become a means for creating assemblages in which such concepts have lost their conventional meaning and significance. It is, admittedly, a world that looks a lot like neoliberalism, since neoliberalism too thrives by muddling the relationship

Friday		Saturday		
Turtle sees dead dog that Ermila saw killed the previous evening	Turtle passes homeless woman who later attends church service	Turtle spends night sleeping in a series of cemeteries	Turtle receives job offer at 6:50 p.m.	Turtle and Santos in police chase at 11:30 p.m.	Turtle kills Nacho at bus station; police kill Turtle
Tranq. and Mama pass Turtle on street while collecting groceries for evening church service		homeless woman attends evening church service; Papa Tomás dies shortly after	Tranq. cooks with homeless woman while waiting for Ana to arrive after work	Tranq. and Ana drive all night looking for Ben	Tranq. has passing encounter with Nacho just before Turtle kills him

FIGURE 2 *Turtle's and Tranquilina's Timeline*

between public and private. The difference, however, is that neoliberalism also requires purified notions of public and private that it can play off each other while Viramontes suggests that objects are already defined and constituted by a core public-private hybridity that makes neoliberalism's oscillations obsolete.[32] Using the ontology of story to complicate the ontology of objects, Viramontes escapes the neoliberal circle without falling into the trap of critique.

Objectifying Race

OR, WHAT AFRICAN AMERICAN LITERATURE IS

Where the demotic masquerades as the democratic and popu-
lism distorts politics, there is good reason to ask whether an
authentic liberatory moment might not reside in postcolonial
peoples and minority ethnic groups being just as selfish, igno-
rant, right-wing and conservative as everybody else.

—PAUL GILROY, *"Fragments for a History of Black Vernacular*
Neoliberalism"

Soon after arriving at Columbia University to begin his freshman year, Macon Detornay, a white hip-hopper from Boston and the protagonist of Adam Mansbach's *Angry Black White Boy,* lands a job as a New York City cab driver and promptly begins robbing the obnoxiously racist white people who are his fares. Macon hopes that his efforts will dispel the dominant culture's reflexive criminaliza-tion of blackness, that being mugged by a white person will shift his victims' racial assumptions. This racial Robin-Hooding backfires, however, when Macon learns that his whiteness is invisible to his victims, all of whom have told the police that they were mugged by a black cabbie. Setting the record straight, Macon instructs his next victim to look closely at his face and report Macon's whiteness to the police. This leads to his quick arrest, but news of a young white man robbing other whites to "give back" to blacks so captures the nation's imagination that Macon becomes an instant media star. With his newfound celebrity he launches the Race Traitor Project, which aims to "make whiteness visible" by encouraging whites to acknowledge their privilege through a national Day of Apology, a day for whites to apologize to blacks in whatever way they see fit (191).

While promoting the Race Traitor Project on a live radio show, a former Freedom Rider calls in to suggest that Macon's work undermines the success of the civil rights movement. When Macon divides the world into white and black, he merely repeats the very segregated thinking this movement veteran fought so hard against. "You're doing more harm than you know," he tells Macon (193). Macon is respectful and sympathetic, but he also pushes back, contending that the civil rights movement "changed laws, not hearts"; its victories have just made "it easier for white people to act like racism is a problem that got solved back in the sixties." Arguing that racism is alive and well today, just more insidious, Macon wonders "where people with [the ex-Freedom Rider's] kind of courage . . . should direct it today" (194). In effect, Macon is stuck between two equally true yet contradictory propositions: the civil rights movement vastly improved the living conditions of blacks in the United States; and yet, the living conditions of blacks in the United States continue to be deplorable. How much credit, then, should the civil rights movement be given?[1] Are its gains canceled out by the ensuing triumph of colorblindness as national ideology, an ideology born out of the movement's explicit focus on equal rights before the law?[2] Are contemporary forms of racism continuous with racisms of the past, or should today's black politics sever its connections to the legacy of the civil rights movement?[3] In short, should we or should we not still pay attention to race; and if we should, what kind of attention does it deserve?

Racial Neoliberalism

Since the 1960s, broad transformations—cultural, economic, and political—have eroded the potency of the civil rights movement's social justice discourse. With the end of segregation, the widespread implementation of affirmative action, and the 1967 repeal of the nation's remaining anti-miscegenation laws, the post–civil rights era triggered substantial upward mobility for many middle and upper-class blacks. At the same time, however, urban gentrification, deindustrialization, the decline of the welfare state, and the rise of finance capitalism disproportionately affected African Americans for the worse. And yet, as Madhu Dubey has observed, such monumental structural transformations—the early social and economic upheavals of a nascent neoliberalism—also ensured that "race [would] no longer form the singular axial principle of all political projects

affecting African-Americans" (*Signs* 30). As economic marginalization and social immobility became decreasingly isomorphic to black
particularity, the role of race and racism in the emerging neoliberal order grew increasingly vexed. Claiming that our contemporary
thinking about these topics "is now severely deficient," for example,
Howard Winant notes that even as "we are pretty sure that racism
continues to exist, indeed flourish, we are less than certain about
what it means today" ("Racism" 757).

Such uncertainty stems not only from the increased visibility
of African American success, but also from the entrenchment of
civil rights liberalism as the dominant model of racial justice. In
the 1960s, blacks fighting for core liberal principles—individual
liberty and equal rights before the law—were a nationally polar-
izing force. Today, when the *legal* barriers to liberty and equality
have been destroyed, such claims feel obvious. No one with any
power and influence in the contemporary socio-cultural main-
stream is against racial liberty and equality; antiracism is a given.
This is a problem, however, because even as racism and racial disparity persist, the givenness of antiracism makes it easy to ignore
race altogether. In its place, economics emerges as the primary
social determinant; policy experts and talking heads recommend
affirmative action for the poor, not for the racialized. The triumph
of neoliberal market rationality confirms that racial inequality is
no longer a problem. It couldn't be; it's irrational. Capitalism has
no reason to be racist; it's bad for the bottom line (Lentin and
Titley 168).

Although neoliberalism seems to divest itself of racism and all
other forms of racial thinking, however, we would of course be wrong
not to see it as a racial project. As Lisa Duggan explains, "During
every phase, the construction of neoliberal politics and policy in the
U.S. has relied on identity and cultural politics. The politics of race,
both overt and covert, have been particularly central to the entire
project" (xii). Neoliberalism does not necessarily articulate a unified
racial agenda, but it does deploy an array of vacillating arguments
about race and racism that ultimately serve its economic interests.
We saw something similar with neoliberalism's relationship to both
human rights and the question of public and private space: depending on the context, seemingly contradictory claims will be mustered
to ensure the reinforcement of market values. Again, Duggan puts
it quite well:

Because . . . the economy and the interests of business can not really be abstracted from race and gender relations, from sexuality or from other cleavages in the body politic, neoliberalism has assembled its projects and interests from the field of issues saturated with race, with gender, with sex. . . . The alliances and issues have changed over time and have differed from place to place. . . . In order to facilitate the flow of money up the economic hierarchy, neoliberal politicians have constructed complex and shifting alliances, issue by issue and location by location—always in contexts shaped by the meanings and effects of race, gender, sexuality, and other markers of difference. These alliances are not simply opportunistic, and the issues not merely epiphenomenal or secondary to the underlying reality of the more solid and real economic goals, but rather, the economic goals have been (must be) formulated *in terms of* the range of political and cultural meanings that shape the social body in a particular time and place. (xvi)

In particular, neoliberal discourse draws heavily on the rhetoric of colorblindness and multicultural diversity, even though those two concepts seem contradictory, with the former asking us to ignore race and the latter directing our attention to it. Despite their divergent treatment of race, however, colorblindness and diversity do share a common effect: the privatization of racism. Whether we ignore or celebrate racial difference, racism can be explained away as the private prejudices of individual bigots. Whether you defend a bigot's first amendment right to his bigotry or, like Oprah Winfrey, you think that the bigots can't die fast enough, racism is shunted to the private sphere where it won't interfere with capital accumulation.[4] Intentional racism is certainly counterproductive to the neoliberal project, but as Sara Ahmed explains, "By saying racism is over there—'look, there it is! in the located body of the racist'—other forms of racism remain unnamed. We might even say that the desire for racism is an articulation of a wider unnamed racism, that accumulates force by not being named, or by operating under the sign of civility" ("Liberal").[5] Intentional racism might be bad for the bottom line, but such privatization of racism also makes it easier to ignore the structural racisms on which a solid bottom line so frequently depends.

Because discourses of colorblindness and diversity are equally good at privatizing racism and leaving structural racism "unnamed," neoliberals are equally comfortable speaking both languages, just never at the same time. Even as neoliberalism "classifies human activity and relationships" according to these terms, it also "actively obscures" the relation between them (Duggan 3). It doesn't make any sense to say that we should simultaneously ignore and highlight racial difference. But structured as a purified neoliberal circle, colorblindness and diversity unwittingly work together to serve neoliberalism's interests. Even more problematically, as we've seen in previous neoliberal circles, the critiques of each position reinforce the neoliberal status quo as well. As long as racial discourse treats race as something that we either should or should not see, something that we should or should not pay attention to, the logics *and critiques* of colorblindness and diversity conveniently reinforce neoliberal goals.

On one side, for instance, those critical of colorblindness charge that neoliberalism's full-throated commitment to the invisibility of race prevents us from talking about race and racism as we properly should. Specifically, the individualization of race and racism (this would be neoliberalism's subjectivizing move) makes it difficult to identify and redress structural racisms born of deep histories, complex institutions, and impersonal social formations. Thus, Pauline Lipman notes that even as "neoliberals frame the post-Civil rights era as 'colorblind,' relieving the state and the general public of responsibility for ameliorating racial inequality and oppression," "neoliberal restructuring has intensified structural inequality based on race" (12–13). Similarly, David Theo Goldberg describes colorblindness, or "racelessness," as "the neoliberal attempt to go beyond—without (fully) coming to terms with—racial histories and their accompanying racist inequities and iniquities; to mediate the racially classed and gendered distinctions to which those histories have given rise without reference to the racial terms of those distinctions; to transform, via the negating dialectic of denial and ignoring, racially marked social orders into racially erased ones" (*Racial State* 221).[6]

At the same time, Goldberg and other critics of colorblindness acknowledge neoliberalism's correlative investment in diversity (its objectivizing move), portraying it as a managed, meaningless approach to racial difference. Thus Goldberg describes the racist state's "superficial celebration of multiculturalism," while Lentin and Titley condemn the way "diversity provides a gently unifying, cost-free form of political commitment attuned to the mediated imaginaries of consumer societies" (183). Distinguishing between the politics of diversity (which merely "valorizes difference") and diversity politics (which "establishes the stratified relations of differences to social legitimacy and individual possibility"), Lentin and Titley want us to keep paying attention to race, just in a smarter way (181). They envision a form of multiculturalism that foregrounds structural imbalances, uneven development, and power discrepancies, thereby inciting meaningful change and provoking new, revolutionary modes of thought. In the face of actually existing racial disparity, we shouldn't be duped by the politics of diversity.

Someone like Walter Benn Michaels would agree that diversity is just a distracting tool of neoliberal expedience, but for him the proper response is not a smarter, more rigorous form of racial thinking. Rather, for Michaels neoliberalism accentuates racial difference, champions diversity and multiculturalism, to distract us from the only difference that really matters: economic difference.[7] Michaels's conclusions about neoliberal diversity thus differ significantly from Goldberg's conclusions about neoliberal colorblindness and its low-risk, for-profit forms of diversity. For Goldberg (as for Lentin and Titley and many other critics of colorblindness), neoliberalized racial thinking prevents us from pursuing the more potent forms of racial thinking that true racial justice requires. But for Michaels neoliberal racial thinking doesn't demand better, more structurally focused racial thinking. Instead, it requires the end of racial thinking altogether and the renewal of class-based thinking.[8] Regardless of where and how we orient our ideas about race, we're always making a mistake as far as Michaels is concerned.

Adolph Reed Jr.'s discussion of race in post-Katrina New Orleans clarifies the point. Reed thoroughly acknowledges that "advantages and disadvantages, social benefits and harms, opportunities and constraints, and everyday civic regard are distributed in American society asymmetrically, in a general pattern in which black people tend to be represented in significant disproportion on the more precarious, more exploited, less privileged end of the distribution" ("Color Line" 289–290). And yet, he also asserts:

> [T]he discourse of racism or racial disparity ... does not help either
> to identify the precise mechanisms through which even many decid-
> edly racialized inequalities are produced or to guide the development

of strategies for challenging them. Analytically, its taxonomic impulse abstracts away from the discrete characteristics of relations and phenomena to extract whichever of their features can be construed as generically racial. To that extent it privileges category over content, labeling over description. (290)

In other words, even when scholars attend properly to diversity politics and resist the frivolous distractions of the politics of diversity, they are still, according to Reed and Michaels, contributing to the neoliberal status quo. The "taxonomic impulse" of any racial justice project can't escape the representational logic that neoliberalism so easily co-opts. And that's why neoliberalism's double commitment to colorblindness and diversity can't be resisted by simply paying attention to race in smarter, better ways—because doing so still runs the risk of reinforcing neoliberalism.[9]

But if it's true that Goldberg's race-attentive critique of colorblindness reinforces neoliberalism in the way that Michaels and Reed describe, then it's also true that Michaels's and Reed's critique of diversity and all other forms of racial thinking might very well reinforce neoliberalism in the way that Goldberg describes. In particular, their implicit promotion of colorblindness dangerously reproduces individualized economic subjects whose interests align with neoliberal values. Taken together, Goldberg's critiques of colorblindness and Michaels's critiques of diversity look a lot like the "complex and shifting alliances" that Duggan's "neoliberal politicians have constructed . . . issue by issue and location by location" (xvi). Together they embody the same kind of argumentative vacillation between colorblindness and diversity that continues to make contemporary racial thinking a deeply vexing problem. This neoliberal circle, which reveals not only the complicities of colorblindness and diversity but also the potential complicities of *critiques* of colorblindness and diversity, makes it extremely difficult to answer the core question of Mansbach's *Angry Black White Boy*, which is also one of the core questions of our post–civil rights neoliberal moment: "It's easy to fight Bull Connor, because he's siccing German shepherds on people. But what do we do about your next-door neighbor, who only says the n-word in his mind? And who just so happens to be a loan officer at the neighborhood bank, and president of the local P.T.A.?" (194).

Literary Racialism

The flip side of that question is equally important even if asking it brings some progressive sacred cows a bit closer to slaughter. To paraphrase Paul Gilroy: What would happen if we took seriously those minority populations who embrace neoliberal values as a viable means of self-improvement and empowerment? Linking the minority/ immigrant "ideology of hustling, and getting by" to neoliberalism's discourse of self-interested, aspirational uplift (26), Gilroy maintains that we shouldn't be surprised that black Atlantic populations are "inclined . . . towards the solutions proffered by neoliberal styles of thought" (35). Most importantly, even as Gilroy clearly loathes neoliberal capitalism, he insists that we must not view those who buy into neoliberalism as dupes. Rather, the real dupes are those who absurdly suppose that black social justice politics should somehow immunize blacks against the seductions of neoliberalism. Thus Gilroy condemns those who would believe "that the trans-national formation of black Atlantic culture is somehow permanently sanctified by its historic roots in the suffering of slaves." Instead, Gilroy asserts, "That noble history offers no prophylaxis against the selfish ecstasy of neoliberal norms" (35). To be clear, Gilroy is not capitulating to neoliberalism. He is not proposing that the achieved economic self-interests of minorities stand as "the measure of redemption from racial hierarchy," but he does wonder "whether it is only a vestigial sentimentality that prevents us from being able to accede to [the achieved economic self-interests of minorities] as a new index of Britain's integration (36). Which is perhaps simply to ask, where is the mode of racial thinking, the approach to racial justice, that can account for Gilroy's black-vernacular neoliberals without critiquing them, without suggesting that they are wrong, misguided, or blind? Gilroy describes a racialized subject who is resoundingly *not* a multicultural subject, a subject whose race links him to the "ideology of hustling" even as his race must not interfere with his economic self-interests. This subject is neither colorblind nor diverse, neither a dupe of neoliberalism nor particularly hostile to it. But where is the theory of race that will provide the space to think meaningfully about this subject?

Unfortunately, the "taxonomic impulse" of contemporary racial thinking—the preoccupation with racial representation common among advocates and critics of colorblindness and diversity

alike—makes it difficult to imagine Gilroy's subject of "black vernacular neoliberalism." Kenneth Warren makes a similar point
in his reading of Michael Thomas's *Man Gone Down*, a novel that
forthrightly asks, "In the absence of a broad movement for social justice, just how do the personal victories and defeats of those with petit
bourgeois aspirations matter in the broadest sense?" (131). Warren
helps us see that African American literary history has also been
dominated by a taxonomic impulse, by the desire to treat literary
representation as an index of the race, even though not all literature written by African Americans can be instrumentalized in that
way. Contending that the particular legal and political concerns of
the civil rights era are no longer germane to contemporary black
literature, for example, Warren suggests that we should reserve
the moniker "African American Literature" for that body of texts
defined by the struggle against Jim Crow segregation in the middle
of the twentieth century. Which is to say, for Warren, things have
changed: "a political and social analysis centered on demonstrating
that current inequalities are simply more subtle attempts to reestablish the terms of racial hierarchy that existed for much of the twentieth century misunderstands both the nature of the previous regime
and the defining elements of the current one" (5). To the extent that
Warren's controversial claims aim to critique and correct, however,
he too ultimately engages his titular question—"*What Was African
American Literature*"—in terms of representational visibility. He
argues that contemporary fiction needn't (and frequently doesn't)
worry so much about making race visible, but this crucial observation doesn't really tell us what it should do, or is doing, instead. One
of the goals of this chapter is to better answer that question.

Warren *is* helpful, however, in identifying not just the juridi-
cal reasons that black-authored contemporary fiction struggles to
represent race coherently, but also the literary-aesthetic causes of
its representational equivocations. Most notably, Warren suggests
that postmodernism's textual turn made it increasingly difficult for
black authors to capture adequately the new socioeconomic realities that defined post–civil rights black experience. Dubey makes
a similar point, noting that poststructuralism's critique of identity
politics in the waning decades of the twentieth century left black
postmodern literature at an impasse between essentialist and antiessentialist conceptions of racial identity and community (*Signs* 5).
Unable to reconcile the political imperative to see race as real and

the intellectual desire to see it as a construct, black postmodernism struggled to reestablish the post–civil rights parameters of African American-ness. At most, Dubey suggests, some authors strike a balance between aesthetics and politics, constructivism and essentialism, that prevents each from undermining the other.[10]

As Macon learns in *Angry Black White Boy*, however, achieving such balance is never easy, and it still makes race and racism a matter of representational visibility. Macon recognizes, for example, that postmodernism's cultural and aesthetic developments make it difficult for him and his generation to engage in overt political struggle: "the ambiguity & dislocation / of the postmodern moment & my left shoulder / prevent me from holding signs aloft // voice too hoarse from rhyming into broken mics to sing along // we shall over sle-e-eep" (167). Macon's sense that postmodernism vitiates politics is echoed in his critique of a professor—a self-described "Academic Gangsta"—who describes hip-hop artists as "postmodern actors interrogating the dislocation of organic sensibilities." "We don't demand responsibility or predicate realism from the characters Arnold Schwarzenegger plays," the professor argues, so "[w]hy can't we just enjoy the fiction." To which Macon replies, "It's easy to celebrate hip hop if you call it fiction, Professor. But if it's fiction, nobody has to answer for anything—not rappers or the people responsible for the problems rap addresses" (101). And yet, as a young white man, Macon requires that same "ambiguity & dislocation," that same recourse to "fiction," to establish himself as a race leader on the national stage. As he quickly learns, however, he also needs a stable notion of racial identity for the Race Traitor Project to affect conditions on the ground in any significant way. Thus, the novel asks, will this "wigger [gone] poststructuralist" (49) ever "[have] to answer for anything" (101)?

Macon hopes that the force of his hip-hop aesthetic will make this question moot. Predicated on the mixing—or as Macon frequently calls it, the miscegenation—of cultural artifacts into new forms, hip-hop builds an aesthetic out of the contradictions that emerge from its juxtaposed constitutive parts. Such cultural productions created from spare parts require an audience that can think allusively, metonymically, and as Mansbach emphasizes, quickly. Distinguishing hip-hop from other collage aesthetics, for instance, Mansbach highlights hip-hop's "hot," "audacious," and "frenetic" energy, an energy exemplified in "the way train pieces and rhymes and musical productions became fodder for what was to come next at the exact moment of their completion, went from innovative to passé in the blink of an eye" ("On Lit Hop"). But when Macon translates this aesthetic of contradicted mixing into the political realm—balancing art and politics, constructed and essential notions of race—his audience can't keep up. They can't bear the contradictions. Thus, instead of healing the community, the Day of Apology erupts in violence, and Macon must flee the city before he is killed. The "miscegenation of frenzied bodies," the guilt, anger, and desire that "smash into one another and explode," these mixtures only bring "death and madness" (253). Clearly, the masses are not prepared to mix their real-life contradictions just yet; or as Macon's roommate Andre rightfully asserts, "[T]his is some irresponsible shit" (222).[11]

Mansbach can't seem to solve this problem either, as the novel's conclusion oscillates wildly between essentialist and antiessentialist approaches to race. As Macon flees New York, he concludes that the failure of the Race Traitor Project reveals the essential intractability of his whiteness. His attempt to construct his own blackness "with spray cans and microphones and brothers in arms" cannot trump the fact that he is "the same as everyone [he's] ever hated" (2). When he arrives in the South, however, this essentialist perspective is challenged by the racial constructivism of a psychiatrist, Dr. Donner, who has made a fortune turning "black people white, white people black, black people blacker, white people whiter" (292). After Macon declines a job offer from Dr. Donner, a group of white racists in a mini-mart recognize Macon as the leader of the Race Traitor Project. Disgusted by his politics, they kidnap him and an innocent bystander, an older black man named Leo. Burleigh, the leader of the group, thinks that Macon can rediscover his essential whiteness by assaulting, and then shooting, Leo. After much horrific violence (Macon punches Leo but refuses to shoot him), Dr. Donner shows up with Nique, one of Macon's black friends from New York, and we learn that Macon's kidnapping was entirely staged by Dr. Donner. Apparently Nique contacted Donner to help Macon become properly white, and Burleigh and his friends are just actors who work for Donner, helping his clients construct new racial identities. Nique, then, who has previously expressed great skepticism toward the antiessentialist construction of race—"Blackness as a state of mind was bullshit" (263)—reverses his position when he hires Dr. Donner to make Macon white again. But Nique's and

Dr. Donner's antiessentialism is reversed by Burleigh, who was hired to *act* like a racist redneck but, as it turns out, actually *is* a racist redneck using his acting job to assault black people: "I guess you could say I been playing myself these past few months," he tells Dr. Donner (334). Then, Burleigh's essentialism is itself reversed when he decides to kill Macon even though, as his friends point out to him, Macon is white. As far as Burleigh is concerned, however, "He ain't been white for a long time" (334). Burleigh's ability to see Macon's black racial construction as a success thus leads to Macon's death. Having previously asserted that he will never really be black until he's willing to die for a cause, Macon's murder perversely grants him the constructed blackness he's always wanted (50 and 124).

In this way, *Angry Black White Boy* perfectly embodies the compromise aesthetics of its post-postmodern moment.[12] Mansbach has clearly learned the lessons of postmodernism (identity is a constructed performance) and the lessons of the world (racial injustice is real and endemic), but he hasn't figured out how to put those lessons together. The novel is about this post-postmodern impasse, this desire to move beyond postmodern constructivism without merely returning to a naïve realism, but the hip-hop tricks it deploys fail to meet the political challenges of its moment because it continues to imagine race representationally, as something that either is or is not there, as something that we either do or do not see. Consequently, the novel not only fails to meet the political challenges of its moment, but it actively reinforces the neoliberal structures responsible for those challenges in the first place. After all, the novel's constant oscillation between, on the one hand, the view that racial difference is not a real difference, and, on the other hand, the view that racial difference is the only difference that matters, is the neoliberal circle par excellence. Even though their goals are politically progressive and committed to social justice, the characters' thinking about race is structurally homologous to neoliberalism's thinking about race: sometimes it matters and sometimes it doesn't, depending on context and expedience. As long as Mansbach and his characters treat race representationally—as a question of reality and artifice, visibility and invisibility—they will remain mired in this neoliberal circle, trapped in a paradox they can't balance.

In its struggle to reconcile the divide between constructivist and realist approaches to race, *Angry Black White Boy* crystallizes a conceptual divide that both Dubey and Warren see as the defining impasse of most contemporary black fiction.[13] The representational logic that treats race as an interpretive problem, as a feature of subjectivity requiring recognition, understanding, and knowledge, circumscribes the discourse of racial justice, leaving it wide open to neoliberal appropriation.[14] The failures of *Angry Black White Boy* thus require us to ask whether African American literature can engage race beyond representation, and, if it does so, what will make it African American if not its arguments about racial representation? Recognizing that the project of racial representation belongs to an earlier historical moment, Warren knows that African American literature needs to move on. But he doesn't tell us what will replace racial representation except its absence. Attempting to fill this blank spot in Warren's argument, I'm interested here in what African American literature is now, in how literature might still be considered African American even as it refuses to make claims about what race represents. This is a literature that manages to be black, but not in any way that we're used to. In refusing to ask what race *means*, it's a literature that escapes the neoliberal circle spinning between colorblindness and diversity, between our inattention and attention to race. Hopefully, it might even prove to be a literature that can speak meaningfully to and about Gilroy's black-vernacular neoliberals who themselves embody a form of blackness that doesn't necessarily always *mean* in the way that we might want it to.

In short, how might we understand race as real without predetermining, overdetermining, or underdetermining its value? An array of contemporary black authors—Colson Whitehead, Percival Everett, Paul Beatty, Mat Johnson, Aaron McGruder, Danzy Senna, Chris Abani, and Teju Cole, to name just a few—have been asking and answering that question in various ways. (Dave Chappelle, along with Key and Peele, are asking something similar through sketch comedy.) All share a desire to engage race in ways that escape the representational logic that has dominated racial thinking ever since DuBois described blackness as an object of recognition, perspective, and consciousness. Beatty, echoing Paul Gilroy's work in *Against Race*, turns to music and affect; Johnson, McGruder and Senna focus on racial mixing; Abani and Cole consider racial formation on a more global scale. My focus here, however, will be on two authors—Whitehead and Everett—who envision race as an object in its own right, not as a feature or characteristic of human subjects. In this way, both successfully extract race from its almost intractable representational logic. Whitehead and Everett acknowledge the existence of race, but they reject the idea that race necessarily bears any representational or referential value. In their hands, race remains substantial; it affects and influences the world, but its value can never be known in advance. Its value is ontological rather than representational; its significance derives from the way it does or does not impact, connect to, link up with, and influence other things in the world. Race is, but it doesn't necessarily mean. Consequently, in contradistinction to the aesthetically and politically compromised post-postmodernism of *Angry Black White Boy*, I align Whitehead's and Everett's works squarely with exomodernism's attempt to think beyond the purified mutual exclusivity of subject and object. In treating something like race, long held to be constitutive of the subject, as an object in its own right, Whitehead and Everett transform the racial subject into a much more muddled subject-object. Imagining race as an object, in other words, "crack[s] open the carapace of human self-concern, exposing [that human self-concern] to the idea, and maybe even the fact, of its external ontological preconditions, its ground" (McGurl, "Geology" 380). When Whitehead and Everett ontologize race and crack open that carapace, we find a form of racial thinking shaped by, but also uniquely resistant to, neoliberalism's easy appropriation of racial representation.

Colson Whitehead and the Catastrophe of Race

In each of his four novels before *Zone One*—*The Intuitionist* (1999), *John Henry Days* (2001), *Apex Hides the Hurt* (2006), and *Sag Harbor* (2009)—Colson Whitehead thoroughly explores the "ontological preconditions" of the world. He does this by replacing the circular distinction between reality and artifice, essentialism and antiessentialism, that so bedevils Mansbach's *Angry Black White Boy* with a material world excessive in its reality. *The Intuitionist*, for instance, describes "traffic lights [that] are unforgiving, ... mysterious and capricious" (75); *John Henry* offers doilies exhibiting "a grim certitude that belied their frilly edges" (130); in *Apex*, a masochistic foot exhibits a "not-so-secret agenda" that involves "dart[ing] toward immovable objects, lunging after collision" (159); in *Sag Harbor*, "houses [wait] all summer for their owners to appear" (33). But it's not just the everyday objects populating these novels that exert a curiously inscrutable agency over their subjects. In addition, each novel is constructed around a single, seemingly mundane object that simultaneously functions as the source of and foil to interpretive desire. An elevator in *The Intuitionist*, a mountain in *John Henry*, a city in *Apex*, a house in *Sag Harbor*, and the plague in *Zone One*: initially each appears to be the key that will unlock its novel's meaning, but ultimately each proves to be little more than a jammed lock. Characters and readers alike struggle to determine the meaningful significance of these things, but, in each case, the things refuse to participate in the symbolic exchange of representation and figuration.

Instead, things throughout Whitehead's novels remain faithful to their "true nature," an idea that speaks neither to an object's essence nor to its constructedness but to a certain materiality that exceeds representation altogether. This, for example, is the protagonist in *Apex*, a nomenclature consultant who excels at identifying the perfect name for new consumer products, meditating on the relationship between things and their names:

> Isn't it great when you're a kid and the whole world is full of anonymous things? ... Everything is bright and mysterious until you know what it is called and then all the light goes out of it. All those flying gliding things are just *birds*. And etc. Once we knew the name of it, how could we ever come to love it? He told himself: What he had given to all those things had been the right name, but never the true name. For things had true natures, and they hid behind false names, beneath the skin we gave them.
>
> ...
>
> A name that got to the heart of the thing—that would be miraculous. But he never got to the heart of the thing, he just slapped a bandage on it to keep the pus in. What is the word, he asked himself, for that elusive thing? It was on the tip of his tongue. What is the name for that which is always beyond our grasp? What do you call *that which escapes*? (182–183)

A similar character in *John Henry Days*, a marketing guru named Lucien, is more confident in his ability to get "to the heart of the thing." Lobbying the mayor of Talcott, West Virginia, for the chance to promote the town's inaugural John Henry Days celebration, Lucien describes his belief in "[t]he inexorable tending towardness of all things." "[T]he world is full of undiscovered treasures waiting to reveal their true light," he tells the mayor (195). "We all have suns in our hands, inner light, every object, and all they need are a little something to initiate the reaction" (194). While Lucien thinks it's easy to "release radiance," the novel's broader search for the true John Henry suggests that we should be more skeptical. The novel opens, for example, with a collection of unattributed first-person accounts of John Henry which, when collated, contradictorily reveal him to be both black and white, 155 pounds or perhaps over 200, a native of Alabama but also of Mississippi, most definitely a real person but also just a tall tale. Like the objects in Helena Viramontes's *Dogs* that both do and do not occupy a specific place and time, things in Whitehead's novels cannot be incorporated into a representational world in which subjects observe and determine the meaning of objects. Thus, another character in *John Henry*, gazing at a statue of John Henry and noting that his arm, frozen in mid-swing, is either about to strike or has just completed a blow, appreciates that the artist has left this point "open to interpretation." But the narrator promptly intrudes to correct her representational approach to the statue: "She is confusing the statue before her with the man, and the man with her conception of the man" (263). Simply put, the statue is a statue, not a representation of something else.[15] In Whitehead's work, subjects never grasp the core truth of objects—not because of some postmodern indeterminacy or misstep of language, but because objects for Whitehead stand outside the self-other dialectic of consciousness altogether.[16] *The Intuitionist*, another Whitehead novel that explicitly thematizes the way subjects understand objects, indicates that this is even true of race. Race in *The Intuitionist* does not signify, refer, represent, or point. It resists, intrudes, and even crashes, but it never means.

The novel, set in an indeterminate place and time with conspicuous echoes of midcentury New York, details a political and ideological conflict between two types of elevator inspectors, Empiricists and Intuitionists. The two groups have competing ideas about how subjects should perceive objects, particularly elevators. The Empiricists inspect every part of an elevator; they look at it, test it, and examine it with a careful eye, paying attention to all its mechanisms and devices. Conversely, Intuitionists merely sense the inner workings of the elevator affectively; they intuit its mechanics and communicate with it on "a nonmaterial basis" (62). Who, then, the novel asks, is best equipped to read the truth of an elevator? Initially, considering Whitehead's interest in the agency of things, it seems that the novel sides with Intuitionism. After all, the founding text of Intuitionism, *Theoretical Elevators,* echoes the subject-object relationships found throughout Whitehead's work: "We conform to objects, we capitulate to them. . . . Nothing we create works the way it should. The car overheats on the highway, the electric can opener cannot open the can. We must tend to our objects and treat them as newborn babes" (38). Given the intractable object world, the author of these words, a black man passing for white named James Fulton, calls for "a renegotiation of our relationship to objects" and insists that elevator inspectors must "separate the elevator from elevatorness." Empiricists err, he suggests, because they "imagine elevators from a human, and therefore inherently alien point of view" (62).

The novel's protagonist, Lila Mae Watson, is unpopular among her colleagues not only because she is an Intuitionist, but also because she is a black woman doing a white man's job. The novel's action is mobilized when an elevator that Lila Mae has inspected—the #11 elevator in the new Fanny Briggs municipal building—plummets and crashes just before the grand opening. In the novel's background, the Elevator Inspectors Guild is electing a new chair. The Empiricist, Frank Chancre, is running against an Intuitionist, Orville Lever. The nation's two dominant elevator-makers have thrown their influence behind the candidates, with United supporting Chancre while Arbo backs Lever. The crash at the Fanny Briggs building emerges as a wedge issue, allowing Chancre to discredit Intuitionism while subtly questioning "colored progress" and the full integration of the elevator guild (115). This layer of political intrigue and corporate malfeasance only enhances our sympathy for Lila Mae and her Intuitionist techniques. Convinced that the elevator crash was a racist Empiricist set-up, Lila Mae tries to clear her name and vindicate Intuitionism; readers are inclined to cheer her on. And yet, we eventually learn that Lila Mae was wrong. There was no racist plot against her and her Intuitionist principles. The elevator was not sabotaged. It just fell, and neither Intuitionism nor Empiricism can explain why.

So despite informing us many times over that Lila Mae is "never wrong," she proves the worst reader in the novel.[17] She is catastrophically wrong about the health of the Fanny Briggs elevator; she incorrectly believes that the Empiricists sent Pompey, the only other black elevator inspector, to sabotage the elevator and discredit Intuitionism (87); a black man named Natchez dupes her into believing he can vindicate her record, but he is actually one of Arbo's corporate thugs trying to discover what Lila Mae knows about one of Fulton's apocryphal elevator designs (211); and like the rest of the world, she falsely believes that Fulton is white when he is actually passing. So what exactly is it about which Lila Mae is "never wrong"? The answer to that question helps us see why the novel actually challenges Intuitionist principles as much as it does Empiricist ones.

As one telling repetition of that phrase reveals, it's not that Lila Mae is never wrong, it's that "Lila Mae is never wrong when it comes to Intuitionism" (227). But really, how could she be? As an affective mode of understanding unmediated by consciousness and rational thought, Intuitionism need not correspond to a given set of facts to be correct. There's nothing for Intuitionism to be wrong about; it's always tautologically correct.[18] This is because, as the only detailed description of an intuitive elevator inspection reveals, the Intuitionist, like the Empiricist, also can't help but "imagine elevators from a human, and therefore inherently alien point of view":

> This elevator's vibrations are resolving themselves in her mind as an aqua-blue cone. . . . The elevator moves upward in the well, toward the grunting in the machine room, and Lila Mae turns that into a picture, too. The ascension is a red spike circling around the blue cone, which doubles in size and wobbles as the elevator starts climbing. You don't pick the shapes and their behavior. Everyone has their own set of genies. Depends on how your brain works. Lila Mae has always had a thing for geometric forms. As the elevator reaches the fifth floor landing, an orange octagon cartwheels into her mind's frame. It hops up and down, incongruous with the annular aggression of the red spike. Cubes and parallelograms emerge around the eighth floor, but they're satisfied with half-hearted little jigs and don't disrupt the proceeding like the mischievous orange octagon. The octagon ricochets into the foreground, famished for attention. She knows what it is. (6)

Lila Mae's reading of the elevator succeeds, but only because she already knows the meaning of her geometric visions. Intuitionism, as much as Empiricism, merely tells us what we already think we know.[19] Both deliver readings that meet our predetermined expectations about how the world works; they just use different tools to do so. In this way, they are structured much like the neoliberal circle and the cycle of critique that Latour describes. Empiricism provides the objective view of the world; Intuitionism offers the subjective;

each critiques the other even though each delivers only a partial and tendentious understanding of a given situation. Consequently, in a catastrophe—which the novel defines as "what happens when you subtract what happens all the time"—neither reading method is adequate (230). Thus, Lila Mae wonders of the crashed elevator, "Did the genies try to warn her, were they aware, twitching at times, forbidden to make plain their knowledge but subtly attempting to alert her through the odd wiggle and shimmy. She wouldn't know what to look for. Whatever signals the genies may or may not have dispatched through the darkness went unread" (227). Lila Mae can't read what she doesn't already know how to read, and yet the world is filled with objects, like falling elevators, that are illegible and opaque to representation. Intuitionists and Empiricists both falter by presuming that objects can be read as if they were representations that deliver meaning about the world. Like the statue of John Henry that is just a statue—not a man or a representation of a man—objects in *The Intuitionist* can be experienced but never read.

If Intuitionism and Empiricism are just two sides of the same misguided coin, then it's not surprising that each constantly turns into the other throughout the novel. First, when Lila Mae learns that James Fulton is actually black, intuitive reading modes replace more empirical approaches. For example, Fulton's writings frequently describe "another world beyond this one." When everyone thought Fulton was white, these words were taken at face value to refer to the new heights that elevator technology could make possible. But once Fulton's passing is revealed, this same phrase is reinterpreted as a neutral façade covering the text's deeper racial allegory (186). Conversely, when Lila Mae learns that the Fanny Briggs elevator crashed of its own accord and not because of a racial conspiracy, empirical reading modes replace more intuitive approaches. As Natchez, whose real name is Raymond Coombs, later explains to a newly illuminated Lila Mae, no one really cared one way or another whether anyone was black (250). Thus, she would have been better served if her reading were more empirical and less intuitively suspicious. In the case of Fulton, then, race is initially irrelevant but later becomes the interpretive linchpin for Intuitionism and its founding texts. Conversely, in the plot of the crashed elevator, racial conspiracy initially explains the apparent sabotage, but then race later proves utterly irrelevant for understanding the catastrophe.[20] Taken together, these plots cancel each other out. If Lila Mae incorrectly reads the crashed elevator as racial allegory, then perhaps she's also wrong to read Fulton's *Theoretical Elevators* as racial allegory. And even though she's absolutely certain that the "luminous truth" of Fulton's race changes everything, the insignificance of race in the elevator plot calls that certainty into doubt. As in the neoliberal circle, race both is and is not crucial depending on what needs explaining; it's impossible to say if and when we should ever pay attention to it.

This is why Walter Kirn's front-cover blurb describing *The Intuitionist* as "the freshest racial allegory since Ralph Ellison's *Invisible Man* and Toni Morrison's *The Bluest Eye*" grossly misreads the novel.[21] To approach *The Intuitionist* as a "fresh racial allegory"—in fact, to read any of Whitehead's novels allegorically—is to read as an Intuitionist. But the whole point of Whitehead's *oeuvre* is that one can never know when to read empirically and when to read intuitively. Consequently, value in Whitehead's novels derives from objects' ontology, from the ways they intrude into, configure, and transmit the world, not from objects' representational capacities. The crucial distinction in *The Intuitionist*, then, is not between Intuitionism and Empiricism—both of which produce meaning "from a human, and therefore inherently alien point of view"—but between those two misguided modes of apprehension and an approach that instead follows the lead of the physical world. That, I would suggest, is the truth of Fulton's "world beyond this one." It's not a world that is transcendent or subterranean; it's a world freed from the referential logic of representation altogether because it understands representation to just be part of the world. Fulton explores such a world in his own writing: "He writes the elevator. His handwriting . . . worsens the closer he gets, as if his words are being pinched and pulled by the elevator on the other side of his writing" (252–253). Notice that Fulton doesn't write *about* the elevator; he doesn't represent it. Rather, his writing invents the elevator, embodies it, transmits it. In Fulton's world things are not other than they are; they are always their "true nature." And Whitehead's novels demonstrate how remarkably difficult it is to reach that apparently simple place.

Regardless of the difficulty, *The Intuitionist* suggests that we should try to think of race in a similar way. It's not a legible mark on the skin, so it can't be read empirically. And it's also not a deeper, more amorphous cultural formation, so it can't be read intuitively. In fact, like the elevator in the Fanny Briggs building, it's simply not a text to be read at all. To be sure, the novel makes it easy to racialize the divide between Empiricism and Intuitionism. The Empiricists' nicknames for Intuitionists are all racially charged "terms belonging to the nomenclature of dark exotica, the sinister foreign" (57–58). In fact, the narrator explicitly reports that "[w]hite people's reality is built on what things appear to be—that's the business of Empiricism" (239). Despite these racial correlations, I'd contend that it's actually the crashed elevator, not Intuitionism, that embodies blackness in the novel. The debate over the cause of the crash is, in effect, a debate about the relative meaning or meaninglessness of race. Cleverly, Whitehead links the discourses of catastrophe and racial passing to establish this connection between race and the elevator. First, the elevator's catastrophic plunge is explained in the language of passing: "The elevator pretended to be what it was not. Number Eleven passed for longevous. Passed for healthy so well that Arbo Elevator Co.'s quality control could not see its duplicity, so well that the building contractors could not see for the routine ease of its assembly coeval doom. So well that Lila Mae Watson of the Department of Elevator Inspectors, who is never wrong, did not see it" (229). In turn, the narrator describes Fulton's racial passing in the language of catastrophe: "It is the moment he has feared since he left his town. When he will be revealed for who he is, the catastrophic accident" (237). As a catastrophe, race remains illegible, an object in its own right. Race cannot be intuitively detected, rooted out, or uncovered; and it cannot be empirically observed, measured, or calibrated. Instead, like an elevator, it is a thing that unexpectedly crashes down on you, but usually doesn't. We should thus not be asking if *The Intuitionist* is a racial allegory, but should instead ask whether race crashes into our attempt to think about the novel. Do we stub our toes against its intractable thinginess, or can we make it through the novel uninjured? The answers to these questions do not tell us if race is constructed or real, superficial or deep. The elevator, like all other things in Whitehead's novels, carries an essential truth, but it's an ontological, not an interpretive truth. *The Intuitionist* speaks of the subsistence and presence of race, but not necessarily of its meaning.

Whitehead's novel thus provides a theory of race in which race asserts itself, demands attention, and invites us into what Bill Brown has described as the "indeterminate ontology" of things—an ontology that blurs the key distinctions between subject and object, culture and nature, on which modernity's operative assumptions

about race are grounded (13). *The Intuitionist* is particularly compelling, I think, because it extends that indeterminate ontology to
the narrative itself, which displays a thingy opacity that frequently
countervails Lila Mae's own attempts to establish the meaning of
her world. This thingy opacity stems from the heterodiegetic narrator's uniquely intrusive interventions into the diegesis of Lila Mae's
story. That is, even though the narrator doesn't walk around in the
world of the plot, he's not entirely removed from it either. Rather
than simply representing a world or telling a story for readers to
interpret, *The Intuitionist*'s narrator concretizes the story's action
by actively intervening in and thwarting Lila Mae's perspective.
Repeatedly asserting that she "doesn't know yet," for example, the
narrator blocks Lila Mae's self-awareness, effectively transforming the novel into an already-determined world of things that Lila
Mae must negotiate, but not on her own terms. For example, we frequently see the narrator rewriting Lila Mae's sense of self: "Ask her
and Lila Mae will not admit that her heart skipped a beat . . ., but it's
true (55–56); "Wishful thinking: that all they want to do is detain
her" (105); "Lila Mae has forgotten this incident. But no matter. It
still happened. It happened like this" (116). In each of these cases, the
world of things—concretized by the narrator—proves more determinant than Lila Mae's perspectival consciousness. The novel is not
about what sense Lila Mae makes of the world; it's about how, by
constantly running up against the world of things—elevators, race,
men, and even the narrator—the sense of Lila Mae is made.[22]

Percival Everett and the Boxed Beetle of Race

Like Colson Whitehead, Percival Everett is a contemporary African
American author who insists on the ontological and non-representational value of race. For my purposes here, Everett's work extends
Whitehead's ontological project more directly to language and literature. In short, much of Everett's prolific *oeuvre* asks: what happens to language and the racialized subjects who use it if we take
quite seriously the idea that words don't represent the world but are
instead just part of it?

Everett is the author of more than a dozen novels and several
poetry and short-story collections, many of which have nothing to do
with race at all. I will focus here on three novels which do explicitly

broach the subject of race—*Glyph* (1999), *Erasure* (2001), and *I Am Not Sidney Poitier* (2009). I read the first two as framing a question about racial value and significance that the third novel effectively answers. In particular, *Glyph* attacks poststructuralism, replacing its perpetually deferred and differentiated modes of meaning production with a Wittgensteinian model of language in which words are tools that yield understanding rather than referents that mean by pointing (or not).[23] Next, *Erasure* wrestles with the implications that this non-referential approach to value production has for two of the most potentially "meaningful" things in the world, a subject and his race. The impasses that stifle *Erasure* are then surpassed in *Not Sidney* where Everett demonstrates how we might move through and thrive in the world while continuing to treat subjects and their race as mere objects. It's this culminating model developed in *Not Sidney* that I propose as an approach to race that exceeds the neoliberal circle of colorblindness and color-sightedness.

Glyph is about a mute infant named Ralph whose father is, as Ralph puts it, "a poststructuralist pretender." Ralph does not talk, but with an IQ of 475, he reads, writes, and understands the most complicated of discourses without ever speaking. The living embodiment of Derrida's famous argument about the precedence of writing over speech, Ralph also articulates Everett's broader dissatisfaction with poststructuralism. Asserting that he has "no problem with the Other, myself the Other, myself, or any bold line drawn between myself and the world, between signifier and signified," Ralph refuses to see language as separate from and striving to point to reality (145).[24] Or as he quips elsewhere, "At the risk of sounding cocky, my gaps are not gaps at all, but are already full, and all my meaning is surface." "If for no other reason than my having claimed it," he adds in a footnote (31). Because language for Ralph is not separate from the world, it also does not stand in for objects in the world. As he explains, "writing . . . [does] not exist 'in the place of,' [does] not seek to address the 'deficiency and infirmity' of speech and thought" (110). Just as a hammer and nails do not occupy an order of reality separate from the house that they are used to build, words do not occupy an order of reality separate from the world they describe:

> [P]erhaps the case is that there is no distinction between the real
> world and that which constitutes real for us in the use of this thing
> called language. There is no split or rupture from the world when it

comes to the reporting of the *real*, as the consciousness of it is on the same side of the paradoxical tape, the Möbius strip of the world, all in the same place, tucked away in the same box in the attic, living in the same cage at the zoo. (177)[25]

Purged of differentiation and fragmentation, freed from Otherness and opposition, objects only "mean" ontologically and superficially, not referentially. In the novel's concluding pages, Ralph extends this idea to fiction. Arguing that "[f]ictive space contains all the possibilities of a given story, its associations and relationships and the set-ordering of its constituent elements," Ralph notes that a story does not represent the world but instead merely "represents itself": "[a] story is neither correct nor incorrect" (200). It's not that the world is language (a frequent mischaracterization of poststructural thought), but that language is world.

Ralph, who happens to be black, recognizes that collapsing the relationship between language and the world in this way has important implications for the "meaning" of subjectivity. This is why he describes his own subjectivity as Wittgenstein's famous beetle in a box, an example Wittgenstein uses to prove, contrary to John Locke, that our inability to know the contents of another's mind does not trap us in our own private worlds (82). To prove this, Wittgenstein imagines a situation in which everyone has a beetle in a box; no one can see inside anyone else's box; and everyone says he knows what a beetle is only by looking at *his* beetle. It's possible, then, that some people have something other than a beetle in their box, or that some might have nothing—we can never know. But Wittgenstein points out that our inability to know what's in everyone's box doesn't make language private; this is not a story about the indeterminacy of meaning or the slipperiness of reference. Instead, it just means that the word "beetle" in no way points to an object in a box; "beetle" is just the word we use to describe something in a box that no one else can know.[26] Or as Wittgenstein notes elsewhere, "The meaning of a word is what is explained by the explanation of the meaning" (sec. 560). Ralph is not the mysterious content inside his head; rather, as with everyone else, he is someone who has mysterious content in his head. In the same way that it's a mistake to think of meaning as something hidden or buried, then, it's a mistake to think of subjectivity as a function of internal consciousness in general and of racial consciousness in particular. Instead, subjectivity is all on the surface, or as Ralph puts it: "I wondered if there was no inside and outside to the spirit of being, no body and soul, no opposite side to any orientation, but that we were Möbius surfaces, our topologies defined by the fact that we can never get around them to the other side" (177).

But what happens when the world insists, contrary to your Wittgensteinian commitments, that your race has meaning and significance beyond its surface topology? Everett considers precisely this question in his next novel, *Erasure*, a story in which the black author Thelonious "Monk" Ellison confronts pressure from his agent and publisher to write novels that are more "black"—a pressure that Everett himself knows something about. As a vocal disbeliever in race as a signifier of value or meaning—"I don't believe in race," Ellison bluntly reports—our protagonist writes a satirical capitulation to the wishes of the publishing industry, adopting the pseudonym Stagg R. Leigh to pen a short novel titled *My Pafology* (2). Saturated with stilted urban black vernacular and egregious stereotypes about black experience, Ellison renames the novel *Fuck* just to press his point all the more. Ultimately, his plan backfires as *Fuck* wins the National Book Award to rave reviews: "The characters are so well drawn that often one forgets that *Fuck* is a novel. It is more like the evening news. The ghetto comes to life in these pages and for this glimpse of hood existence we owe the author a tremendous debt. The writing is dazzling, the dialogue as true as dialogue gets and it is simply honest" (260).[27] As far as Ellison is concerned, there's not a single honest representation in the entire novel; it merely reinforces what a general readership—whites and blacks alike—think blackness signifies.

Basically, Ellison's satirical novel gets the better of him. A woodworker in his spare time, Ellison explains that he intended *Fuck* to be like a chair: "a chair *is* its space, is its own canvas, occupies space properly" (208). But an audience of symptomatic readers committed to the idea of black racial pathology fails to treat *Fuck* merely as "a functional device, its appearance a thing to behold" (209). Readers have not learned, as Ellison apparently did at an early age, that words do not conceal meaning: "It used to be that I would look for deeper meaning in everything," Ellison reports, "Thinking that I was some kind of hermeneutic sleuth, but I stopped that when I was twelve. . . . I have since come to recognize that I was abandoning any search for elucidation of what might be called subjective or thematic meaning schemes and replacing it with a mere delineation of specific case descriptions" (26). Increasingly subjected to the "subjective or thematic meaning schemes" of his readers, however, Ellison eventually becomes Stagg R. Leigh, intentionally behaving, dressing, and speaking like a hardened young black man from the urban underbelly. Ellison points out the irony: "I was a victim of racism by virtue of my failing to acknowledge racial difference and by failing to have my art be defined as an exercise in racial self-expression." Prevented from treating race as a surface effect, he feels increasingly compelled "to wear the mask of the person [he] was expected to be" (212). Trapped in the racial neoliberal circle, Ellison's tale is not about overcoming double-consciousness but about his inevitable subjection to it.

Ellison decides to reveal his ruse at the National Book Award ceremony, but as he walks to the podium and "look[s] at the television cameras looking at [him]," he can only mutter, "Egads, I'm on television" (265). With this, the novel abruptly ends. The television cameras absorb Ellison into the mediated reflexivity of racial reference and foil his desire to reveal the truth. Ellison simply can't figure out how to make his race, and his novel, into a chair. As earlier set-pieces in *Erasure* make clear, Ellison has few good options. When Van Go Jenkins, the protagonist and first-person narrator of *Fuck*, is invited to appear on a talk show, for example, he initially believes that he will be asked serious questions about his life. At the studio, however, the makeup department wants him to "shine like a proper TV nigger," and it's quickly apparent that he's only on the show to reinforce the audience's assumptions about black pathology. Conversely, Tom, the black protagonist of a short story embedded in *Erasure*, correctly answers a series of arcane questions on a game show called *Virtute et Armis*: he knows what a serial distribution field is, and he correctly quotes the Latin opening to Emerson's "Self-Reliance." In doing so, however, he doesn't give the audience what they want. In fact, when he gazes out at them at the end of the show, they have all died (178). Taken together, these two fictional television appearances frame the very limited options confronting Ellison: he can fulfill audience expectations and achieve fame, or he can craft literary chairs and lose his audience altogether.

Ellison can't turn his racial subjectivity into a chair because he has written a satire. What he intends as a joke, the audience reads as realism. The form of his novel is not its own space, it doesn't "occupy space properly." Instead, as ironic satire, it opens up a surface-depth dialectic in which readers find the very racial assumptions they already hold. Once Ellison engages in a debate about the *meaning* of his work, once he writes in a genre that assumes a distinction between surface and depth, he's done for. And in this novel, at least, so is Everett, who, like Ellison with his chairs, frequently talks about "making books," not writing them (Stewart 302). But as satire, *Erasure* fails to occupy its own space just as Ellison's work does. Like *Fuck, Erasure* is a novel about how stupid it is to expect novels by black authors to be about race, but in making that point satirically, it's consistently read and taught as an African American novel about race. There is, however, a curious story included in *Erasure* that points us toward the solution Everett develops in his later novel, *I Am Not Sidney Poitier.* The story is about a parrot who says, "Who is it?" whenever someone knocks on the door. One day, a plumber knocks on the door, and when the parrot asks, "Who is it," the plumber responds, "The plumber." Not knowing that his interlocutor is a parrot, this exchange continues until the man, violently exasperated, breaks down the door and promptly dies of a heart attack. The parrot's owner returns home, sees the dead plumber, asks, "Who is it?" and the parrot responds, "The plumber." Ellison asks if the parrot answers the owner and concludes that "he does and he doesn't" (227). This story of course highlights Everett's sense that querying the referential value of language, as of race, is a futile task. Instead, as Wittgenstein puts it, "[T]he meaning of a word is its use in the language" (sec. 43). Understanding results when words link to or bounce off the other component parts of a given scenario. In this case, the parrot, the plumber, the owner, the words "Who is it" and the words "the plumber" are all equivalent parts of a language game that either does or does not produce knowledge depending on how those parts come into contact with each other.

This is the non-representational model of meaning-making that reigns in *I Am Not Sidney Poitier.* Throughout the novel, the name of the protagonist and first-person narrator, Not Sidney Poitier, crystallizes the difference between treating language as a thing to be used and treating it as a sign that refers. This curious name—Not Sidney is the first name, Poitier the surname—occasions much humor, but the humor makes a specific point about the non-referential nature of language. For example, great confusion arises for Not Sidney when he introduces himself as "Not Sidney," prompting people to ask what his name is if it is not Sidney. Once that confusion is cleared up, however, the homophonic "knot" intrudes. As one character asks, "Knot, with a k?," to which Not Sidney appropriately, if unhelpfully, responds, "Not with a k" (139). Like the parrot responding "the plumber," Not Sidney frequently delivers truthful answers to questions that a given interrogator does not even realize she's asking. For example, because Not Sidney Poitier looks identical to Sidney Poitier, people frequently comment, "But you're not Sidney Poitier, are you?" To which Not Sidney Poitier replies, "I am" (198).

Of course, these indexical travails only emerge when characters treat language referentially, as a correspondence between words and world, as if words were not already world. Not Sidney achieves much greater understanding whenever he attempts to discern, not the referents of language, but the connections it establishes in the larger collection of things it networks. For example, when a police officer in Peckerwood County pulls him over for being black in Peckerwood County, the police officer's accent renders his words, save the opaque "Hey boy," utterly unintelligible to Not Sidney. And yet, Not Sidney understands everything perfectly. Not because the garbled words point to his reality, but because the words, combined with the black-and-white patrol car, the sheriff's mirrored sunglasses, the desiccated landscape, the hand resting on the holstered pistol, all interconnect to produce Not Sidney's understanding of the situation. The words in this scene don't represent meaning or refer to the world; instead, they bounce off, link to, and affiliate with their ontological peers.

Elsewhere Everett deploys tautology to emphasize the non-referential thinginess of language: for example, the narrator describes "screams that filled the streets like screams" (5); a dream that "spiraled like all things spiral" (63); a woman who stands "on the veranda wearing a veranda-standing dress" (68); a Reverend who displays great "reverence" and offers a prayer in which "free men are free to live freely" (159); a bank where "bank people did bank work and talked bank talk and walked bankly back and forth" (192); and the "hooded heads" of the KKK that "walk around doing hooded things" (195). These descriptions do not reference secondary properties that objects in the world commonly display. Instead of pointing to properties, these adjectives link to objects—spirals, banks, hoods—to acquire their value; the words join a wider network of objects to produce meaning. Such sentences literalize Wittgenstein's notion that a word's meaning "is explained by the explanation of the meaning" (sec. 560).

Everett pursues a similar anti-referential regime at the level of plot as he models nearly every event in the novel on a Sidney Poitier movie. *Band of Angels* (1957), *Lilies of the Field* (1963), *Guess Who's Coming to Dinner* (1967), *In the Heat of the Night* (1967), *Buck and the Preacher* (1972), and many more provide the content to the majority of the novel's plot. Curiously, however, the specific referential structure that the text has to the films remains opaque. Little is gained by reading the relation literally, allusively, satirically, metaphorically, ironically, metonymically, etc. This is again because the text does not refer or point to these movies, producing meaning vis-à-vis the specific stance it adopts toward them. Instead, the text treats the movies as its equals, expecting readers to assemble understanding by linking them together, or not. The strongest thing we might say about the text-film relation is that the plot of chapter six proceeds very *In the Heat of the Night*-y. Truth, meaning, and value are achieved through linking and connecting, not through correspondence.[28]

The same is true of Not Sidney's very subjectivity. As I've already noted, Not Sidney looks increasingly like Sidney Poitier as the novel proceeds. But just as the presence of Ted Turner, Jane Fonda, and Percival Everett doesn't "mean" anything particularly deep or symptomatic about the characters who share their names, neither does Not Sidney's uncanny resemblance to the famous black actor. We see this significance which is not one as Not Sidney arrives at LAX and is mistaken for the real Sidney Poitier. A driver whisks him away to the Academy Awards where his good friends Harry Belafonte and Elizabeth Taylor present him with an award for the "Most Dignified Figure in American Culture." In his acceptance speech, Not Sidney shares with the audience the key lesson he has learned on his journey from Georgia to Los Angeles: "I came back to this place to find something, to connect with something lost, to reunite if not with my whole self, then with a piece of it. What I've discovered is that this thing is not here. In fact, it is nowhere. I have learned that my name is not my name. It seems you all know me and nothing could be further from the truth and yet you know me better than I know myself, perhaps better than I can know myself." Here, unlike in *Erasure*, we finally have a black man who can speak to his audience. And he can do so because, as his speech indicates, he has abandoned the surface-depth model of subjectivity. He abjures subjectivity both as a function of consciousness (there are no missing parts or deeper layers of the self that will make Not Sidney complete) and as a function of reference (his name is not equivalent to his self). Like a chair, there is no difference between who he is and what the audience sees. He is who and what the networks in which he is immersed configure him as being; his identity is explained by the explanation of his identity. Thus, in a culminating rejection of subjectivity conventionally conceived, Not Sidney declares that he would like the headstone of his grave to read: "*I AM NOT MYSELF TODAY*" (234). Not Sidney is not his self because there are not two things, a person and a self. There is just Not Sidney, another object in the world. Like Ralph's stories that are neither correct nor incorrect, like the parrot that both does and does not answer the woman's question, Not Sidney Poitier both is and is not Sidney Poitier. It depends on his use in the language.

And if this is true of Not Sidney's subjectivity, then it's also true of his race. Notably, while the rest of the world reads his race as a sign or symptom of something else—the officer sees it as a crime, many white women see it as a turn-on, his girlfriend's bougie parents see it as a problem—Not Sidney simply refuses to see race as anything other than a thing. He acknowledges that race exists; he admits that there might be a beetle in the box. But for Not Sidney, this means that race, like Wittgenstein's beetle, "cancels out"; it's just another object in the world. Crucially, we should distinguish Not Sidney's position on race from Ellison's claim in *Erasure*: "I don't believe in race." When Ellison denies the very existence of race, he merely articulates the ideological inverse (i.e., colorblindness) of those who insist on its inherent meaning and value. Both positions accept that race is a matter of representation; they just disagree about whether or not that representation is an artificial construct or an inherent truth. Not Sidney, however, is speaking a different, non-representational language. For Not Sidney race is not a representation—an object of recognition, consciousness, or meaning—it's just another thing in the world. As such it both does and does not mean, depending on its use. Consequently, even though Not Sidney meets racism at every turn, he adopts a rigorously neutral stance toward it. The novel does not condemn, critique, or seek to correct racism because there is not a correspondingly appropriate or virtuous attitude that one should adopt toward race. Race is real to the extent that it produces material effects in the world, and those material effects are what race means—nothing more and nothing less. It doesn't follow, in other words, that we *must* see race as deep and significant. Instead, race is real because people choose to see it as such, but it is, just

like everything else in the world, merely what it is. Its significance
lies not in what it hides or conceals but in the ways it does or does
not connect to and translate other ontologically equivalent things in
the world.

What [Is] African American Literature?

Together, Colson Whitehead and Percival Everett claim this space
beyond racial meaning and meaninglessness, beyond diversity and
colorblindness, for twenty-first-century African American literature. Far from the compromised aesthetic of *Angry Black White Boy*
that merely balances realist politics and formal experiment, essentialist and constructivist worldviews, Whitehead and Everett break
the circle altogether when they refuse to see race as a sign—as an
object of meaning, interpretation, or consciousness—and instead
render it as a thing resistant to the ascription of significance
or value. Doing so takes away the doubled approach to racial
justice—sometimes emphasizing diversity and at other times
preferring colorblindness—that neoliberalism deftly deploys to
perpetuate its own interests. True, race remains a matter of visibility, but for Whitehead and Everett, it's a visibility that doesn't
signify (much like the tropes in *Tropic of Orange* that refuse to
turn). And without meaningful signification, neoliberal rhetorics
can't manipulate race and racial value so easily. If the meaning
of race were merely indeterminate, the door would remain wide
open for neoliberal appropriation. But if meaning is nothing but
use, then whatever claims neoliberalism might make about race
are defused. Neoliberalism, race, and anything else in the world
become networked actants as susceptible to reconfiguration—or
to use Wittgenstein's language, to alternative uses—as any other
network of objects might be.

Consequently, neither Whitehead nor Everett delivers a politics,
much less a politics of race, standing over and against an unjust state
of affairs. Their novels do not set out to critique racial injustice or
racial representation; they do not hope to replace one understanding
of the meaning of race with another. Rather, they imagine a world
in which race doesn't mean at all. But thinking about race absent
of meaning is not the same thing as colorblindness. Colorblindness
says, "Race doesn't mean anything to me; race is meaningless." But

Whitehead and Everett make a slightly different point: race has nothing to do with the question of meaning in the first place. It can provide value to a given configuration of objects in the world, but it doesn't mean anything representationally. Whitehead and Everett imagine a world in which race is a thing rather than a referent, a world where we no longer require critique to reveal or achieve racial truth, justice, or utopia because there is no racial truth, justice, or utopia that neoliberalism has hidden or suppressed. There's not something missing or hidden that a universal language of rights, or a postmodern discourse of difference, can replace or reveal. Instead, there is just a homogenous plane of reality, part of which includes neoliberalism, and it's all guaranteed to look different from one day to the next.

Finally, Whitehead and Everett offer a partial answer to a question that goes largely unasked in Warren's *What Was African American Literature?* Namely, what *is* African American literature? The evidence provided here suggests that it has overcome the divide between political realism and aesthetic experimentation that defines postmodern African American fiction. And it has also moved past the attempt to balance those literary modes, a project that Dubey associates with later postmodernism and which I have been describing as uniquely post-postmodern. It also displays a notable commitment to objects, ontology, and presence, although when placed against the backdrop of recent African American literary history, I think we can see that those commitments are not exactly assertions of truth about the way the world really is as much as they are expedient ways to escape postmodern impasse. That is, I don't think these authors are suggesting that they have discovered the truth of race; rather, they seem to be asking us to consider the possibilities that arise when we think about race in this different way, as a thing. Ultimately, then, while Warren correctly suggests that contemporary black authors like Whitehead and Everett are not particularly focused on racial injustice and civil rights, hopefully my readings have demonstrated that they are not postracial writers either. There is still something distinctly "black" about their writing, even if it's only in an ontological sense. That is, in the same way that "the meaning of a word is what is explained by the explanation of the meaning," this literature is still African American literature because it's understood in terms of its African American-ness (sec. 560). Or, as I said of the connection between *Not Sidney* and the many Sidney Poitier movies

constituting its plot, this literature is still African American literature because it's very African American-y. Crucially, however, in
its shared refusal to tell us what race *means*, this literature thinks
beyond colorblindness and diversity to an object-oriented notion of
race that can't be swallowed by the neoliberal circle.

Welcoming the World

POST-ECOLOGICAL FICTION

That's the thing about nature. There's so much of it.
—THE DOWAGER COUNTESS, *Downton Abbey*

The year is 1855. Erasmus D. Wells, naturalist, is preparing the *Narwhal* for an Arctic voyage commandeered by his imperious brother-in-law Zechariah (Zeke) Voorhees. With a small crew, they hope to learn the fate of Sir John Franklin's Arctic expedition, missing since 1845. As he stands on the dock peering at the Delaware River, Erasmus has a distinctly postmodern vision: a "partial reflection trapped between hull and pilings ... the planks wavered, the railing bent, the boom appeared then disappeared." After a moment, however, his vision adjusts—"the image filled the surface without concealing the complicated life below"—and he again gazes with the eye of modern science: "He saw, beneath the transparent shadow, what his father had taught him to see: the schools of minnows, the eels and algae, the mussels burrowing into the silt; the diatoms and desmids and insect larvae sweeping past hydrazoans and infant snails" (16). As the watery refraction of the world above accedes to science's view of the ecological order below, the opening lines of *The Voyage of the Narwhal* signal that postmodernism's representational epistemologies of difference and deferral are being left behind. And yet, text quickly proves thicker than water. A submerged oyster, for instance, reminds Erasmus of the fantastical Pliny the Elder stories his father once shared with him. And later, recording the harbor scene in his journal, language foils his desire *"to show things both sequentially, and simultaneously."*[1] Worse, his subjective perspective—his "single pair of eyes" and "single voice"—intrudes into his account, compromising the scientific objectivity of his descriptions.

Stuck with this singular view, Erasmus covets an impossible vision: "*I wish I could show it as if through a fan of eyes. Widening out from my single perspective to several viewpoints, then many, so the whole picture might appear and not just my version of it. As if I weren't there. The river as the fish saw it, the ship as it looked to the men, Zeke as he looked to young Ned Kynd . . . : all those things, at once. So someone else might experience those hours for himself*" (26–27).

As Erasmus realizes when he moves from observing the world to writing about the world, the question of ecology is also a representational problem. Struggling with language to represent the world, the nature writer must determine the amount of culture nature can brook before it ceases to be nature.[2] If his writing includes his voice and vision, will the human skew and taint the true natural order Erasmus aims to crystallize in text? This is the micro-version of a tension between culture's subjectivity and nature's objectivity that frames the major debates within political ecology and environmental policy more broadly. On the one hand, deep ecology presents a view of nature distinct from the generally exploitative incursions of human culture, capitalism, development, and so on. Embedded in a previously existing natural order, humans must keep their disruptive presence to a minimum. Culture should become like nature—we should "be green"—so that nature can remain itself. On the other hand, sustainability advocates refute the myth of pristine nature and assume that human culture must learn to mediate the environment effectively. Deep ecology essentializes nature, objectivizing it as a given always threatened by the contingencies of culture; but sustainability views nature as a construct able to accommodate and partner with the subjectivizing force of human culture, with its particular voice and vision.

As we've seen in previous chapters, neoliberalism gains purchase on political ecology by co-opting and manipulating each of these competing environmental discourses.[3] Of course, as with human rights, public space, and race, it makes sense that neoliberalism also has a vested interest in the nature-culture relationship. For example, contending that "environmental change and environmental politics" are "constitutive" of neoliberalism (2), Heynen et al. observe that neoliberalism seems committed to any ecological thinking that allows it "to expand opportunities for capital investment and accumulation by reworking state-market-civil society relations" (10). Consequently, neoliberalism speaks the language of sustainability just as fluently as it does the language of deep ecology even though those two discourses tend to be at odds with each other. The trick, as we've seen in previous chapters, is that neoliberalism can't speak both at the same time. Rather, it alternates between the two, deploying whichever serves its interests best at the moment. This in turn creates a rhetorical and representational circularity immune to critique and allows neoliberalism to proceed with its primarily ontological (not representational or ideological) reconfiguration of the world.

For example, deep ecology's biologism, its commitment to a natural wilderness untrammeled by human artifact, its desire to maintain a holistic natural order: all of these values align perfectly with the laissez-faire economic principles of neoliberal capitalism. This is why Darwin emerges as a crucial figure for both deep ecology and neoliberalism. His thinking simultaneously sanctions a nature that is "red in tooth and claw" and an equally bloody and riven version of political economy.[4] In this view, humans are just as natural as nature; all of our bad decisions and loathsome creations are self-justifying because they all contribute to the natural evolutionary order. Karl Polanyi observes this dangerous overlap between economic and ecological worldviews when he warns at the beginning of *The Great Transformation*, an ur-text of anti-neoliberal thought, that "a self-adjusting market ... could not exist for any length of time without annihilating the human and natural substance of society; it would have physically destroyed man and transformed his surroundings into a wilderness" (3). Perversely, then, whenever deep ecology suggests a retreat from the self-interested consumerism of human culture back to the earth, it tacitly endorses the laissez-faire motivations of neoliberal capital.

Meanwhile, the sustainability agenda, aiming to identify an equilibrium between production and consumption that will avert the inevitable entropic death of unrestrained capitalism, also tends to reinforce the economic status quo. After all, neoliberals would love to make the earth's natural resources infinitely sustainable too. Sustainability might preserve the current environmental configuration, but it sustains the current economic configuration as well.[5] Sustainability "promotes and facilitates the continuation of the established socio-economic practice, while at the same time confirming the belief that society is performing the ecological U-turn" (Blühdorn 198).[6] Particularly egregious is neoliberalism's rhetorical yoking of sustainability and capitalist development under the notion of "sustainable development." In using this term "to cloak policies of expansion and accumulation," Rachel Greenwald Smith explains, "champions of neoliberalism have taken up even the very rhetoric of sustainability that environmentalists use to demand that the growth of global markets occurs with attention to the consequences for both class divisions and ecological health" (549). With equal access to the rhetorics of deep ecology and sustainability, then, this ecological neoliberal circle makes it difficult for activists and intellectuals to ground a viable political ecology that can effectively critique and differentiate itself from the neoliberal status quo.[7]

Erasmus senses that a "fan of eyes" might resolve these divides between culture and nature, word and world. Maybe objective science need not be at odds with subjective perspective. Perhaps he might accrue enough subjective perspectives—"[t]he river as the fish saw it, the ship as it looked to the men"—to achieve an objective and totalized view. Barrett seems to share Erasmus's hope. Equally invested in scientific inquiry and imaginative fiction, Narwhal also struggles to break from a postmodern epistemology that has tended to view those projects as mutually exclusive: language compromises knowing; culture taints nature; subjective mediation foils objective truth. Indeed, Barrett gives Narwhal its own "fan of eyes," multiplying historical and narrative perspectives throughout the text in an attempt to produce a thicker vision of the novel's action.[8] It's a valiant effort to think beyond postmodernism, but it's also a strategy which, as we've already seen in the compromised aesthetics of Adam Mansbach's Angry Black White Boy, doesn't entirely succeed. It doesn't succeed because Barrett's attempt to balance objective and subjective, essential and constructed, never fully dismantles the value of those concepts. Helpfully, the "fan of eyes" does avoid postmodernism's tendency to dwell on the inadequacy of representation and instead emphasizes the positive content that representations do achieve. Nevertheless, this approach continues to presuppose the purified divide between nature and culture so easily exploited by neoliberal discourse.

Speaking for the Fishes

As Erasmus speculates on the best way to turn representation into a "fan of eyes," he can't decide if the fan should include his perspective as one among many others or if his subjectivity should be purged from the representation altogether. Which method would achieve the most accurate portrait of the aqueous environs, he wonders. Initially, Erasmus intends the "fan of eyes" to conjure a scene "*as if [he] weren't there.*" But as soon as he pens those words in his journal, he admits that he's not being honest with himself: "He *did* want his own point of view to count, even as he also wanted to be invisible" (27). Rather than a balanced accumulation of multiple perspectives, these thoughts introduce two alternative solutions to Erasmus's representational difficulties. First, if Erasmus were to suppress his subjective perspective entirely, the resulting representation would be performative. All mimesis and no diegesis, Erasmus's text would immanently embody the marine life and its surroundings.[9] The second possibility, that he might be invisible yet still count, describes what I will be calling (following Bruno Latour) the spokesperson model of representation, or, representative representation. In this scenario, Erasmus must be present to speak for the creatures of the sea even as he keeps his unique subjectivity at bay. Ultimately, *Narwhal* doesn't adopt either of these methods. Instead, it proliferates subjective viewpoints, hoping they will add up to a portrait greater than the sum of its parts. Along the way, however, the novel does include several instances of these alternative representational forms that are worth exploring. For my purposes here, I will argue that turning representation into immanent performance does not resolve Erasmus's representational impasse or the ecological neoliberal circle, but representative representation just might.

First, performance and immanence. In an echo of Erasmus's initial thoughts on underwater representation, the narrator describes the dream of an Inuit youth named Tom. In the dream, Tom experiences tribal members pulling his drowned uncle from beneath the Arctic ice. I say he "experiences" rather than witnesses this event because throughout the dream Tom merges with and becomes an array of different objects and people: "He was the hook; he was the line; he was the strong body above, pulling delicately. He was the woman wailing as the boot broke the surface of the water, and he was the man watching as the body was born, feet first, from the sea" (390). Here Tom knows the event not by multiplying perspective, but by multiplying being. He doesn't just see as these things see; he is as these things are.[10] Yet another submerged vision in the novel, however, reveals the limitations of Tom's immanent becoming. During the voyage north, Erasmus's colleague Dr. Boerhaave falls beneath the ice and dies. Chapters later, the narrator tells us:

> [N]either Ned nor anyone else would be haunted by the sight of Dr. Boerhaave's head, which in the months since his drowning had been severed from his body by a passing grampus and then swept south in the currents, coming to rest face up on the rubble below a cliff. Among the rounded rocks his head was invisible to his friends, and the singing noise made by the wind passing over his jaw bones was lost in the roar of the waves (232).

By emphasizing all that remains unseen and unknown about Boerhaave's severed head, this passage demonstrates that immanent performance only works if someone is there to witness and record it. We still require a narrator to see the severed head go unseen if we ever hope to know about it, and Tom requires the dream's diegetic structure to experience his immanent performances of being.

Analogous to Boerhaave's head is a screw-studded sole from a leather shoe that Erasmus discovers among a remote group of Inuit. Remember, Erasmus's Arctic expedition is searching for evidence of what might have befallen the Franklin exploratory team a decade earlier, and this strip of leather is the only relic that might teach them the fate of Franklin and his men. However, when an Inuit woman gives Erasmus the shoe fragment, he selfishly keeps it as a personal souvenir of the trip and doesn't reveal its existence to anyone. Like Boerhaave's severed head, it too goes unseen. Consequently, when Erasmus finally does reveal the relic as material evidence of an important discovery, no one in Philadelphia believes him. Because he neglected to "include it on [his] list of the items [they] found," reporters charge that he "could have found it anywhere, and that it might be anything." As he explains to his brother, because "there's no one who witnessed me finding it, no written evidence of how I got it," it carries no meaning or value (294). Despite being "real," without documentation and empirical observation, it's worthless. In this way, the immanence of being is too severed from diegetic representation to be effective.

Instead, Erasmus's sense that the sole's value depends on itemization, witnesses, and written evidence brings us to the second, more productive representational alternative to the "fan of eyes":

representative representation. Writing that itemizes, documents, and describes—the representative representations of a writing that speaks for, not of, its objects—treats representation as an act of inclusion, in the political sense, not as an act of reference.[11] It takes Erasmus a while to appreciate this idea. At first, he so fears the corrupting influence of subjective perspective that he purges all humans from his initial account of the voyage. By the novel's conclusion, however, he realizes that suppressing human subjectivity, producing nature writing that is only "about the *place*—a natural history of the place through the seasons" (306), has left the Inuit excluded from his account, as if they were not part of the place and its natural history too (385). "The best thing to do might be never to visit such places," Erasmus admits, but having visited, he concludes that he was wrong to "avert his eyes" from the human and study "the plants and animals instead."[12]

Although the novel ends before Erasmus can apply this lesson, *Narwhal* leads us to imagine that Erasmus—having realized that he can see the world without imposing himself on it, that one need not choose between nature and culture, deep ecology and sustainability—will return north, spend time with the Inuit, and write a more proper "representation" of the Arctic environment. Functioning as a spokesperson, Erasmus will not filter the world through his subjective perspective but will instead speak for a world that cannot speak for itself. As Latour puts it, "If I speak in the name of another, I am not speaking in my own name" (*Politics* 64).[13] Crucially, this idea helps us see that we can escape mere perspectivalism without having to embrace the performativity of immanent becoming. We don't have to choose between knowing the fish without being it, or being the fish without knowing it. Instead, when we speak for the fish, we treat it as our ontological equivalent. It is, quite literally, represented. Or as Erasmus thinks of the work produced by Alexandra, a superb illustrator of nature's flora and fauna: "Nothing she rendered was new to him, yet each stroke of her pencils . . . was like a chisel held to a cleavage plane: tap, tap, and the rock split into two sharp pieces, the world cracked and spoke to him" (392). It would be wrong to see Alexandra's art—the art of the spokesperson giving voice to the world—as either merely subjective or wholly objective. It's not the mediated artifice of culture, but it's also not the pure reality of the natural world. Instead, it occupies a representational domain beyond that distinction precisely to the extent that it replaces the problem of knowing with the fact of existence. Or to be more exact, the art of the spokesperson makes knowledge a function of existence, not a function of referential resemblance. Knowledge is not about how close we over here can get to the world over there; it's about how much of the world over there can be brought into and included in the world over here until we fully appreciate that it's actually all one world.

After examining two other contemporary novels that wrestle with the question of how best to represent the environment—Mat Johnson's *Pym* and Kim Stanley Robinson's *Antarctica*—this chapter concludes with a text that I see as a paradigmatic example of the spokesperson's art: Tom McCarthy's *Remainder*. *Pym* will do important work challenging typical forms of environmental representation—that is, the belief that our words can conjure and critique the world. *Antarctica* will then replace those word-world forms of critical representation with representative representations achieved through the scientific method. Robinson's novel will also prove instructive, however, because even as it replaces linguistic representation with scientific representation, it can't resist the lure of performance. That is, Robinson's prose not only describes the slow accumulation of scientific knowledge by diligent spokespeople, it also painstakingly enacts that process for its readers. But the great thing about the spokesperson's art is that it absolutely does not require such performative modes of becoming, it doesn't force us to choose between being and knowing, which is precisely what *Remainder* will show in the chapter's culmination. Recognizing that difference per se is not a problem and that it's just the entrenched difference between subjects and objects that traps us in undecidable circles, *Remainder* proves that knowing and talking about the world require neither our distanced critique of it nor our immanent merging into it. Instead, McCarthy's novel reorients the production of knowledge and value around a different kind of difference: the difference between excluded and included objects, between objects that do and do not have spokespeople. I'll argue that in doing so, by replacing *subjectivized* difference with the difference among ontologically equivalent objects, *Remainder* avoids recourse to more reductive forms of immanence and instead models a political ecology that stands outside the circular debate between deep ecology and sustainability, expanding the known world by embracing non-identity.

A Monstrous World

While Alexandra, the nature illustrator in *Narwhal*, embraces the spokesperson's art, the novel itself, which remains committed to a project of critique, cannot. The perspectival distance between subject and object that critique requires is difficult to maintain when writing as a spokesperson. But because Barrett sees a lot to critique in the nineteenth century—namely the patriarchal, colonial, and racist assumptions that fueled the era's ostensibly neutral pursuit of knowledge—the same gap that confounds Erasmus's writings intrudes into her narrative representations as well.

Whether highlighting the injustices suffered by nature or the afflictions of marginalized populations subjected to environmental crisis, this impulse to critique has motivated ecological writing and ecocriticism since its inception. And this compulsion to critique has in turn elevated the status of representation in political ecology. Because showing the world always entails a particular, usually political, framing of the world, representations matter. As Richard Kerridge argued in the 1990s, "the real, material ecological crisis . . . is also a cultural crisis, a crisis of representation. The inability of political cultures to address environmentalism is in part a failure of narrative" (4). In turn, nature writing and other representations of the environment are opportunities to set the terms of debate, reveal environmental injustice, and articulate a better future. This idea abides, as Rob Nixon's *Slow Violence* insists that we must "convert into image and narrative the [ecological] disasters that are slow moving and long in the making, disasters that are anonymous and star nobody, disasters that are attritional and of indifferent interest to the sensation-driven technologies of our image-world" (3).[14] In his attempt to find those representations that will do justice to ecological violence, Nixon unapologetically focuses on "writer-activists" who "are enraged by injustices they wish to see redressed, injustices they believe they can help expose, silences they can help dismantle through testimonial protest, rhetorical inventiveness, and counterhistories in the face of formidable odds" (6). As this righteous description of writer-activists demonstrates, however, "they" form a large part of these representations. They are revealing what *they* find unjust, exposing arrangements *they* deem problematic. But by separating the perceiving subject from the object of critique, such critical representations reinforce the purified culture-nature divide that enables and exacerbates the very environmental degradation they're supposedly challenging.[15]

This is the argument of Mat Johnson's *Pym*, a novel that moves us from Barrett's nineteenth-century Arctic expedition to a twenty-first-century Antarctic one. Instead of situating the period's scientific advances against the backdrop of modernity's constitutive racism and sexism, Johnson's characters discover a colony of subterranean ice monsters in the context of contemporary neoliberalism. Whereas Barrett critiques nineteenth-century culture for interfering with the scientific process, Johnson suggests that neoliberalism has made critique redundant. In *Pym* all attempts to comment on or gain knowledge of the natural world fail because they all ultimately reinforce the neoliberal project. For Johnson the only alternative is to abandon the illusion that we over here are different from, and thus qualified to say something about, the natural world over there.

Johnson's speculative fiction works from the premise that the shocking events recounted in Poe's *Narrative of Arthur Gordon Pym* are true, and it deploys Antarctica as an ecology of radical otherness to emphasize the futility of maintaining the old purified divides between subject and object, human and non-human, culture and nature, word and world. The zany plot in brief: A black but very light-skinned English professor, Chris Jaynes, finds archival evidence suggesting that Poe's famously bizarre novel is historically accurate. To verify his discovery, he recruits his adventurous cousin Booker Jaynes to lead an expedition to Antarctica. Booker agrees, but only because he plans to harvest glacial ice, bottle it, and sell it as drinking water in the States. Chris's Little Debbie–loving friend Garth joins the expedition when he learns that his favorite artist, Thomas Karvel, has retreated to Antarctica to wait out what vague reports scattered throughout the novel suggest are the end times.[16] Chris fills out the crew with two men who run an "Afro-Adventure Blog," his ex-girlfriend Angela, and her new husband Nathaniel, an entertainment lawyer. Shortly after their arrival in Antarctica, they discover the all-white race of Tekelians—massive hairy monsters living in caves below the ice—alluded to at the end of Poe's novel. They also meet Arthur Gordon Pym who, mistaking the light-skinned Chris as a slave trader (the rest of the crew has darker skin, and Pym knows nothing of human civilization since his disappearance in the early nineteenth century), facilitates their enslavement at the hands of the Tekelians. Chris and Garth escape and eventually find Karvel's Antarctic retreat, a biosphere in which he exactingly re-creates the "natural" beauty of his artworks. Eventually the Tekelians show up because the boilers heating Karvel's biosphere are melting their caves. Instead of working things out, the humans serve the Tekelians a dinner riddled with rat poison. But when the Tekelians discover the genocidal plot, they kill everyone except for Chris and Garth, who escape with Pym in search of the all-black island nation of Tsalal (also described in Poe's novel). As Pym dies, Chris and Garth reach the island where they are greeted by a gregarious group of loincloth-wearing "brown people."[17] We learn nothing of the "Armageddon" that befalls humankind while the group is isolated in Antarctica, but a framing preface in which Chris Jaynes retrospectively details the process of bringing his tale into print suggests that, at the very least, Mat Johnson has survived to author "these revelations under the guise of fiction," and apparently Random House is still around to publish them as *Pym* (4).

Throughout *Pym*, Johnson mocks and derides the notion that humans control and determine their relationship to nature, and he does so by conjuring an external world that resists his characters' every attempt to know it representationally. The majority of Chris's crew, budding neoliberal entrepreneurs that they are, approaches the world economically: Booker wants to sell bottled water; the bloggers hope to gain fame and increase traffic to their site; Nathaniel, the entertainment lawyer, hopes to sell the movie rights to the narrative of their adventure; and his wife, Angela, dreams of opening an ice hotel and developing a new fad diet based on Tekelian cuisine. When the group first discovers the Tekelian caves, they haggle over naming rights to the subterranean ice formations; when they discover the Tekelian monsters, they negotiate their "respective stakes in intellectual property and other rights of exploitation," including action figures (132); and when they realize that Pym must be over two hundred years old, they immediately approach this "fountain of youth" from "a business standpoint" (142). Even when enslaved, neoliberal Nathaniel, noting that "life is all about improving your assets," accepts his status as a commodity among the Tekelians and learns their language to increase his value (197). Although Chris and Garth do not share these economic interests, Chris eventually realizes that their motivations are not substantially different from the rest of his profit-oriented team:

> Garth and I were no better. Our goals, what had brought us down here, were out there on the ice like shining oases, luminescent to us individually. Now, frozen, trapped, I couldn't help thinking that maybe they didn't matter. That what really mattered is what our ambitions had led us to. That we were in this moment because of the future we imagined for ourselves. That even without the snow beasts, we were enslaved. By our greed, our lusts, our dreams. (188)

But it's not just the economic and utopian visions of nature that are untenable and ultimately destructive. In *Pym* aesthetic representations of nature also lead inevitably to its demise. Johnson makes this point with Karvel, whose biosphere, originally intended to improve nature representationally, ultimately triggers a series of boiler explosions that implode the entire Tekelian habitat. As with the crew's pervasive neoliberalism and Chris and Garth's utopianism, Karvel is trapped in his own subjectivized distance from the natural world: "There is only one look. There is only one vision. Perfection isn't about change, diversity. It's about getting close to that one vision" (251). Johnson's particular insight here is to demonstrate that utopian politics (Chris's search for an all-black island untouched by white colonialism) and aesthetic treatments of nature (Karvel's biosphere) are structurally homologous to and thus ultimately complicit with neoliberalism's relationship to nature.

As far as Johnson is concerned, all of these acts of seeing, all of these representations of the world, are inherently greedy and inevitably dangerous to the extent that they force the world over there to comport with us over here. Such representational acts can only lead to our mutually assured destruction, as we see when Chris and his crew, all descendants of slaves, immediately move to enslave the Tekelians. Notice, for example, how Johnson's description of an early encounter reiterates the discourse of the slave trade: "[W]e were at a disadvantage in choosing who among them to take as samples of this species, having just that day been introduced to their existence" (147). Chris's cousin, claiming expertise in "the art of ice monkey commerce," even instructs his comrades to "[i]nspect their teeth . . ., poke a finger into the backs of their mouths to see if they're missing any. . . . Check their hair, make sure it's not falling out" (148). These humans, it turns out, are as monstrous as the monsters. They might have a lot to say about the natural world, but the lesson of Johnson's novel is that none of them should be saying it. Their visionary representations, their self-important critiques, are monstrosities one and all.[18]

This has crucial implications for our approach to both neoliberalism and the environmental destruction it exacerbates. If we over here are not much different from the world over there, then our fears of neoliberal dominance and ecological disaster are misplaced. We should not be afraid of nefarious forces afoot in the world; we should be afraid of ourselves. We should be afraid of no longer having any monsters to fear. In place of neoliberalism as bogeyman, Brenner and Theodore helpfully remind us of "the constitutively uneven character" of neoliberal environmentalisms which are rarely "singular," "homogeneous," "stable," or "self-regulating" (158). Neoliberalism is neither other to us nor other to the natural world. This is partly why contemporary environmental scientists have begun referring to our current geological period as the Anthropocene. We don't affect nature and geology; we are nature and geology, and we have been at least since the industrial revolution. Capitalism is not the enemy of world ecology; it is world ecology. And to the extent that critique's representational structures keep us thinking as humans rather than as one of many ecologically interconnected species, our representations of the environment might actually be hurting more than they help (Chakrabarty 217).

Dropping Science

Confronted with monstrous, irreducible nonidentity, what alternatives do we have for relating to the world? Embracing the representative representations of the spokesperson in lieu of critique, Kim Stanley Robinson suggests that we would be well served by a turn to science. The science Robinson has in mind, however, is not that set of objective facts that short-circuits political discourse with its apparently exclusive access to the truth of the world. Instead, science in Robinson's novels always increases uncertainty and doubt. It doesn't unify knowledge; it complicates it.[19] The primary object of scientific inquiry in Robinson's *Antarctica* is the geological history of the continent. The only continent without sovereign territory and a native population, Antarctica is an apt choice for speculating about how a government run by science would operate. The territory is governed by the Antarctic Treaty System, an international treaty that preserves the continent as a demilitarized land of peaceful scientific inquiry. In the novel, this harmony is threatened by advances in resource extraction which have piqued the economic interests of various nations and corporations.[20] This triggers a series of confrontations that reveal just how factionalized the continent has become. In addition to the scientists and the large bureaucracy of supporting staff and institutions loosely coordinated by the National Science Foundation, there are: private companies running adventure tours for wilderness lovers; private oil and gas companies doing exploratory drilling for natural resources to commodify; politicians who want to use the scientists to develop climate change policies while simultaneously maneuvering against their ideological opponents in Washington; a group of "ferals" who live nomadically on the continent with the ultimate goal of becoming "native" to Antarctica; and ecoterrorists who see all human presence in this sacrosanct wilderness as anathema. When the ecoterrorists stage a coordinated series of attacks that threaten all of the other interests operating in Antarctica, the stage is set for Robinson to re-build this world from the bottom up, with science.

Some of the factions are suspicious of science, worrying that the scientists will use their exclusive access to objective truth to steer negotiations in their favor. For example, Carlos, a Chilean who grew up in Antarctica and now works for a private company investing in methane extraction, contends of the scientists: "They know that knowledge can become power, and with the power that science wields in this world, they control things. Control even the political realm, but without the hassle of politics per se" (347). But the scientists in *Antarctica* do not hold the trump card of pure facts. If their knowledge surpasses that of the other interest groups, it's only because they are painfully aware of all that they don't know. Robinson dramatizes this point by staging a scientific controversy between stabilists (scientists who claim that Antarctica's eastern ice cap formed "forty or fifty million years ago") and dynamicists (those who think that the same chunk of ice was nonexistent as recently as three million years ago) (171). Even as the novel's dynamicists believe that the evidence supports their conclusions, they also acknowledge that they are not necessarily more correct than the stabilists, who also have evidence

supporting their conclusions. Wade, an aide to a Washington senator hoping to lead the policy charge on climate change, looks to the
scientists for facts and figures that will allow the senator to make his
case. But the scientists insist that the only thing he can justifiably
tell the senator is that "nobody knows" (175). As the lead dynamicist admits, the stabilists "are trying to prove a hypothesis, they are
down here gathering data every season, they're publishing results in
peer-reviewed journals. They're wrong, I think, but they are still scientists. Many scientists are wrong, perhaps most. . . . Even we may be
wrong" (176). In this way, science's production of doubt and uncertainty ensures that its conclusions cannot be deployed in the service
of any particular ideological interest.

Even as the content of scientific knowledge can't determine the
facts of the world once and for all, the process by which scientific
knowledge is produced holds more potential. That is, the content of
science will not support one set of interests over the others, but the
formal processes of science can mediate the overarching relationship
among all interests. An invented text that Robinson inserts into his
novel—*The Ethical, Political, and Utopian Elements Embodied in the
Structure of Modern Science*—observes, for instance, that "science is
self-organizing and self-actualizing, and always trying to get better,
to be more scientific, as one of its rules." Moreover, "various features of normal scientific practice, the methodology and so on, are
in fact ethical positions. Things like reproducibility, Occam's razor,
or peer review—almost everything in science that makes it specifically scientific . . . is utopian" (350). The dynamicists out in the field
agree, as they constantly emphasize the slow and ongoing process
of transforming empirical observations into knowledge, a process
that could take generations since Antarctica doesn't provide "a cliff
of facts, but of stone" (307). Because those stones, of course, do not
speak, the scientists have to "translate" them, to speak for them (311).
This in turn requires "making alliances to help you to show what you
wanted to show, and to make clear also that what you were showing was important" (309). It's all horribly complicated. To ultimately
"locate [their evidentiary objects] in dense meshes of history [and]
turn them into facts, facts that would then support a theory," the
dynamicists must first enlist "an array of paleobotanists, paleobi-
ologists, geomorphologists, geophysicists, paleoclimatologists, and
glaciologists . . . all bringing their specialty to bear on the subject at
hand, all of whose own careers, if they took part in this effort, would

then become at least somewhat connected to the success or failure of
the dynamicist view" (386). But then . . .

> the lab work on the samples would have to be done, and the litera-
> ture would have to be researched, and other scientists asked to make
> contributions possibly; and the papers would have to be written, and
> revised, and submitted to the most prominent and appropriate jour-
> nals, where anonymous reviewers would no doubt suggest further
> revisions, which, as they often strengthened one's case, were usu-
> ally incorporated; and only then would the papers be published. . . .
> And in that state they would be read, and would add to the dialogue
> among the small groups of people who had the expertise to judge
> the arguments, to probe them for weaknesses; people who would
> indeed make judgments and criticisms; and later their own scien-
> tific assumptions about the field would take this new set of facts into
> account, and engage the theory, and they would design their own
> projects accordingly; and see different things than they would have
> otherwise, out in the world, and the dialogue would go on, as it had
> ever since Lyell, or Newton or Aristotle or the first talking primates.
> (387–388)

This due diligence that the scientific method demands, according to
Robinson, gives science its utopian impulse and political potential.

No one has laid out this idea more methodically than Bruno
Latour in *Politics of Nature*, where he describes the due process
involved in composing a common world. Instead of dividing the
world into subjects and objects, values and facts, Latour suggests that
the most relevant distinction is between that which is excluded and
that which is included: "We no longer have a society surrounded by a
nature, but a collective producing a clear distinction between what it
has internalized and what it has externalized" (124). To achieve this
new organization, Latour deconstructs values and facts only to reas-
semble them in a more productive fashion. First, Latour observes
that values-oriented arguments are deployed in two different ways.
Either they emphasize that something has been left out of a given
configuration (e.g., homosexuality should be included in anti-bias
laws) or they argue that a new arrangement does not comport with
currently accepted standards (e.g., legalizing marijuana does not
align with the values of our community). Facts-oriented arguments
exhibit a similar distinction. Either we use facts to argue against
simplification (e.g., your praise for the decline in unemployment

ignores the fact that thousands have merely stopped looking for work) or we deploy them to suggest that something cannot be challenged (e.g., climactic records clearly demonstrate that humans are making the planet warmer). Latour next notes that these four conceptual moves should be regrouped. Using values to emphasize that something has been left out and using facts to argue against simplification are now grouped together under the category, "the power to take into account." Meanwhile, using values to argue that something new doesn't accord with the existing order of things and using facts to suggest that something cannot be challenged are now grouped together under the category, "the power to arrange in rank order." The first two gestures are different ways of determining what should be brought into the fold, and the second two gestures are different ways of determining the relative importance of those newly included things.

This is, of course, precisely how Robinson describes the scientific process in *Antarctica*. First, the information must be gathered, the interested parties must convoke, and only then does the collective determine who makes the cut. Then, after new candidates have been admitted, specialists must determine how much significance each should bear in the world. Perhaps previously held beliefs, scientific or otherwise, will be abandoned, jettisoned from the current version of reality to make way for the new candidates. Perhaps none will make the cut and they will have to return later with stronger arguments and better evidence if they hope to gain admission.[21] The process is ongoing: "[W]e are allowing the articulation of propositions in the successive states of their natural history to emerge, from the appearance of candidate entities to their incorporation into the states of the world" (*Politics* 116). Everything, whether value or fact, is an equal candidate for admission into, or rejection from, the world we compose together.[22]

Politically, this is clearly not a revolutionary project, and it's not an ideological one either.[23] In the novel, for instance, the stabilists and dynamicists do not offer competing representations of reality; they offer differently networked and allied pieces of the world. When the dynamicists "translate" the stones one way and the stabilists another, at issue is not whose subjective representation most closely approximates the scientific truth of the objective world. Rather, as substitutions for the stone, their translations go out into the world and either do or do not find allies to corroborate a specific configuration of evidence and objects. Their words are functioning ontologically, not referentially; they are speaking for the world, not of the world. Accordingly, meaningful truth becomes a function of inclusion in the world, of being represented in the "parliament of things."

When the competing interests in *Antarctica* finally sit down and hash out a new arrangement for the continent, this is precisely how most of them use language. Starting from scratch, each faction is allowed to speak, including the two main antagonists: a lawyer who speaks for the ecoterrorists and their radicalized deep ecology and Carlos who speaks for the corporate drilling interests that employ him. The ecoterrorists' lawyer condemns corporate and governmental despoliation of "this last wilderness continent" (561), and Carlos, emphasizing the safety of resource extraction, speaks the language of sustainability, suggesting that the benefits of feeding the world outweigh the environmental damage: "We have to provide [the poor] with food and the energy to make food and shelter and clothing and schools and hospitals and you *cannot do it* with your deep-ecology wilderness dream." As the conversation proceeds, we see that Carlos speaks as a spokesperson while the lawyer speaks as an ideologue. In other words, the lawyer transforms a conversation about one form of representation (who and what should be included) into a debate about a different form of representation (whose vision is most true, the least ideologically mystified). Thus, the lawyer tells Carlos that his "brain has been overdetermined by [his] structured position in the global hierarchy" (566). Certain of the purity of his own vision, the lawyer critiques Carlos as a naïve pawn of his corporate overlords. This lengthy exchange is particularly instructive, however, because it demonstrates how the voice of the scientific spokesperson short-circuits the representational logic of ideology critique. The lawyer speaks the mutually exclusive, all-or-nothing language of the ecoterrorists, a language of critique that relies on the purified divide between subject and object, culture and nature, word and world. It's a discourse committed to revealing Carlos's complicity, his inauthenticity, his blindness. But for Carlos, none of those things matter. He is not worried about selling out, only about making sure that the reality for which he speaks will be included in the final dispensation. In defending his company's exploratory drilling, he is, in short, defending sustainability with the language of science:

[T]here are new pipelines now, flexible and unbreakably strong, designed to lie under the surface of the ocean. . . . The materials are fantastic, they're made of meshes like Kevlar, and include plastics grown in soy plants. . . . So these new technologies make methane a more useful fuel. And burning these methane hydrates could actually help the global climate situation. You see, if the polar caps melt, like we see them starting to, then this methane below us will be released into the atmosphere, and kick off a greenhouse warming that makes the one we have now look like nothing. We think now that some of the great rapid climate warmings of the past were caused by the release of methane hydrate deposits. So it's possible we can capture this gas, and burn it for our own power, and reduce greenhouse gases at the same time. It's very elegant in that way. (220)

Here Carlos defuses neoliberalism—or what the novel repeatedly calls "*Gotterdammerung* capitalism"—not with critique, but with science. It's not proven wrong, unjust, or ideologically mystified; it's proven to be another thing in the world that must, in effect, make it through peer review if it wants to be taken seriously.

This scientization of politics, the extension of the scientific method to all the world's objects, beliefs, humans, even economic systems, leaves the representational arts in a tricky position. What would literature that tried to include rather than represent look like? Robinson's novel raises this question through the figure of Ta Shu, a Chinese poet in the novel who is "baffled" by the representational challenges that Antarctica presents to his art. Notably, Ta Shu abandons text altogether and instead wears a camera that provides a live feed of his Antarctic escapades to his audience in China. Excluding himself from the frame, the video allows Ta Shu to embody, not show, his adventures. As I intend the admittedly lengthy and tedious quotations earlier to demonstrate, Robinson seems similarly committed to the immanent mode of Ta Shu's performance. That is, *Antarctica* doesn't just tell us that science takes a long time to work; it takes a long time to tell us that science takes a long time to work. Science must go through all the proper channels and cover all its bases, it must exert its "power to take into account," and apparently so must Robinson's prose.[24]

But as I suggested before in discussing immanent performance in Barrett's *Narwhal*, such performances preclude the key difference between excluded and included that motivates a deliberative scientific (and political) process. To be sure, making literature performative—producing a text with formal features that enact and embody its content—ontologizes literature and wrests it away from the representational paradoxes and impasses of postmodernism so easily exploited by neoliberalism. Performance most certainly solves the problem of literature's inability to represent the world. But it does so by conflating being and doing, by reducing world to event. It's too easy, and it doesn't fully account for discrete, ontological difference. In other words, Robinson's belabored performance of deliberation actually obscures the inside/outside difference that deliberation requires in the first place.

This is why I propose a different approach, an approach in which literature abandons the project of speaking accurately about the world, but it does so without necessarily retreating into immanent performance. Instead, literature, just like all those scientific spokespeople in *Antarctica*, might be seen as one of many possible ways to speak for a world that cannot speak for itself. This is what Latour recommends, for example, when he describes literature as a site for the "redistribution of agencies" ("Attempt" 489, n. 25). Functioning more like a lobbyist for the world's excluded objects, literature might locate agency where previously none had been granted while denying agency where it had previously seemed obvious and given. In this scenario, words might still refer to things, but the standards and stakes of that referential act would concern literature's incorporative capacity, not its mimetic accuracy.[25] Literary truth, value, and meaning would derive from a text's ability to expand the world that gets taken into account and included in the already-existing world. Literature would thus become one of many different ways that humans have to expand their world.

I mean this, however, not in the humanistic, Nussbaumian sense, but in an antihumanist, ironic sense.[26] Irony, at least a specific form of irony, is foundational to any attempt to reimagine literature as a non-referential "redistribution of agencies," as a cataloguing and expansion of the connections among human and nonhuman worlds. Timothy Morton provides the definition of irony I intend here: "the refreshing and consistent noncoincidence of what is in our heads with what is the case." Because irony is all about "a willingness to be wrong," it becomes a crucial aesthetic mode in any literary pursuit of "nonidentity" (*Ecology* 193). Irony is, in effect, the mode of science and of a truly deliberative democracy. It's the attitude toward the world that allows us to compose the world, to take it into account *and* to arrange it in rank order. Irony's commitment to what's not known, not said, and not there makes it an ideal tool for establishing a relationship between the excluded and the included, and its tenacious skepticism aids in discerning where new things belong in relation to the old.[27] In addition, irony foils immanence—or at least what I've referred to as the Deleuzian/Bergsonian immanence of becoming—by insisting on a deliberately speculative moment in which excluded and included meet. As Morton points out, irony's commitment to non-identity undermines what he describes as a broad structural homology among an algorithmic, organic sense of nature; an "automated capitalism" devoted to free-market logic; organicist literary forms that conflate content and form; and those leftist politics that continue to believe in "self-organizing labor" (*Ecology* 188–193). Only irony places the necessary hiccup in these various forms of emergent becoming and institutes a speculative moment of ecological, aesthetic, economic, and/or political deliberation that stands obliquely to neoliberalism's frequently automated and algorithmic immanence.

Antartica

Tom McCarthy's *Remainder* shows us what a world filled with such speculative hiccups looks like. The novel begins with a name-less first-person narrator struggling to recall the details of a recent trauma. Apparently some detritus fell from the sky, landed on his head, and left him partially amnesic. The corporation responsible for the accident awards him 8.5 million pounds to never mention the incident again, which is easy because he doesn't remember it. Unsure of how to spend his money, he has an epiphany while standing in a bathroom at a party. A crack in the bathroom wall reminds him of an apartment that he can't quite place—perhaps he even lived there once—but he does remember feeling comfortable and at ease there. Having been consistently and uncomfortably alienated from his physical environment ever since the accident, he decides to re-create and then inhabit the apartment building, precisely replicating every last detail he can recall. This includes artificially distressing newly purchased materials, hiring a woman to cook liver in a downstairs apartment, and arranging for black cats to walk on the roof of the adjacent building, all in an attempt to match life in the "re-enacted" apartment with his memory. The experiment is so successful that he re-enacts other events as well, an obsessive habit that culminates in the re-enactment of a bank heist. At the last moment, however, he switches the setting of the robbery from a constructed set in a warehouse to the bank itself, transforming the staged event into an actual one. When events don't go as planned—one of his re-enactors ends up dead—he flees with his facilitator, Naz, on a private jet. Informed that the aircraft has been ordered to return to the airport with its fugitive passengers, the narrator hijacks the plane and orders the pilot to repeat a figure-eight pattern in the sky. Presumably they will run out of fuel and crash, but the book ends before that happens.

The narrator's compulsion to re-enact stems from his desire to erase the self-conscious distance that intrudes between him and the world. Unable to behave with transparent authenticity, he feels like he's playing a role, like he can't inhabit space properly. In an irony apparently lost on the narrator, he locates the ideal form of authentic behavior in cinema, specifically in Robert De Niro's performance in *Mean Streets*: "Every move he made, each gesture was perfect, seamless. Whether it was lighting up a cigarette or opening a fridge door or just walking down the street: he seemed to execute the action perfectly, to live it, to merge with it until he was it and it was him and there was nothing in between" (23). The accident only exacerbates the narrator's awkwardness, requiring him to relearn the most foundational physical motions: the "twenty-seven separate manoeuvres involved" in lifting a carrot to his mouth (20), the "seventy-five manoeuvres involved in taking a single step forward" (22). For De Niro, thinking never intrudes into being or doing; he's all immanent performance. But the narrator cannot be or do without thinking getting in the way. The re-enactments solve this problem by doing the thinking ahead of time. Once they are set in motion, the narrator inhabits them seamlessly, immanently.

The dilemma that the novel thinks through, then, is both ecological and postmodern: vexed by the relationship between authenticity and inauthenticity, truth and illusion, reality and artifice, a subject struggles to establish the proper relationship to his environment. Meaning, ethics, knowledge, connection—they're all foiled by the intractable divide the narrator suffers between knowing and being, representation and performance. Even the culminating bank heist echoes Jean Baudrillard's meditation—from that most canonical of postmodern handbooks, *Simulacra and Simulation*—on the implications of organizing "a fake holdup." Predicting the plot of *Remainder*, Baudrillard contends that any attempt to simulate a bank robbery will fail because reality will inevitably intrude: "a policeman will really fire on sight; a client of the bank will faint and die of a heart attack" (20). In Baudrillard's postmodern vision, this conflation of illusion and reality traps subjects in iterative structures of epistemological indeterminacy. (Think *White Noise.)* *Remainder's* narrator wants out of those structures, and the constant pursuit of immanence defines his escape plan. By merging into the flow of events around him, he erases epistemology's subject-object difference and achieves the immersive truth of pure being, which always seems to make him feel "tingly": "I stared at her and felt the edges of my vision widening. The walls around her door, the mosaicked floor that emanated from its base, the ceiling—all these seemed to both expand and brighten. I felt myself beginning to drift into them, these surfaces—and to drift once more close to the edges of a trance" (226).

The narrator makes this sound delightful. The constant "merging" and "emerging," the hyper-awareness of micro and macro movements, patterns, connections, and interconnections, the harmonious consonance between the human and non-human world: so much wonderfully pure being and becoming. But all of this seductive tingling is a red herring. *Remainder* begins with the tragic alienation of a subject from his world, but the novel is also quite skeptical that such self-consciousness can be overcome with the immanence of pure flow. Instead, *Remainder* demonstrates that the representational logic responsible for a subject's distanced self-consciousness from the world needs to be radically reconceived. The novel shows that representation and performance, diegesis and mimesis, are just two sides of the same coin, echoes of a broader antinomy between transcendence and immanence that doesn't help us think about the environment or our place in it.

We should thus be suspicious of the narrator's sense that there is no finer merging, no better way to collapse the distance between thinking and being, than death. Speaking of a murder victim the narrator plans to embody in a future re-enactment, the narrator reveals:

The truth is that, for me, this man had become a symbol of perfection. It may have been clumsy to fall from his bike, but in dying beside the bollards on the tarmac he'd done what I wanted to do: merged with the space around him, sunk and flowed into it until there was no distance between it and him—and merged, too, with his actions, merged to the extent of having no more consciousness of them. He'd stopped being separate, removed, imperfect. . . . The spot that this had happened on was the ground zero of perfection—all perfection. (197–198)

More disturbingly, when a fellow re-enactor is shot during the bank robbery, the narrator's only response is to whisper, "Beautiful," while lowering himself beside the corpse to observe how "parts of his flesh had broken through the skin and risen, like rising dough" (294). Similarly, when his assistant Naz proposes killing everyone involved in the bank robbery to prevent any "leakage" that might lead to their arrest, the narrator agrees, noting how "*really* beautiful" it will be when their "plane bec[omes] a pillow ripping open, its stuffing of feathers rushing outward, merging with the air" (276). Despite the elegant and evocative simplicity of the narrator's observations, we should see his obsessive desire to transubstantiate himself (and others) into the world as a clear indictment of an algorithmic immanence entirely free of deliberative agents and speculative hiccups. Because enacting the immanence of death proves rather dangerous and irresponsible, *Remainder* asks whether the alienating divide between self and world might be reconciled without succumbing to the lethal seductions of pure, immanent merging. We need difference to save us from immanent death, but we don't want a schismatic difference that alienates subject from object, thinking from being. Where might we find a nonalienating difference that still allows things to be what they are?

Answering this question requires some parsing of McCarthy's thinking about death. Obviously not a numbly callous murderer, McCarthy nevertheless remains a great advocate of death. Co-founder (with Simon Critchley) of the International Necronautical Society, an avant-garde agitprop organization that releases aesthetic-philosophical statements that manage simultaneous sincerity and absurdity, McCarthy proclaims the following in the group's manifesto, originally published as a paid advertisement in the London *Times*: "1. That death is a type of space, which we intend to map, enter, colonise and, eventually, inhabit. 2. That there is no beauty without death, its immanence. We shall sing death's beauty—that is, beauty." This obviously sounds a lot like the project that *Remainder*'s narrator pursues, except McCarthy and his friends are not dehiscing their colleagues with psychopathic calm.

We should thus make a distinction between the narrator, who is necrocorpic, and McCarthy, who is just necronautical. The narrator produces and embodies death; McCarthy sails toward it: "Our very bodies are no more than vehicles carrying us ineluctably towards death. We are all necronauts, always, already." As an artist, then, McCarthy's job is not to kill, but "to bring death out into the world." He will "chart all its forms and media: in literature and art, where it is most apparent; also in science and culture, where it lurks submerged but no less potent for the obfuscation." Thus, he implores his readers to "deliver [them]selves over utterly to death, not in desperation but rigorously, creatively, eyes and mouths wide open so that they may be filled from the deep wells of the Unknown." McCarthy is, in effect, death's spokesperson, its representative. His job is not to destroy, but to fill up the world as it already is with all that we've excluded from it. This requires the narrator's heightened attunement to space, his subjectivity-annihilating relationships with objects, his proclivity for tracing the networked interconnections of events large and small, but it won't require death per se. Which means it also doesn't require pure immanence either. To be sure, the manifesto's second proposition explicitly connects death to immanence—"there is no beauty without death, its immanence"—but it also implies that we need not become death. Instead, "We shall sing death's beauty"; we shall speak for it as its representatives in the world. Difference—in the form of the distinction between excluded and included—abides.

In turn, necronautical literature avoids standard representational modes of reference without succumbing to performative immanence either. In a recent interview, for instance, McCarthy envisions a textual mode beyond those alternatives when he describes literature not as representation but as transmission, like a set of radio signals that can be "picked up and warped and mutated into something else" (Hart 672).[28] Notably, McCarthy suggests that this materialization or mattering of literature, this ontologization of text, overcomes the alienating and self-conscious distance the narrator experiences in *Remainder*, but it does so without reducing the subject to immanent flow. Instead, it erases the subject-object divide altogether. It "push[es] away from perspectivism and all the attendant ideologies about subjectivity, Cartesianism, and depth," effectively "rethinking . . . personality, character, and so on as a set of surfaces and planes" (670). This "two-dimensional geometry" makes matter matter (to borrow from the title of the Necronauts' collected writings, *The Mattering of Matter*). It transmits and materializes those remainders that have been excluded from prior consideration, not by painting their pictures, but by including them.

Consequently, even as McCarthy's novel evokes dazzling scenes of pure becoming, a stray bit of "messy, irksome matter" always intrudes and undoes the narrator's transubstantial project (17). From the champagne cork that won't properly pop (25) to the refrigerator door that sticks (131), from the kitchen counter that snags the narrator's shirt (140) to the windshield wiper fluid that disappears from its reservoir only to gush from the car's dashboard components after ignition (171), "everything fucks up" (24). Including the bank robbery, which falters when Robber Five, a re-enactor who has grown accustomed to stumbling over a kink in the fake carpet of the fake bank, falls during the actual heist because the real carpet at the real bank has no kink. The ensuing Rube Goldberg–esque chain reaction—Robber Five collides with Two who fires his gun killing Four—ensures the robbery's fatal failure (290–291). As the narrator notes, "Matter, for all my intricate preparations, all my bluffs and sleights of hand, played a blinder. Double-bluffed me. Tripped me up again" (282). And yet, despite the robbery being a "fuck-up," the narrator reports that "it was a very happy day" (282). Because ultimately the point is not to transubstantiate matter. That would not be a rigorous delivery unto death, but a naïve and desperate one. Instead, the point is to include matter in all of its obdurate immediacy. It's precisely when the re-enactment does not go according to plan, when the narrator is not immersed in becoming one with the world, that he is fully necronautical. Thus, it's not surprising that the narrator's most authentic feelings arrive in "a moment that had come about not through an orchestrated re-enactment, but by chance" (241). In the breach of pure accident, from matter's pure unaccountability, death comes into the world. Not to annihilate, but to teach us that "matter's what makes us alive—the bitty flow, the scar tissue, signature of the world's very first disaster and promissory note guaranteeing its last. Try to iron it out at your peril" (304).[29]

In McCarthy's world, it's not just matter that matters, but people too. Not because they are uniquely significant, but because they also occupy space. The narrator learns this truth shortly after his injury forces him to slow down human action and motion, breaking it into its component parts, "filling up time with space," until he is little more than an assemblage of interconnected things in the world. The necronautical nature of this human mattering is aptly captured in the narrator's description of that one chance occurrence in which he felt the "least unreal": "I'd come out of the tube just as rush hour was beginning, and commuters—men and women dressed in suits—had hurried past me. I'd stood still, facing the other way, feeling them hurrying, streaming. I'd turned the palms of my hands outwards, felt the tingling begin" (241). The experience of "being in that particular space, right then, in that particular relation to the others, to the world," he says, gave him the sensation of "having passed onto the other side" (242). In other words, it's not just the non-identity of external matter that makes him alive, it's his own constitutive non-identity, his own being towards death, that produces life's value too. Unlike Henry James's "Figure in the Carpet," which treats meaning and value as an epistemological effect of reference and representation, McCarthy's various kinks in the carpet establish meaning and value as an ontological effect of the inescapable truth of non-identity—not just other objects' non-identity with us, but also our own non-identity with ourselves.

Immanence, which loathes non-identity, can't get us there; but irony's commitment to non-identity, its necessary inclusion of the excluded, can. And it's this ironic structuring of *Remainder*, its willingness to take into account what's not there, that makes this a quintessentially ecological novel. To be sure, *Remainder* has nothing to tell us about nature, and it certainly doesn't provide a roadmap out of environmental crisis and catastrophe. But it does consistently transform the typically is-not into what most resolutely is. If McCarthy had provided my chapter with a fourth novelistic account of a polar expedition, for example, it would highlight, as McCarthy himself emphasizes, "not the imperial dreams in the head of the polar explorer Ernest Shackleton but rather his blackened, frostbitten toes which, after the white space into which he'd ventured and on which he hoped to write his name solidified and crushed his boat, he and his crew were forced to chop from their own feet, cook on their stove and eat" ("Joint Statement"). "Necronauts," McCarthy writes in a "Joint Statement on Inauthenticity," "are poets of the antipodes of poetry, artists of art's polar opposite, its Antartica." Perversely, this is a life-giving, conservationist ethos. As the narrator speculates of a man shot shortly after exiting a phone booth, heightened attention to the space around him—including more stuff in his world and filling up time with more space—might have saved his life: "Inside the phone box this time I examined every surface it had to present. My man, the victim, would have taken all these in—but then his brain would have edited most of them back out again, dismissed them as mundane, irrelevant" (212–213). Such failure to take into account is not just life-threatening, but also an affront to ecology. On the other hand, including more matter, appreciating one's own status as matter, constitutes an ecological movement toward life. Admittedly, it's a dark ecology, but it's also an ecology of abundance.[30] Accepting the muck of the world necessarily entails a bounteous expansion of the world:

> Chewing gum, cigarette butts and bottle tops had been distributed randomly across the area and sunk into its outer membrane, become one with tarmac, stone, dirt, water, mud. If you were to cut out ten square centimetres of it like you do with fields on school geography trips . . . you'd find so much to analyse, so many layers, just so much *matter*—that your study of it would branch out and become endless until, finally, you threw your hands up in despair and announced to whatever authority it was you were reporting to: *There's too much here, too much to process, just too much.* (201–202)

As befits the ecology of our contemporary risk society in which crisis and catastrophe are increasingly everyday phenomena, the mode here is one of constant overwhelming.

While it's not necessarily true that *Remainder* is so overwhelming that there's just "too much to process," it is true that the novel asks its readers to process things—gum, fried liver, windshield washer fluid, a crack in a wall—that most novels, particularly the twenty-first-century, neo-realist novel, would edit out. But *Remainder* is actually more real, and thus more ecological, precisely to the extent that it requires us to delve into the stuff of the world: "As she set [my coffee] down on the polished table I noticed that it was a two-part construction: the cup itself, then, slotted into that, a plastic filter section where the coffee grains themselves were. . . . There was a saucer too, of course: three parts. The receptionist lowered the whole assemblage gently down onto the table's surface" (48). As the novel fills up its own time with space, so too is the reader's time filled up with space, transforming the text into an archaeological dig that readers must excavate and configure rather than interpret.[31]

Such excavation requires a certain kind of immersion, but it's definitely not a temporal one. It requires heightened attention, not going with the flow. The radical inclusion of the world still requires deliberation, agency, a certain culling, even as that deliberation comes not from a distanced subject but from an actant who is already part of the assemblage at hand. In this way, we will not be tripped up by the kinks in McCarthy's novelistic carpet, kinks that we "iron out at [our] peril" (304). I am thinking in particular of three different remainders, or kinks, that matter quite conspicuously throughout the novel. First, there is the persistent smell of cordite that the narrator complains about during the first re-enactment. His facilitators assume it will dissipate as the cast-iron skillet being used to fry liver in a downstairs apartment gets broken in, but they are wrong. Instead, the smell endures and no one can account for its origin. Even more curious, when Naz asks the narrator when and where he first encountered cordite, the narrator reports that he has actually never been near it. Second, there is a man, a borough councillor, who helps Naz facilitate the narrator's re-enactment of a drive-by shooting. Later, the "short councillor" appears in the narrator's apartment, speaking of the narrator in the third person. But the narrator does not remember sharing any of the copious information the short councillor knows about the narrator, and later, when the narrator speaks to Naz about the short councillor, Naz just asks, "What short councillor?" (270). Finally, the "short councillor," who happens to be the only other person in the novel to smell cordite, is also connected with a word, "residual," that might actually be the word "recidual" (270). "Residual" makes no sense in the context it's used (on pages 236 and 259), and "recidual" is not a word (273). Just as McCarthy devotes several pages to the short councillor only to vaporize him with Naz's question, the narrator also diligently traces down the meaning of this word, only to abandon the search.[32] These intrusions of textual matter are not Derridean supplements, always both (and undecidably) additions and substitutions. Instead, they are the text's agency, its means of asserting that, like the carrot the narrator struggles to lift shortly after his accident, it is not "a no-thing" and is actually "more active than [us]" (21). These are the things that readers must take into account and then put in rank order. How do these things fit into the novelistic configuration we've excavated? Should they be included in that assemblage, and, if so, how and where? To answer these questions, we must join the novel in its mud and muck. McCarthy asks us to relinquish our transcendent subject positions, sail toward death, and forge connections not just with the stuff in the text but with the text itself as stuff.

Emptied of plot, character development, interiority, meaningful symbols, and all the other hallmarks of the novel, *Remainder* matters. A man is hit on the head; he loses himself. Not only does he not return to himself, but he doesn't even bother to build a new self. He just re-enacts. It's not Beckett, but it's also not Franzen. In between those two, we find a novel that is a configuration, an assemblage, but not a representation, of the world. *Remainder* stands and speaks for a previously unconsidered world, and in doing so, it also stands and speaks for a new trajectory for the twenty-first-century novel.[33] With their various textual ontologizations, most of the novels discussed throughout *After Critique* coalesce around this trajectory, which, as I've been arguing all along, is marked most conspicuously by neoliberalism. Their collective embrace of various forms of ontological thinking has stuck a wrench in an array of neoliberal circles, but it's also important to remember that this move is only made possible by neoliberalism as well. That is, even as these novels shun the purified divide between subjects and objects that neoliberalism deploys in its representations of the world, they are turning to and embracing the subject-object hybrids that neoliberalism proliferates. This is why these texts, risking complicity and capitulation, so frequently mirror neoliberal structures. And yet, because these novels refuse to grant neoliberalism its purified distinction between subject and object, culture and nature, word and world, the hybrid subject-objects they describe are free to establish new relations, new configurations, and even new modes of meaning-making that potentially undermine neoliberal dominance. In so doing, this newly exomodern literature produces an ecological vision of radical inclusion and a textual surface impermeable to critique and to neoliberal appropriation. Rather than wringing such texts of meaning, we can only survey them top to bottom, like forensic scientists whose grids and diagrams explain and discover a world. Or as the narrator of *Remainder* puts it, "Forensic procedure is an art form, nothing less. No, I'll go further: it's higher, more refined, than any art form. Why? Because it's real" (185). To read as forensic scientists, to write texts that demand to be read by forensic scientists, is to non-critically engage our neoliberal moment without capitulating to it. Like Wile E. Coyote, a great idol of the necronauts, it is to "die almost without noticing, again and again, repeatedly" ("Joint").

Accounting 101

READING THE EXOMODERN

Nearly everything in David Foster Wallace's unfinished novel *The Pale King* is complex: aspects of the law are "so complicated as to almost defy description" (205); the IRS Regional Examination Center in Peoria, Illinois, is "too overwhelmingly complex and repetitive to describe" (289); "there are complex psychodynamics involved in taxation" (110). When an IRS recruiter explains the institution's bureaucratic structure to Chris Fogle, the young recruit reports:

> the whole thing was so complicated, and consisted of so many branches, sub-branches, divisions, and coordinating offices and sub-offices, as well as parallel or bilateral sub-offices and technology support divisions, that it appeared impossible to comprehend even the general sense of well enough to take a real interest in, though I obviously made it a conscious point to look as attentive and engaged as possible, if only to show that I was someone who could be trained to herd and process large amounts of info. (245–246)

The reader can sympathize. What's funny is that Fogle signs on with the IRS after growing disillusioned with college courses—psychology, political science, literature—in which "everything was fuzzy and abstract and open to interpretation and then those interpretations were open to still more interpretations," classes in which "nothing meant anything" (155). Such is the burden of reading in the twenty-first century: having finally closed the door on poststructural indeterminacy, we find ourselves newly threatened by the enormous complexity of massively intricate assemblages. The vast scope and scale of the exomodern intrudes, posing an entirely new set of interpretive dilemmas for the human whose hermeneutics are dwarfed by deep time and fractal space. Despite their common production of interpretive opacity, however, *The Pale King* indicates a fundamental difference between the literature classroom and the IRS. The indeterminacy of the literature classroom is humanist, derived from the insuperable gulf between self and other, word and world. Perspective compromises value ad infinitum. But the indeterminacy of the IRS is posthumanist and exomodern, derived from an overwhelming magnitude, an impenetrable totality. Wallace stakes *The Pale King* on the idea that, while we've exhausted all options for coping with the former, we can actually do something productive with the latter.[1]

When confronted with vast complexity, we can, in particular, take a cue from Nate Silver and separate the signal from the noise, although doing so runs two distinct risks. First, there is the threat of subjective bias: the possibility that the signal one discerns is merely the signal one wants to see, that we inevitably compromise the texts we read. (This was Erasmus's fear in *Narwhal*.) This accusation hounded Silver's statistical tracking of the 2012 presidential election as his critics, insisting that his predictions were biased toward the left, saw too much Nate Silver in the numbers. Such critiques, if they are accurate, land us right back in the humanist indeterminacy of relativized perspective. Second, there is the distinct possibility that, having replaced the human with the quantitative, the signal one discerns will further exacerbate neoliberalism's economic rationalization of living, breathing individuals. How can we sort for relevance without adopting the bottom-line thinking of for-profit corporations? And what does the text look like that will allow us to do so?

The first problem—the threat of subjective perspective, of self-conscious reflexivity—preoccupies the bulk of Wallace's work. It also appears in *The Pale King*, but he offers a different solution to it there. Wallace's pre-*Pale King* work pursues new forms of sincere belief in an attempt to overcome irony's soul-crushing cynicism and self-reflexivity's circular mediations. A certain magical thinking always intrudes into these forms, however, requiring readers to risk credulity, accept truth as a Derridean gift, or locate authentic value deep in our hearts.[2] Notably, when the same paradoxical relations between authenticity and inauthenticity, sincerity and irony, emerge in *The Pale King*, no one has to leap over any abysses of meaning to find the truth. Instead, Wallace has moved everything to the surface.

A lengthy conversation between Meredith Rand and Shane Drinion, two IRS employees out for a drink after work, demonstrates this crucial shift in Wallace's thinking about how best to overcome the gulf of reflexive self-consciousness. Rand suffers from being so pretty that she can never tell if people like her for her surface looks or for who she really is deep inside: "I wanted people to look past the prettiness thing and the sexual thing and see who I was, like as a person, and I felt really mad and sorry for myself that people didn't" (499). Paradoxically and self-defeatingly, her perception of other people's superficiality makes her angry inside, thereby sabotaging the possibility that anyone would ever actually like her true inner self because that true inner self is really angry.[3] Instead of prescribing an ethical leap of faith or a trusting belief in others' ability to see the real her, however, Rand overcomes this paradox by accepting that the surface-depth distinction fueling her insecurity is entirely specious. Her prettiness *and* her anger about only being loved for her prettiness are both right there on her surface for everyone to see: "in reality everything was the surface" (499).

Rand's interlocutor, her reader, Shane Drinion, reinforces this insight. Rather than forging an affecting connection with Rand's inner self, Drinion's engagement with Rand's story entails "merely absorbing information and adding it to himself" (504). Drinion's approach to Rand's information strikes her as peculiar and disarming. He appears to have "no natural sense of whether something was sarcastic or not" (457); he never compares "anything to anything" (463); his "face remains composed and neutral without seeming in any way to be trying to stay neutral" (468); and he's incapable of irony (481). A perfect antidote to Rand's surface-depth circularity, Drinion is "both interesting and really boring at the same time" (461). He refuses to critique, judge, condemn, analogize, or even emotionally connect with Rand. At most, he incorporates what other IRS employees might call Rand's relevant "fact-pattern" into his understanding of her (16).[4] Displaying some residual surface-depth angst, Rand interprets Drinion's surface reading as a sign of his boredom. But Drinion assures her that despite the repetitive parts of her story which "add no new information" and consequently "require more work to pay attention to," he actually finds her narrative quite interesting. As he explains to Rand:

> In fact, to be honest, in those parts where you do repeat the same essential point of information in a slightly different way, the underlying motive, which I get the feeling is a concern that what you're

imparting might be unclear or uninteresting and must get recast and resaid in many different ways to assure yourself that the listener really understands you—this is interesting, and somewhat emotional, and it coheres in an interesting way with the surface subject of what Ed, in the story you're telling, is teaching you, and so in that respect even the repetitive or redundant elements compel interest and require little conscious effort to pay attention to, at least so far as I'm concerned. (502)

As with Rand's pathological pulchritude, here Drinion demonstrates that her "underlying" concern about how Drinion is receiving her narrative is actually just all part of the surface of the story. The story is simply a vast collection of information that Drinion must sort, process, and scan for relevance. This is reading exomodernism. This is reading like an accountant.[5]

Replacing the hermeneutic circle with a form of reading that attentively takes into account, Wallace must also determine whether such attentive accounting can be distinguished from the bottom-line thinking of neoliberal capital. This question emerges in the context of a drastic transformation sweeping through Wallace's fictionalized IRS in the mid-1980s. According to several different employees, Reagan's trickle-down economics have failed to raise sufficient revenues for the federal government, but there's also a pervasive reluctance to increase taxes. With few good options, the executive branch asks the IRS to squeeze more revenue from the already-existing tax code. As one employee explains, "[T]here was compelling reason to conceive, constitute, and operate the IRS as a business—a going, for-profit concern type of thing—rather than as an institutional bureaucracy" (112–113). This free-market model radically changes the way examiners process their never-ending stream of paperwork. Prior to this neoliberal corporatization of the IRS, examiners were evaluated on throughput. Now, these new "revenue agents" are exclusively judged on their "return on audit" (332). "In essence, in today's IRS, you're businessmen" (338).[6]

This shift at the IRS changes the way its examiners and accountants read. Before the overhaul, they were expected to pay close attention to the documents they processed, but it was difficult to tell who was attentive and who was zoning out. As one examiner explains, "From outside the examiner, there was no guarantee that anyone could distinguish the difference between doing the job well and being in what she called the stare, staring at the returns but not engaged by them, not truly paying attention." But now that examiners must maximize revenue instead of throughput, it's easy to see who's doing a good job. As the same examiner notes, "This helps us pay attention" (117). So here's the problem. Without reintroducing the subjectivity of the hermeneutic circle, can we pay close attention to and make an adequate accounting of the vast amounts of data coursing through the world? And if so, then how do we ensure that our attentive search for relevance, meaning, and value in an overwhelming swarm of information remains immune from capital's similar commitment to bottom-line value? Do we really require a profit incentive to pay attention?

Wallace asks and answers these questions by challenging his readers to assess their own ability to pay attention. With different chapters narrated by various IRS employees with wildly divergent voices, we have plenty of opportunity to determine whether we can sort for relevance without reducing the intricately complex material to something other than what it is. Of the many narrative voices, two in particular—Chris Fogle and David Wallace—crystallize this challenge for readers. Taken together we see Wallace asking if we can read like accountants without constantly searching for profit.

Fogle's narration is a massive information dump, unsorted, constantly digressive, always threatening to devolve into irrelevance.[7] Selecting almost at random, we learn, for example:

> Both TACs [Training and Assessment Centers] are divisions of what is commonly known as Treasury School, as the Service is technically a branch of the US Treasury Department. But Treasury also includes everything from the Bureau of Alcohol, Tobacco, and Firearms to the US Secret Service, so 'Treasury School' now stands for over a dozen different training programs and facilities, including the Federal Law Enforcement Academy in Athens GA, to which those posted to Criminal Investigations from the TAC are sent for specialized training which they share with ATF agents, the DEA, federal marshals, and so on and so forth. (178)

David Wallace, a character earnestly purporting to be the author himself, has no patience for Fogle's irrelevant narrative information.[8] Describing Fogle, his "logorrheic colleague," as a "maundering grandstander," David Wallace assures us that he has "no intention of inflicting on [us] a regurgitation of every last sensation and passing thought [he] happen[s] to recall." "I am about art here," David Wallace insists, "not simple reproduction." What Fogle fails to appreciate, according to David Wallace, "is that there are vastly different kinds of truth, some of which are incompatible with one another. Example: A 100 percent accurate, comprehensive list of the exact size and shape of every blade of grass in my front lawn is 'true,' but it is not a truth that anyone will have any interest in. What renders a truth meaningful, worthwhile, & c. is its relevance, which in turn requires extraordinary discernment and sensitivity to context, questions of value, and overall point" (259). Just like the revenue agents at the newly corporatized IRS who "process and reduce the information in [their] file[s] to just the information that has value," David Wallace promises a payoff (342). The time we spend with him as readers will be time well spent. Consequently, David Wallace punctuates his narrative with self-reflexive observations about the processes by which he has guaranteed its value. He reports that his descriptions, for example, are forged from "artful compression" (276); other observations are "condensed from an unusually long, intense, unpunctuated notebook entry" (277); elsewhere he only shares "some specially selected relevant portions of" his memory (261).

And yet, because David Wallace's world is just as "extremely involved and confusing" (256) as the "highly complex" (242) world that Chris Fogle never "know[s] how to describe" (217), David Wallace struggles to find the profitable bottom line of his narrative. He tries quite hard, insisting that *The Pale King* is a memoir, that it's entirely true, that his firsthand experiences and observations are the valuable takeaway from the text.[9] But he ultimately spins off into digressive complexity just like Fogle. Unlike David Wallace, who tells us that he won't go on and on about irrelevant and arcane details only to then go on and on about irrelevant and arcane details, I actually won't quote at length the exhaustive description he provides of the IRS building's convoluted traffic patterns and parking complexities. You can just see for yourself by carefully examining every last word of the eleven pages he devotes to such minutiae (270–280). In short, David Wallace's attempt to reduce *The Pale King* to himself, to his own subjectivity, is deeply misguided. Not only is it impossible—there is simply always too much detail to tell—but it's also unwittingly complicit with the market-driven logic ascendant at the IRS. The bottom line that is most in line with the neoliberal project is one that derives its value from the entrepreneurial subject himself. Not surprisingly, then, David Wallace attempts to prove that he is actually David Foster Wallace and not just "some abstract narrative persona ... rather like a corporation" by providing that most corporately efficient of identifiers, his social security number (66). It's 975-04-2012.

David Wallace's inability to escape Fogle's tendencies for digressive irrelevance, coupled with David Foster Wallace's clear embrace of the Foglesque (section 25, for example, drolly informs us, "Howard Cardwell turns a page. Ken Wax turns a page. Matt Redgate turns a page," and so on), indicates that we need new ways to sort for relevance, new approaches to meaning and value that don't reduce to the neoliberal subject (i.e., to David Wallace). Once again, as with the conversation between Meredith Rand and Shane Drinion, bringing meaning and value to the surface proves crucial, or so Chris Fogle gradually realizes over the course of three different epiphanies he has in college. The first comes from drugs, the second from television, and the third from a substitute accounting professor.[10]

Providing the "first glimmer" of the worldview that would eventually lead him to the IRS, Chris Fogle develops a proclivity for a popular diet drug called Obetrol (187). Fogle isn't fat, but he enjoys that the drug makes him self-aware without being self-conscious (181). That is, instead of separating from himself and falling down a reflexive rabbit hole, the drug allows him not just to be in a room, but to "be totally aware that [he is] in the room, seated in a certain easy chair in a certain position listening to a certain specific track of an album whose cover was a certain specific combination of colors and designs" (181). Eventually Fogle learns to choose what he pays attention to—he's not just overloaded by tedious, blade-of-grass detail—which opens onto the realization that his "realest, most profound parts" are not "drives or appetites but simple attention, awareness" (187).

Building on the attentive awareness Obetrol provides, Fogle experiences a second epiphanic truth one afternoon while watching *As the World Turns* on CBS. Fogle had slowly become hooked on the soap opera, but he never appreciated that the announcer, who after each commercial break would declare, "You're watching *As the World Turns*," was speaking the literal truth. One day, however, the "bare reality" of the announcer's observation strikes him: "the announcer

was actually saying over and over what I was literally doing." Fogle
carefully notes that he's not reading the statement as a "humanities-
type ironic metaphor." He's not highlighting "the obvious double
entendre," "the show's almost terrifying pun about the passive waste
of time sitting there watching something" while life in the real world
continues. Instead, Fogle insists, the insight "was more literal, which
somehow had made it harder to see" (222).

These two attunements prime Fogle for the most transformative
event of his young life, a speech that a substitute accounting professor delivers to a class in which Fogle isn't enrolled but has stumbled
into because, of course, he's not paying attention. The professor's
message is revelatory for Fogle: "Enduring tedium over real time in
a confined space is what real courage is." Welcoming the students to
"the world of reality" where "there is no audience," he exhorts the
truth: "actual heroism receives no ovation, entertains no one. No one
queues up to see it. No one is interested" (229). Notably, as with the
previous epiphanies, the professor's speech makes Fogle "aware of
how every detail in the classroom appeared very vivid and distinct,
as though painstakingly drawn and shaded" (230).

In each of these cases, and much like the narrator in McCarthy's
Remainder, Fogle becomes aware of what's there, of the surface
reality hidden in plain sight. Previously, the surface was inscrutable, equally obscured by layers of self-conscious duplicity (e.g.,
the iterative interpretations of the humanities classroom) or
non-differentiated oblivion (e.g., Jimmy Carter's late 1970s "mal-
aise" that left Fogle "free to choose 'whatever' because it didn't
really matter" [223]). The trio of epiphanies, however, teaches him
how to differentiate without distancing, how to find value in the
world without having to search beneath it or hover above it: "If
I wanted to matter—even just to myself—I would have to be less
free, by deciding to choose in some kind of definite way" (224).
Such definite choice also happens to define the task of accounting. As the professor professes, "In today's world, boundaries are
fixed, and most significant facts have been generated. Gentlemen,
the heroic frontier now lies in the ordering and deployment of
those facts. Classification, organization, presentation" (232). Being
aware of, paying attention to, and bringing order to swarms of
information—these are the tasks of an ethical reader, even if that
reader happens to work for the profit-driven IRS. In this arrangement, profit is a potential byproduct of reading but in no way

governs it. Again, the professor explains: "To attend fully to the interests of the client and to balance those interests against the high ethical standards of the FASB [Financial Accounting Standards Board] and extant law—yea, to serve those who care not for service but only for results—this is heroism. . . . Effacement. Sacrifice. Service. To give oneself over to the care of others' money—that is effacement, perdurance, sacrifice, honor, doughtiness, valor" (231). These are the posthuman possibilities of a neutral and non-profit engagement with neoliberal institutions. Such acts of courageous reading produce not-necessarily-bottom-line value, a form of value that is definite, precise, and real, but not deep.[11]

As *The Pale King* demonstrates, this mode of value production requires not just readers who take into account, but also authors who write texts that require readerly accounting. Throughout *After Critique*, I have tried to read attentively, organizing the disparate surface features of texts and presenting them in configurations that deliver value to those texts. I paid attention to the different types of transformation in *Beasts of No Nation*; I tracked the extraneous objects and skewed chronology of *Their Dogs Came with Them*; I defended Whitehead's and Everett's novels from the racial allegories threatening to make them other than they are; and I re-enacted the matter of McCarthy's *Remainder*, kinks and all. But I was only able to do so because all of these texts were already predisposed to remaining as they are, already hostile to readers searching for a critical politics in them. These works are all quite skeptical of the human and its supposed value. On the other hand, texts that fetishize their memoiristic truth (*A Long Way Gone*), that view race through the lens of representational reflexivity (*Angry Black White Boy*), or that thematize perception as a surface-depth paradox (*The Voyage of the Narwhal*), almost beg to be read and critiqued symptomatically. The burden for escaping critique's complicity with the neoliberal status quo, then, falls not only on readers, but also on authors. Post-symptomatic reading methods aren't enough; we must also appreciate the burgeoning body of contemporary literature asking to be read post-symptomatically. Perversely, David Foster Wallace's suicide left us one such novel, unfinished and disorganized, ideal for this project. Perhaps the completed version of *The Pale King* would have been even more "involved and confusing," even more "complex and puzzling," even more "complicated and idiosyncratic" than the one Wallace left us. We might imagine a final text that would "require far more time and energy to ferret out and truly understand than any sane person would want to expend" (256–257). I hope to have demonstrated, in my many descriptions of exomodern fiction, that reading such texts can avoid forms of critique conducive to the neoliberal project without becoming tedious. By my own accounting, this is what literature today asks of us.

{ NOTES }

Introduction

1. David Harvey's *A Brief History of Neoliberalism* continues to offer the clearest description of neoliberalism as an economic phenomenon.

2. See Lisa Duggan's *The Twilight of Equality?* for an excellent analysis of neoliberalism's politicization. Other examples of this more political take on neoliberalism would include Walter Benn Michaels's "Plots Against America" and *The Trouble with Diversity*, David Theo Goldberg's *The Threat of Race*, and Costas Douzinas's *The End of Human Rights*.

3. Because I will be using this formulation—the production of meaning and value—throughout *After Critique*, a clarifying note seems in order. I intend this phrase in the broadest of ways. I use the word "meaning" because my primary focus will be literature, particularly how texts mean. It's conventional to think of literature's meaning as a function of what literature represents; a text's meaning is whatever that text shows us or tells us about the world. Such representations might be mimetic, polemical, experimental, satirical, and so on, but they all share a common belief that language means by referring (sometimes successfully and sometimes not) to beliefs, people, events, ideas, or things in and of the world. I use the word "value" because, in discussing neoliberalism, I'm not just talking about books but will also be discussing people, space, race, and the environment. These things don't necessarily mean in the way books do—they are not signs that refer—but their value is still a function of how they are represented. What they mean to us, how significant we take them to be, depends on perception, recognition, framing, and so on. Finally, I talk about the *production* of meaning and value to insist that representation is just one particular way that we achieve our knowledge and understanding of the world.

4. This doesn't necessarily mean, however, that Brown subscribes in full to Foucault's thinking about neoliberalism. See in particular the second and third chapters in *Undoing the Demos*.

5. This hands-off administration of the social sphere that doesn't actually intrude into the social sphere is one way of understanding Foucault's notion of governmentality, although the degree to which governmentality should be seen as continuous with or distinct from Foucault's earlier work on the power-knowledge nexus of the disciplinary society remains a matter of considerable debate. Expansive discussions can be found in Stephen Collier's "Topologies of Power" and Vanessa Lemm and Miguel Vatter's *The Government of Life*. See Winnubst for more on Foucault's post-normative treatment of neoliberal rationality, but also see Patton for a competing take on Foucault that views his stance on neoliberalism as more in line with his earlier treatment of madness, sexuality, medicine, and discipline as normative social formations. For a broader view, Larner helpfully distinguishes among scholars who treat neoliberalism as a policy, those who conceive it as ideology, and those who analyze it as post-normative governmentality.

6. Not surprisingly, the right has taken a fair amount of glee in Zamora's claims, reveling in the notion that an *apparent* lefty like Foucault might actually be in love with the free market. See, for example, Drezner and also Doherty. Steinmetz-Jenkins and Arnold do a good job stamping out much of this nonsense.

7. In this regard, *After Critique* comports with Michael Clune's *American Literature and the Free Market, 1945–2000*, which identifies a non-complicit fascination with deregulated markets among late twentieth-century authors. But while Clune's archive of authors supersedes the economic by catalyzing readers' phenomenological encounter with the aesthetic, my archive of authors does so by exploring literary ontology and the unique modes of value production it makes possible.

8. The first commercial can be viewed here: http://www.youtube.com/watch?v=FBP-korQD9o. The second is here: http://www.youtube.com/watch?v=1U-9ZgHIpsc.

9. The Infiniti Q50 commercial can be seen here: http://www.youtube.com/watch?v=5ClTs094jwU. The Prius ad can be viewed here: http://www.youtube.com/watch?v=HFIYlDEpLcQ.

10. This take on the semiotic square is more in line with Fredric Jameson's sense—outlined in his foreword to Greimas's *On Meaning*—that it actually "constitutes a virtual map of conceptual closure, or better still, of the closure of ideology itself" (xv). For Jameson, such conceptual closure requires the dialectic's immanent critique, but I will be suggesting that such closure actually requires a more radical shift from the field of "concepts" to the terrain of being.

11. Of course, the continued proliferation of prisons, discriminatory policing, and other forms of state violence suggest that there's still plenty of room for normative manipulation and control under the regime of neoliberal governmentality.

12. A story Adam Gopnik told for The Moth, a live storytelling radio show, makes the point about post-normative ontology in less economic terms. Gopnik's story, "The Pieties of Perspiration," recounts the moment he and his teenage son encountered two men having sex in the sauna at their New York City gym. Whereas Gopnik's father would have made a moral judgment about the scene, Gopnik notes that his own reaction concerned the "appropriateness" of what the men were doing. This is a normative judgment: the action isn't morally wrong, but it's not being done the right way (or in this case, in the right place). The point of the story, however, is to register the teenage son's different response, which declares the scene not immoral or inappropriate, but "awkward." Here we find a post-normative view concerned only with the relative grace of a given configuration. The morality, appropriateness, or meaning of the act are all irrelevant; all that matters is the way it occupies space.

13. See, for example, Clive Barnett ("Publics and Markets"), Jamie Peck, and Peck's work with Nik Theodore and Neil Brenner.

14. A similar argument can be found in Daniel Stedman Jones's *Masters of the Universe: Hayek, Friedman, and the Birth of Neoliberal Politics*. Challenging the left's belief that greedy capitalists have intentionally pursued neoliberal policies and the right's belief that neoliberalism emerged as a natural response to the collapse of the welfare state, Jones insists that it's just not that simple. Instead, as Michael Clune ably explains in his review of the book:

> [Jones] shows neoliberalism's ascendance to be the result of a series of more or less
> ad hoc moves on the part of politicians, activists, media figures, and economists in

response to a series of political and economic shocks that began in the 1970s. The image of a dramatic face-off between neoliberals and proponents of the postwar center-left consensus is largely an artifact of retrospective right-wing propaganda, which the left seems to have accepted in its essential features. (par. 5)

Clune's review prompted a defensive, and counter-defensive, exchange with Jasper Bernes and Joshua Clover that crystallizes this debate (at least within the intellectual left) about the exact nature of neoliberalism. Their exchange can be found here: http://lareviewofbooks.org/ article.php?id=1463&fulltext=1.

15. This is sometimes misunderstood as a Hobbesian war of all against all, but the strength and influence that accrues to actants is not the result of brute force motivated by self-preservation. Violent actants would inevitably fare quite poorly in a Latourian universe. Instead, the process of establishing alliances and forging networks is always very deliberative, reasoned, and considered. Latour describes the process at length in *Politics of Nature*, which I discuss more thoroughly in chapter four.

16. Jane Bennett has done valuable work thinking about how politics changes when we view the world as "as a confederation of human and nonhuman elements" (21). However, Bennett never fully collapses the subject-object distinction, ultimately regrounding her work in the human (104). In this way, although she draws heavily on Latour's thinking, Bennett's theory of "vibrant matter" is quite at odds with Latour's metaphysics of concrete actants. Bennett's vision is vitalist, immanent, and Bergsonian in a way that Latour's refuses to be. Whereas Latour only sees an ontological equivalence of actants, Bennett highlights an object world that is *more* alive than we think, and in this way her treatment of objects aligns more with Deleuzian virtuality and becoming than it does with Latour, whose model certainly allows for change, but not through the flow of becoming. (See chapter five in Graham Harman's *Prince of Networks* for an extended explanation of why Latour is not an immanent thinker like Bergson or Deleuze. See Bennett's "Systems and Things" for a defense of her Deleuzianism.)

Nevertheless, the politics that emerge from Bennett's analyses are in line with the arguments I make here. She too identifies a political mode in which moral outrage at neoliberal injustice makes little sense. For example, she concludes of the massive blackout affecting much of the northeastern United States, including New York City, and parts of Canada, in 2003:

Though it would give me pleasure to assert that deregulation and corporate greed are the real culprits in the blackout, the most I can honestly affirm is that corporations are one of the sites at which human efforts at reform can be applied, that corporate regulation is one place where intentions might initiate a cascade of effects. Perhaps the ethical responsibility of an individual human now resides in one's response to the assemblages in which one finds oneself participating. (37)

17. Admittedly, I am generalizing here. I do not intend to dismiss all of affect theory, or the very interesting work on embodiment and becoming that grows out of Deleuze's thinking. That mode of immanent vitalism is helpful and illuminating in many instances, but its ability to account for the production of value strikes me as rather thin. This is, in effect, the same point that Badiou makes when he suggests that for all of its schizophrenic multiplicity, Deleuze's work, committed as it is to "the univocity of being," is actually best understood as a "philosophy of the One" (xiii). Because I don't find such "univocity"

particularly effective against the neoliberal circle's representational duplicity, my argument privileges Latourian over Deleuzian immanence. This preference is also informed by the fact that *After Critique*'s literary archive proves much more interested in discretely differentiated objects than it does in the immanent ongoingness of process and flow.

18. Defending immanent dialectical critique against the ascendance of surface reading, Carolyn Lesjak actually enlists Latour to her cause, although this probably says more about Lesjak's admirable reconception of "dialectical reading" than it does about Latour, who is not a dialectician. For Latour's concerns with dialectical thought, see *We Have Never Been Modern*, pages 55–59.

19. But this is certainly why so many descriptions of the dialectic actually sound so Latourian. Merleau-Ponty's *Adventures of the Dialectic* comes to mind. As does Fredric Jameson explaining the dialectical process of watching "Identity turn into Difference and Difference back into Identity" so often that one eventually understands not only that "they must always be thought together," but also that "in some other sense, they are one and the same as each other" (454–455). I often wonder why, with his insistence on the intractable and permanent ambivalence of the dialectic—"The dialectic is an injunction to think the negative and the positive together at one and the same time, in the unity of a single thought"—Jameson persists in even calling this dialectical thought (421). Progress, change, and utopian content have been so purged from his thinking that Jameson's descriptions of the dialectic seem to depict the ontological conditions of being more than they do the developmental processes of thought.

20. J. L. Austin walks right up to the edge of this question about the ontological equivalence of word and world, but then pulls back, ultimately granting representation a provisionally distinct ontological status. That is, for Austin, word and world are ontologically equivalent up until the point that words are called on to be about the world: "There is no reason why the world should not include the words, in every sense except the sense of the actual statement itself which on any particular occasion is being made about the world" (quoted in Danto 81).

21. As Walter Benn Michaels points out in *Shape of the Signifier*, poststructuralism's preoccupation with the materiality of the signifier is another kind of ontological turn, one Michaels criticizes for its abandonment of intentional meaning. I find Michaels's critique of poststructuralism perfectly compelling, but I also contend here that the ontological turn I identify in contemporary fiction differs crucially from what poststructuralism attempted in the second half of the twentieth century. In particular, poststructuralism's ontological critique of representation, and Michaels's critique of that critique, both maintain the distinction between subjects and objects that standard forms of representational meaning-making require. The texts I examine, however, tend to collapse the distinction between subjects and objects. Consequently, the ontological turn described in *After Critique* is not a critique of the possibility of representation, which is how poststructuralism's fetishization of the signifier's materiality was intended. Instead, it's an attempt to produce new forms of value in a neoliberal landscape that obscures the doubleness of subject-object ontology with either subjective or objective representational modes.

22. Wai Chee Dimock's *Through Other Continents* stands as a paradigmatic example of such work, and Mark McGurl's "The Posthuman Comedy" notably expands Dimock's claims. Much of Timothy Morton's thinking is also in this vein, insisting for example

that "poems do something as physical as what happens when my car scrapes the side-walk" ("Object-Oriented" 206). Rita Felski also treads this path when she imagines texts as "nonhuman actors" (574). And surely Franco Moretti's trees, maps, and graphs empha-size textual ontology in this way as well.

23. Scientific texts would be an obvious exception to this claim. As I'll discuss at length in chapter four, it's plausible to imagine the kind of writing we find in scientific journals as acts of transmission rather than instances of representation. Latour, in fact, predicates the entire notion of circulating reference on the communicative procedures of a group of soil scientists working in South America.

24. See "Model Minorities and the Minority Model—The Neoliberal Novel," Michaels's contribution to *The Cambridge History of the American Novel*.

25. This is why Michaels not only links identity-oriented literature to neoliberalism (see *The Trouble with Diversity*, "Model Minorities," and "Plots Against America") but also highlights the connections between neoliberalism and more poststructurally inclined postmodern forms (see *Shape of the Signifier* and "The Beauty of a Social Problem").

26. Of course, as numerous scholars have observed, this divide was always a false one. See, for example, Chow, Dubey (*Signs*), Steiner, Michaels (*Shape*), Huehls (*Qualified*), Hungerford, McGurl (*Program*), and Heise.

27. According to this narrative, then, the advent of exomodern fiction stems from con-ceptual shifts within the literary-cultural terrain, not from any monumental historical event such as 9/11. Neoliberalism is continuous across postmodernism and exomodern-ism; it provides the historical backdrop of both periods. The difference is that postmod-ernism's romance with difference and absence prevented it from making any substantial claims about or interventions in the neoliberal project while exomodernism's rejection of critique and embrace of presence gives it a traction that postmodernism could never muster.

28. See Jason Gladstone and Daniel Worden's introduction to *Twentieth-Century Literature*'s special issue on postmodernism for a thorough treatment of the periodization issues swarming around the notion of postmodernism. See Andrew Hoberek's introduc-tion for a similarly stellar aggregation of dominant themes and trends in literature after postmodernism.

For arguments about how we should think of literature after postmodernism, see Green (who prefers the term "Late-Postmodernism"), Burn (*Jonathan Franzen*), Freitag, Holland, Timmer, and Toth. Also see the Toth and Brooks collection as well as articles by McLaughlin and Giles. Other attempts to categorize literature after postmodern-ism emphasize the increasingly postnational character of contemporary fiction. See, for example, Adams, Murphy, Robbins ("Worlding"), Medovoi, Mukherjee, and Song.

29. Post-postmodernism began in the 1990s, but it's certainly not confined to that decade. Authors continue to produce texts today, well into the twenty-first century, that are still worried about the relative adequacy and inadequacy of language. See Nealon for a description of post-postmodernism that sees it as an "intensification" of postmodernism.

30. This is also frequently viewed as post-postmodernism's return to reference. See, for example, Elliott, McLaughlin, and Dubey ("Post-postmodernism").

31. The snarky-suspicious reading of all this sees post-postmodernism as a trick that white male authors have devised so that the world will finally pay attention to their feelings. That is, post-postmodernism gives Franzen that "tribe" that he so desperately

yearned for in his now infamous *Harper's* article from 1996, but which, as a white guy, he felt he wasn't allowed to have. This is certainly one way to overcome postmodern impasse.

32. Franzen of course begins the quarrel, not with Marcus, but with Gaddis, in the *Harper's* essay "Perchance to Dream," and another in *The New Yorker* several years later. Marcus then tweaks Franzen's nose in his 2005 *Harper's* essay, "Why Experimental Fiction Threatens to Destroy Publishing, Jonathan Franzen, and Life as We Know It: A Correction." Lee Konstantinou ably chronicles the whole saga in his review of Marcus's *The Flame Alphabet*.

33. The important work that Ramón Saldívar is doing in ethnic literature on what he calls the "postracial aesthetic," and that Caren Irr is doing in world literature on what she calls the novel of the "new nomad," are the critical counterparts to this emerging body of fiction. Each has a piece in *American Literary History's* special issue on the twenty-first century novel, and Irr has another fascinating piece in *Twentieth-Century Literature*. In that essay Irr connects the white-male, neo-realist sincerity of Jonathan Franzen (and others) to the fiction of global writers of color through the form of the national allegory. Also see Irr's *Toward the Geopolitical Novel*.

Chapter 1

1. This is the underlying premise of Pheng Cheah's compelling *Inhuman Conditions*, which identifies human rights and cosmopolitanism as "the two primary ways of figuring the global as the human" (3).

2. For an extended discussion on the specific normativity of human rights discourse, see Cheah, 149–152.

3. In addition to Dawes, Slaughter, and McClennen, expansive treatments of the relation between human rights and representation can be found in Goldberg and Moore, Elizabeth Goldberg, Cubilié, and Anthonissen and Blommaert.

4. Critical scholarship reveals a range of arguments about the utility and potency of representations petitioning for the recognition of human rights. In their foundational work on narratives of testimony and witness, Schaffer and Smith allow that representations seeking to establish an "ethics of recognition" with their audience might inhibit human rights more than they help, but in general they see that as a risk worth taking. James Dawes does as well, although he too cautions that every act of storytelling is a kind of theft, an invasion of privacy that transforms personal experience into a generalized narrative that always risks reinforcing the dominant culture's view of the long-suffering, human rights victim ("Human" 409). Hesford views human rights representation as "spectacle," emphasizing the crucial role that visual representation plays in the "social and rhetorical process of incorporation and recognition ... that underwrites the discourse of human rights" (7). Even more skeptically, Judith Butler observes: "It is not just that some humans are treated as humans, and others are dehumanized; it is rather that dehumanization becomes the condition for the production of the human to the extent that a 'Western' civilization defines itself over and against a population understood as, by definition, illegitimate, if not dubiously human" (91).

5. See, for example, Douzinas, who argues that the potency of human rights "comes from their aporetic nature" (21); Mullins, who contends that "paradox does not necessarily impede human rights, but actually gives them form, shape, and purpose" (122); and Slaughter, who explains, "If we recognize paradox's figurative role in human rights

instead of treating it as a shameful limitation of human rights discourse and practice, then we can attend to its productive possibilities" (*Human Rights* 13). Slaughter's claim extends and expands on Wendy Brown's thinking in "Suffering the Paradoxes of Rights."

6. See, for example, Schaffer and Smith, for whom the "asymmetries of power" that grow out of an "ethics of recognition grounded in identity" can be overcome by "readers and listeners [who] accept and relate to difference at the expense of a certain and secure sense of self" (232). Although she's much less sanguine about the chance of that ever happening, Spivak describes an "activating of democratic structures" that occurs whenever teachers "take children's response to teaching as [their] teaching text" ("Use" 179–181).

7. See Ignatieff.

8. This is the poststructural approach—universality becomes a "constitutive lack"—Ernesto Laclau favors, and it dominates the essays in the *South Atlantic Quarterly* special issue on human rights, many of which adopt what the editors of that issue, Ian Balfour and Eduardo Cadava, describe as "aporetic praxis" (293). The Derridean take on human rights outlined in Cheah's *Inhuman Conditions* makes similar moves. But see Stanton for a critique of the limitations of a rights regime grounded in constitutive absence.

9. Upendra Baxi's *The Future of Human Rights*, Noam Chomsky's *Profit over People*, and Thom Hartmann's *Unequal Protection* all broadly imagine global capital and human rights in oppositional terms.

10. Inderpal Grewal sees 1981 as a crucial turning point since that's the year that "the International Commission of Jurists met at the Hague to argue that human rights and development needed to work together" (132).

11. As Karen Faulk describes in her ethnographic study of human rights under Argentinian neoliberalism, even the very nature of what counted as human rights abuse gradually changed. For example, Faulk finds that under neoliberalism, human rights petitioners tended to be less concerned with transgressions against the "physical integrity" of the human and more preoccupied with violations "against the nature of the neoliberal subject itself." Thus, complaints of "corruption and impunity" emerged as a dominant discourse for condemning the state's failure "to create the conditions in which neoliberal subjectivity-as-citizenship can adequately flourish" (x). Also see Joanna Fax's "Vulnerability as Hegemony" for an astute analysis of the way neoliberalism replaces potential *victims* of human rights abuse with populations that are *vulnerable* to the state's encroachment on their autonomy and liberty.

12. For more on this transition in development see David Craig and Doug Porter's *Development Beyond Neoliberalism?* A more skeptical assessment of development can be found in Baxi's *Human Rights in a Posthuman World*.

13. See Paul Bové's "Rights Discourse in the Age of U.S./China Trade" and Bruce Robbins's "Temporizing: Time and Politics in the Humanities and Human Rights."

14. Tim Jensen and Wendy Hesford's brilliant rhetorical analysis of the Beijing Olympics describes an even better example of the human rights version of the neoliberal circle. In examining the mutually reinforcing rhetorics of human rights, neoliberalism, and Chinese nationalism, Jensen and Hesford identify a tendency to "collapse a prepolitical articulation of human rights with its antipode—human rights as political, bestowed upon those who are citizens of a particular nation-state" (128). This conflation made it easy for institutional power—specifically the Chinese government and its corporate partners—to deploy human rights as "both sword and shield for the expansion and further entrenchment of neoliberal ideologies and economic doctrines" (133).

15. See Nick Mansfield's "Human Rights as Violence and Enigma" for a thorough critique of the logic of recognition underpinning standard human rights discourse.

16. Baxi borrows the idea from Agnes Heller, who describes the "dual contingency" of humanity. Not only is the contingent person thrown into the world in a place and time not of his choosing, but he also "does not receive the destination or telos of his life at the moment of birth as happened in premodern times" (55). The contingent person's absent telos poses trouble for the tautological-teleological project of human rights as Joseph Slaughter describes it.

17. Cheah makes the opposite argument. Even though he contends that standard approaches to human rights "are grounded in a rationalist conception of normativity that the actually existing capitalist world system renders untenable" (151), he nevertheless wants "to rethink normativity otherwise, from the ground up" (161). For Cheah this involves locating normativity in "the absolute surprise or chance of the event that reopens and keeps time and history going" (173). To my mind, little is gained from describing the constitutive absence of *différance* as the antifoundational foundation of normative thinking. Because neoliberalism exploits the normativity of human rights, capitalizing on the paradoxical relationship between the morally derived universal norms of the human rights object and the legally derived particular norms of the human rights subject, I think we should be wary of *any* normative conception of human rights, no matter how contingent and radically temporalized it is.

18. See Schaffer and Smith's interesting discussion of prisoner narratives for a thorough consideration of the difficulties that attend any attempt to represent individuals whose ambiguous status as both victim and perpetrator pushes them "beyond the boundaries of citizen-subject" (161).

19. For a thorough analysis of the limitations of truth and reconciliation commissions in general, see Hayner. Also see Schaffer and Smith for a detailed account of the "limited success" of the truth-and-reconciliation process in South Africa.

20. The timelessness of catachrestic violence in *Beasts* only further reinforces Bruce Robbins's important call for a more fully temporalized approach to human rights. That is, *Beasts* identifies a disturbing coincidence between the universalizations that justify human rights abuse and the timeless universals that are so frequently invoked to redress such abuses. See Robbins's "Temporizing."

21. I don't really think it matters if we describe this as posthuman or not. To be sure, this is not a standard humanism that locates inherent and inalienable value in the subject, but it's also not a standard posthumanism in the vein of Donna Haraway or Kate Hayles. Perhaps, by emphasizing the complicated subject-object doubleness of the human, I'm describing a quasi-humanism. For more thorough considerations of human rights in the age of posthumanism, see Baxi's *Human Rights in a Posthuman World* as well as the conclusion to Hesford's *Spectacular Rhetorics*.

Chapter 2

1. See Jason Hackworth's *The Neoliberal City: Governance, Ideology and Development in American Urbanism*.

2. While irrelevant to the legal decision, it's worth noting that in 2009 Pfizer merged with Wyeth and relocated its research facilities from New London to Groton,

Connecticut. At that time, none of the land transferred to the New London Development Corporation had been developed. For newspaper accounts, see "After the Homes Are Gone" and Patrick McGeehan.

This possibility actually came up in the court proceedings. Claiming that "the City had failed to adduce 'clear and convincing evidence' that the economic benefits of the plan would in fact come to pass," Kelo and her neighbors asked the court to consider the contingency of the redevelopment plan's future outcomes. Writing for the majority, however, Justice Stevens asserted that the actual future use of the land was immaterial. Citing an earlier eminent domain decision, Stevens wrote, "'It is only the taking's purpose, and not its mechanics' . . . that matters in determining public use" (11).

3. For a comprehensive and non-partisan legal overview of *Kelo*, see Merriam and Ross.

4. See Nadler, Diamond, and Patton whose polling found *Kelo* to be one of the most controversial Supreme Court decisions ever, with 80–90 percent of those polled disapproving of the result. Notably, they report that variables such as political affiliation, age, sex, education, income, and home ownership made only marginal difference in respondents' negative views of the decision.

5. See, for example, Machan's "Betrayal at the Supreme Court" and commentary from The Institute for Justice.

6. See Calfee for an analysis of the discrepancy between the public's collective outrage and the legal academy's collective yawn toward the decision.

7. O'Connor's dissent suggests that this expansion stems from "errant language" in *Berman* and *Midkiff*—that it was, in effect, an unintended oversight—but Benjamin Barros's analysis of conference notes from those two cases convincingly contends that the expansion resulted from the court's entirely intentional "deference to the legislature" in each case. In short, the court knew what it was doing when it expanded public use to include public purpose.

8. Nicholas Blomley locates a similar muddling in the curious collection of *amici curiae* filed on behalf of Susette Kelo, which came, on the one hand, from conservative groups like "the Property Rights Foundation, the Cascade Policy Institute, the Cato Institute, the Tidewater Libertarian Party, the Mountain States Legal Foundation and the Institute for Justice," and on the other, from left-leaning institutions like "the Congress for New Urbanism, Jane Jacobs, the National Association for the Advancement of Colored People, and the American Association of Retired People" ("Legal" 202).

9. Amazingly, despite his well-known hostility toward all forms of preferential treatment for minorities, Thomas's disgust at the majority opinion leads him to claim, "If ever there were justification for intrusive judicial review of constitutional provisions that protect 'discrete and insular minorities,' . . . surely that principle would apply with great force to the powerless groups and individuals the Public Use Clause protects" ("Justice Thomas Dissenting" 17). In other words, the only minority rights that Thomas can imagine protecting are those of individual homeowners (not actual minorities).

10. The idea that property rights are *natural* rights comes from John Locke, who argued that private property acquired through labor is a "natural right" that precedes and sanctions the social contract, and not the other way around. (See Locke's *Second Treatise on Civil Government*, but also see Shrader-Frechette for a provocative rethinking of Locke as the father of unbridled, laissez-faire capitalism.) This is the theory favored by the Hoover

Institution, which launched a "property rights initiative" designed to defend and propagate the notion that "the institution of the right to private property is perhaps the single most important condition for a society in which freedom, including free trade, is to flourish" (Machan, *Right* 2). Contending that private property is the *precondition* for government, social order, and moral values, the Hoover initiative denounces those who would treat private property as an artificial construct. This constructivist position descends from Marx's dismissive reduction of property rights to "the right of self-interest" (42); Pierre Proudhon's famous claim that "property is theft" (38); and John Maynard Keynes's insistence "that enlightened self-interest [does not] always operate in the public interest" (sec. IV, par. 1). For a contemporary constructivist analysis, see Murphy and Nagel, but also see Grey who argues that the decline of property rights is a natural development of late capitalism and not a symptom of creeping socialism.

11. See Wolfe for a thorough account of the various affinities and inclinations that typically align the left with public values and the right with private ones.

12. Hackworth's *The Neoliberal City*, Harvey's *Rebel Cities*, and Chase's *The Spaces of Neoliberalism* are all premised on this oppositional relationship.

13. Ginsburg; Hackworth; Kohn; Dear and Scott; Roweis and Scott; Hirsch and Mohl; and Hodge and Greve all contend that the public half of urban planning's public-private partnerships is a ruse.

14. See, for example, Marc Mihaly who contends that contemporary "mixed-use" redevelopment projects are "the product of hard-won sophistication among city officials, regulators, and public and private development advocates" (43) and are "undertaken in a manner that renders almost quaint the very concept of distinct, clearly separable 'public' gain and 'private' gain" (57).

15. Peck's work is always at the center of these discussions about neoliberalism's contingent heterogeneity. In addition to *Constructions of Neoliberal Reason*, also see "Neoliberalizing Space," with Tickell; "Neoliberal Urbanism," with Theodore and Brenner; and "Squaring Up to Neoliberalism," with Leitner and Sheppard.

16. See, for example, Farías and Bender's *Urban Assemblages* and McCann and Ward's *Mobile Urbanism*.

17. See, for example, Ash Amin and Nigel Thrift's *Arts of the Political*.

18. This is also the premise of Latour's "From Realpolitik to Dingpolitik: or, How to Make Things Public."

19. In the same way that Yamashita refuses to deploy nature as a critique of private property, she is also refreshingly cynical about the ability of multicultural diversity and ethnic identity to function as a tonic for Anglo cultural hegemony and homogeneity. The novel's multi-ethnic cast of characters absolutely refuses to speak the language of cultural particularity. Both Hsu and Rody see great political promise in Yamashita's radical de-essentialization of ethnic identity while Lee uses the novel to theorize a "romantic universalism" that productively negotiates the tension between collective identity and the impossibility of universality.

20. This should be read as a rebuke to those geographers—e.g., Henri Lefebvre, David Harvey, Don Mitchell, Neil Smith—whose ideological approach to late capitalism faithfully trusts that its internal theoretical contradictions will eventually lead to its demise. This trust in immanent critique does not adequately account for capitalism's contingencies of value.

21. William Gibson's Bridge trilogy—*Virtual Light, Idoru,* and *All Tomorrow's Parties*—explores this phenomenon in great detail. Set in a more technologically advanced future, the Bay Bridge that connects Oakland and San Francisco is abandoned after an earthquake, and the region's homeless occupy it, transforming it into a city. One character, Tessa, romanticizes the bridge as an "interstitial space," but Gibson emphasizes its purely ad hoc nature: the bridge "had occurred piecemeal, to no set plan, employing every imaginable technique and material" (*Virtual Light* 69), and its occupants function by "common sense," not "consensus" (280). Given an explicit reference to Gibson's most famous novel, *Neuromancer*, in *Tropic of Orange*, I would not be surprised if Yamashita's thinking about the freeway was influenced by Gibson's representation of the Bay Bridge (245).

22. Lee takes Manzanar as an example of what universalism looks like after post-structuralism: "Manzanar alone supersedes the paradox of urban coexistence—the dense, physical proximity counterbalanced by the atomistic nature of the population's movements and the division of spaces by race and class" (515). Hauser sees Manzanar as an avatar of Yamashita: "The 'strangely organic vision' is not only Manzanar's but also Yamashita's. Their positions parallel in the creation of an aesthetic compendium out of 'the residue of . . . the city'" (*TO* 56).

23. Most criticism on the novel highlights its unique narrative structure: Bénézet, Cooney, and Adams focus on genre while Hauser and Hsu highlight narrative structure and character interaction. Very little attention, however, has been paid to the novel's tropological commitments.

24. See Smith and Katz for an argument about metaphor's complicities with the ownership model of private property.

25. Although the Dodgers controversy does not appear in the text, the novel is set directly in its wake. The freeway construction, which began in the 1950s and lasted through the 1960s, is historically accurate in the novel, but the 1970 rabies quarantine is a fabrication. However, following the Chicano protests of August 29, 1970, the Los Angeles Police Department did impose a curfew in East Los Angeles, which required citizens to clear checkpoints and prove their place of residence to the authorities. In an interview with Michael Silverblatt, Viramontes explains that the rabies quarantine is a metaphor for the state's post-protest treatment of East Los Angeles residents.

26. Such language clearly invokes Viramontes's previous novel, *Under the Feet of Jesus,* which is also concerned with law and the land. For that novel's matriarch, just pointing to the earth under her feet is enough to justify her family's presence in the United States (63). For an extended reading of these themes in that novel, see my "Ostension, Simile, and Catachresis."

27. Of course, as these dynamics are not new, the novel should also be read as a broader critique of lost Chicano land, lost Chicano history. The freeways and the quarantine repeat the loss and ensuing marginalization of Mexican land, history, and identity after the Mexican-American war, which repeats the loss and ensuing marginalization of indigenous land, history, and identity under Spanish colonization, and so on. In fact, an excerpt from *The Broken Spears*—an Aztec account of Spanish colonization—provides the novel's epigraph and its title: "They came in battle array, as conquerors, and the dust rose in whirlwinds on the roads. . . . Their dogs came with them, running ahead of the column. They raised their muzzles high; they lifted their muzzles to the wind. They raced on before

with saliva dripping from their jaws." Although the quarantine plot reverses the dogs' role in the Aztec account of colonization (i.e., the dogs, along with the residents of East LA, are the victims, not the colonizers), the structural parallel and historical continuity between the two colonial acts is clear—as are the territorial parallels between the local quarantine and the US-Mexico border. With the quarantine, the indignity and injustice of the border—the "shifting weight of bodies, hushing children, hours passing, backs aching, only to be told certain papers were unacceptable as proof of residency, including rent receipts"—come nightly to the streets and sidewalks of East LA (63).

28. The language of the lizard scene makes the connection to Tranquilina's rape perfectly clear, as Ermila's required viewing of the tail-snipping reads like mild sexual assault. After Luis severs the tail, for instance, the lizard is "stiff and silent" like "stone." He then makes Ermila "touch it" and its "rings of wrinkled skin." As the narrator reports, "The cold sensation never left her fingers, his clamp around her wrist as he pulled her behind the toolshed never left her, his dirty rough clasp where the lizard's head poked in and out never left her" (6).

29. Kevane sees Tranquilina's belief in a more religious vein, departing from Mama's blind Catholic faith but nevertheless insisting on the continued relevance of the sacred for Chicanos in East Los Angeles. I would suggest, however, that what Viramontes describes, in personal correspondence with Kevane, as "the sacredness of the written word" (24) is not a blended or "*mestizo*" form of belief that combines Papa's Aztec traditions and Mama's Catholic ones, as Kevane argues (30). Instead, I see Tranquilina's textual turn as a categorically different form of belief—a form of belief that is actually more a form of ownership—that should be distinguished from rather than included in Kevane's treatment of Latino religious traditions.

30. Other evidence corroborates the idea that the execution occurred on Saturday night. For example, when Jan reports the vandalism of his car to the police, he hints that the McBride Street Boys might be responsible. This leads the police to investigate their prime suspect, Santos, the gang member Turtle encounters just after receiving her job offer. She's then with Santos when the police helicopters begin chasing his car. Suggesting that this chase occurs Saturday night, readers are given access to "the police report filed on *Sunday* morning after the incident" (296). Although we know that the vandalism must have occurred on Friday because the girls had to skip school to do it, it's still possible that the police did not begin searching for Santos until Saturday. (Perhaps Jan did not even report the vandalism until Saturday.) These events, then, plausibly corroborate Nacho's Saturday-night demise.

And yet, still other evidence, besides the Ermila-Nacho plot, contradicts the idea that Nacho dies Saturday. Tranquilina arrives at the bus station and witnesses Nacho's murder on the same night that she and Ana drive around Los Angeles searching for Ben. But we also know that Tranquilina cannot begin that search until Ana finishes at work. So why is Ana working on Saturday? Unless Ana is dressed in the fancy business attire of her "strict office dress code" to work all day and late into the evening on a weekend night, with her boss present until closing time, it seems much more likely that this night, the night of Nacho's death, is a Friday night (272). This is also corroborated by the horrible traffic Ana encounters upon leaving work, suggesting that she is stuck in rush-hour gridlock. If Ana and Tranquilina search for Ben and witness Nacho's death on Friday, however, then those events are discrepant with the Friday-Saturday events of Tranquilina's and Turtle's plots (see Figure 2). Thus, in her connection to Ana and their search for Ben, Tranquilina inhabits Ermila's and Nacho's Thursday-Friday plot, but in her connection to Turtle via the homeless woman, Tranquilina inhabits Turtle's Friday-Saturday plot.

31. I am admittedly making quite a bit out of what might very well be a mistake. Because Viramontes worked intermittently on the novel for nearly fifteen years and then wove together different parts of different drafts, it's plausible that the chronology was shuffled somewhere along the way. However, the careful placement of the suturing objects, the selective inclusion of enough days of the week to piece together the chronology but not enough to nail it down precisely, and the attention to coincident detail, all equally suggest the presence of Viramontes's intent. After all, the book is about freeways and earthquakes, quarantines and community—which is to say it's about how property and the people who own it either do or do not come together.

32. I intend this public-private hybridity to echo Graham Harman's suggestion, which I discussed in the introduction, that "the literal and the nonliteral . . . are two distinct sides of every point in the cosmos" ("Well-Wrought" 190).

Chapter 3

1. Having internalized antiracism, the right avoids criticizing the civil rights movement for fear that they'll appear racist. Instead, most explicit criticisms of the movement actually come from the left. Some contend, for example, that the civil rights movement was so inspiringly successful that it has overshadowed and atrophied all subsequent black politics. (Glaude, Gillespie, and the introduction to Reed and Warren discuss this point.) Others contend that the movement was not radical enough, that its fight for the bourgeois rights of liberal individualism was misguided. These critics suggest that the movement should have confronted the deeper structural racism endemic to social institutions throughout the United States, or that it should have pursued a more revolutionary, class-based agenda. For examples of the former perspective, see Singh 212–224 and Dubey (*Signs* 4–6). A more moderated version of the class-based perspective can be found in West 271–291; its more radical articulation appears in Macedo and Gounari. See King for a subtle and compelling defense of the civil rights movement.

2. As Michael Omi and Howard Winant write, "The racial reforms won by our movements were not only real victories; they also marked a defeat of our more radical aspirations. The incorporation of our demands (equality, justice, inclusion) in the warped and denatured form of 'color blindness' reinforced the underlying racist system we set out to destroy" (1570). For more on the direct link between the civil rights movement and the ideology of colorblindness, see Winant (*New Politics* 39–49) and Cochran 28–30 and 46–53. Also see Bonilla-Silva for an empirical analysis of the right's appropriation of the movement's values, an appropriation that was perhaps never so mind-bendingly perverse as when Glenn Beck, suggesting that it was time "to reclaim the civil rights movement," held his rally to "restore honor" in front of the Lincoln Memorial exactly forty-seven years after King delivered his "I have a dream" speech there.

3. As Adolph Reed Jr. describes it, this question frames a debate between those whose historicization of race and racism allows them to acknowledge that racial difference in the United States has and will continue to change and those who see race "as sufficiently durable as to be ultimately impervious to essential transformation, either by dissolution or

radical revaluation" ("Color Line" 262). In this latter camp, Reed places Stuart Hall, Henry Holt, Michael Omi, and Howard Winant, and he makes two particularly pointed assaults on their position. First, Reed notes that despite their enlightened acknowledgement of the social construction of race, their apparent inability to let race go suggests that "when the chips of actual historical possibility are on the line, they do accord race an ontological status" (262). And more personally, Reed suggests that such scholars benefit materially from maintaining "the race line," which he contends "is anchored within a political economy of race relations that delivers material and symbolic benefits disproportionately to members of the professional-managerial strata who occupy the status of brokers or representatives and who insist on it as the default language of black political aspiration" (288).

4. In a 2013 interview, Winfrey noted that "there are still generations of people, older people, who were born and bred and marinated in it, in that prejudice and racism, and they just have to die." Paradoxically, Winfrey was skewered by the right for "playing the race card" even though her understanding of racism is deeply conservative—that is, privatized. For Winfrey's comments and the requisite skewering, see Sheppard.

5. For a more extensive version of Ahmed's thinking on this topic, see "The Nonperformativity of Antiracism" where she smartly describes statements in support of multicultural diversity as nonperformatives—that is, as statements that actually maintain racism by intentionally failing to do what they say. Also see David Theo Goldberg's *The Threat of Race*, particularly pages 331–339, for an excellent discussion on the privatization of racism.

6. Goldberg reinforces these arguments in *The Threat of Race*. Also see Shih, Eng, Mills, and Ishiwata for more critiques of neoliberal colorblindness.

7. According to Michaels, the second and equally important step in this process involves reducing class to an identity on par with race, because once we see class as an identity, the only responsibility we have to the poor is not to discriminate against them for being poor. Michaels makes all of these arguments most explicitly in "Plots against America," "The Neoliberal Imagination," and in chapters two, three, and five of *The Trouble with Diversity*.

8. It's important to appreciate, however, that Michaels's preference for class over race is not Marxist. In fact, his personal politics seem to articulate a radical, classical liberalism. Michaels favors equal opportunity over equal outcomes, but he takes the idea of equal opportunity quite literally. In his preferred scenario, every child would have an equal opportunity to succeed, but this would require the elimination of all inheritance, the absolute equal funding of all public schools, the elimination of private education, and so on. Such a position is ultimately part of Michaels's attempt to force conservatives to admit that they're not actually all that committed to equal opportunity, and, by extension, to force them to defend economic inequality in its current form. (See Michaels's interview with Yasmin Nair for an extensive discussion of his personal politics.)

9. Reed elaborates these arguments in his essay on *Django Unchained* and *The Help*.

10. For Dubey, Samuel Delaney's science fiction embodies this ideal mixing of aesthetic and political domains. Less successful, Dubey notes that the sheer antiessentialism of Trey Ellis's New Black Aesthetic fails because it admits that it's not real while more essentializing black literature like Toni Morrison's, which turns to nostalgic settings from blacks' rural and southern past, fails because the vernacular that it deploys is a fantasy.

11. Given the violent descriptions of hip-hop's creative process, however, Macon's spectacular failure to convert miscegenated contradictions from an aesthetics to a politics should come as no surprise. This, for example, is how Macon describes rap: "Rappers raped music of its musicality, threw a few cents' retribution and a deadpan nod of respect to its parents and then saddled up, riding the unholy metalwork contraption toward the apocalypse as it bucked and snorted fire underneath them" (60). This "[b]uild and destroy" (36) process leaves hip-hoppers with a shallow sense of history—"you'd think hip hoppers / would be natural historians correct / but only for eight digital seconds at a time" (80)—and little game plan for the future (two major liabilities when it comes to political protest).

12. This is not exactly the kind of compromise Rachel Greenwald Smith has in mind in her crucial essay, "Compromise Aesthetics," but I think the phrase aptly describes texts like Mansbach's that can't outrun the neoliberal circle.

13. Adam Mansbach is Jewish, not black. But given the racial project of his novel, it strikes me as perfectly reasonable to describe the text as African American literature (Warren's arguments notwithstanding).

14. See Jodi Melamed's *Represent and Destroy* for a thorough description of the limitations and complicities that dominate race writing in the twentieth century precisely because of our pervasive inability to think of race as anything other than a problem needing a solution.

15. The statue scene in *John Henry Days* clearly alludes to the Booker T. Washington statue that the Invisible Man can't interpret in Ralph Ellison's novel. Crucially, Ellison's entire novel turns on that interpretive indeterminacy—it's impossible to tell if Washington is lifting or instituting a veil over the kneeling slave—while Whitehead leaves such representational questions behind.

16. For examples of postmodern (mis)readings of Whitehead, see Ramsey, Tucker, Bérubé, Russell, and Inscoe.

17. The phrase appears on pages 9, 197, 227, 229, and 255.

18. The implications of this clearly challenge the privileged position that Lauren Berlant assigns to Intuitionism's affective knowledge production in her reading of the novel.

19. It's remarkable how much this debate echoes the disagreements among Enlightenment empirical philosophers. David Hume, for example, endorsing a more skeptical empiricism, suggested that John Locke's attempts to deduce universal truths from empirical experience always presupposed the knowledge Locke thought he was discovering.

20. Adding another reversal to this surface-depth oscillation, it's worth noting that the racial conspiracy is both a hidden thing that Lila Mae intuits, but it's also something corroborated by Natchez, the friendly face who turns out to be a corporate spy. So when Natchez tells Lila Mae that the elevator crash is likely part of a vast racial conspiracy, he's lying to her. But when she believes him, she's actually reading empirically, even though she thinks they're reading suspiciously together. Thus, if Lila Mae were more suspicious of Natchez and less suspicious of the elevator crash, then she might have figured things out. Of course, the point of such vacillation is that it's impossible to know when one should read empirically and when one should read intuitively. The only actionable lesson seems to be that we should stop reading for meaning altogether.

21. See Rambsy for a discussion of Kirn's quote that comes in a broader analysis of the cultural and economic institutions that have made Whitehead the "literary" author that he has always wanted to be.

22. Jennifer Egan's *A Visit from the Goon Squad* comes to mind as another novel in which narrative perspective functions in this overdetermined way.

23. As will become clear in the ensuing discussion of Everett's work, I see him making a key distinction between meaning—which is concerned with the referential relationship between word and world—and understanding, which is instead concerned with whether or not communication occurs. Debates about meaning worry about the connection between the signifier and the signified; debates about understanding worry about the connection between the speaker/author and the audience/reader. Wittgenstein of course talks a great deal about meaning, but not as a union of signifiers and signifieds. Instead, meaning for Wittgenstein is a function of use, not reference. Thus, "Interpretations by themselves do not determine meaning" (sec. 198).

24. It's worth remembering that both Saussure and Wittgenstein reject the Augustinian model of language in which signs point to things. But what perhaps goes underappreciated is that Wittgenstein, in effect, rejects it more. Saussure's structuralism and its poststructural offspring maintain the sign-thing model; they just complicate it and point out that it doesn't work. But Wittgenstein makes the much more radical claim that language is not a sign system separate from things; it's just another part of the world of things, and within that world, we communicate not referential meaning, but a set of rules and expectations about the way the world is ordered and can be arranged.

25. The Möbius strip is of course an ur-image of poststructurally inflected postmodern fiction, but Everett deploys it here much differently. For someone like John Barth, whose *Lost in the Funhouse* begins with instructions for turning the book's opening story into a Möbius strip, language remains referential even when it can only point to itself. For Everett, however, there simply is no pointing. Put differently, Barth worries that the world has been reduced to language while Everett contends that language is simply another part of the world. This would be one way to understand why so much of Bruno Latour's work echoes poststructuralism's preoccupation with the materiality of the signifier even as he draws the entirely opposite conclusions about language and the world.

26. For Wittgenstein, having minds that others can't know doesn't mean that our mental experiences are intractably private. Instead, the question of their content is a moot point—he says it "cancels out"—and we simply move on to talk about minds that have things in them (sec. 293).

27. One such "honest" exchange goes like this:

"Fuck you," I say.
"Fuck you," Yellow say.
"Fuck you," I say.
"Fuck you," Yellow say.
"Fuck you," I say.
"Fuck you," Yellow say.
"Fuck you," I say.
"Fuck you," Yellow say.
"Fuck you," I say.

"Fuck you," Yellow say.
"Fuck you," I say.
"Fuck you," Yellow say.

28. Here I am suggesting that Everett basically develops a model of meaning-making and knowledge production identical to Bruno Latour's notion of circulating reference, which I discuss in the introduction.

Chapter 4

1. Barrett uses italics to indicate non-narrated speech or writing. These words are italicized because they are from Erasmus's journal.

2. Lawrence Buell, for example, wondering why "literature [must] always lead us away from the physical world, never back to it" (11), worries that the scholarly emphasis on "the distinction between text and referent" has prevented readers from finding nature in literature (10). Dana Phillips, on the other hand, contends that text inevitably precludes our access to nature.

3. Strong treatments of the relation between neoliberalism and the environment can be found in Heynen et al., Peet et al., Nixon, and Harvey ("What's Green . . ."). For a more polemical account, see Foster.

4. Of course, both read Darwin tendentiously, finding necessity and determinism where there is only contingency and randomness. Emphasizing the latter over the former, thinkers such as Elizabeth Grosz and Tim Morton describe evolution in ways that counter deep ecology's and neoliberalism's use of Darwin. See, for example, Grosz's *Becoming Undone* and Morton's *The Ecological Thought*, which notes that evolutionary traits do not develop teleologically, or "in order to" adapt in a specific way (45). Or as Greg Garrard has it, because evolution "just depends," we're wrong to find meaning and value in its proliferating processes (86).

5. Witness, for example, two recently published books—one by two outspoken sustainability advocates (L. Hunter Lovins and Boyd Cohen) and another by two more neutral academics (Peter Newell and Matthew Paterson)—both titled *Climate Capitalism*, as if the two terms were the most natural of bedfellows, as if we can't sustain one without the other.

6. For an extended critique of neoliberalism's engagement with the discourse of sustainability, now commonly referred to as "greenwashing," see Shiva.

7. David Harvey offers environmental justice as a third term between deep ecology and sustainability. Explaining that environmental justice substitutes pure moral outrage for sustainability's cost-benefit discourse and deep ecology's "mother earth" discourse, Harvey contends that it alone ekes out a space immune to neoliberal appropriation. Harvey wants environmental justice to "radicalize" sustainability, functioning as the conscience of economic modernization by articulating "a nonco-opted and nonperverted version" of its ideals ("What's Green" 352). But here Harvey merely updates outmoded Old Left thinking about capitalism's internal contradictions, replacing class difference with the racial, gender, ethnic, and national differences that concern environmental justice movements. That is, he still believes that capitalism has a "nonperverted" outside. The literature I read here suggests that he's wrong. We're all perverts now.

8. See Caren Irr's *Pink Pirates*, pages 94–103, for an extended analysis of Barrett's techniques.

9. Drawing on Richard Schechner's introduction to the concept, I use performance here to describe an immanence that renders being and knowing coextensive and non-differentiated. Immersed in the flow of time, sutured into the folds of space, the immanence of performance tends toward unification and holism. Henri Bergson (*Duration*), Gilles Deleuze (*Bergsonism*), and Elizabeth Grosz (*Nick of Time*) all use the concepts in this way.

10. Tom's mother, Annie, who dreams of herself as a seal, has similar powers of mimetic performance, but this connection highlights an unfortunate aspect of *Narwhal*. Barrett consistently associates the Inuits' perspectiveless vision with regrettably romanticized notions of their otherness. For example, in explaining Zeke's intrusion into the Inuit community, the narrator tells us that Annie's "tribe was one great person, each of them a limb, an organ, a bone. Onto the hand her family formed, Zeke had come like an extra finger. They'd welcomed him, but he'd had no understanding of the way they were joined together. He saw himself as a singular being, a delusion they'd found laughable and terrifying all at once" (319). While "singular beings" like Zeke suffer the compromised knowledge of their isolated perspective, apparently inhabitants of the Arctic wilderness, holistically imbricated with the land, suffer no such distance.

11. I take this idea from Latour's maxim, "No reality without representation!" (*Politics* 86). This does not mean that things become real through figuration, but by acquiring standing amongst other actors in the world.

12. Throughout *Narwhal*, Barrett highlights the absurdity of "discovering" people and environments that the people living in that environment already knew existed (386). Thinking about writing as an act of representative inclusion requires a shift from narratives of discovery (in which things don't exist until we find them) to narratives of existence (in which things already exist even if we don't know about them yet).

13. Of course, Latour also insists that being a spokesperson doesn't necessarily make representative representation objective and true: "with the notion of spokesperson we are designating not the transparency of the speech in question, but the *entire gamut* running from complete doubt . . . to total confidence" (*Politics* 64).

14. One of the rare exceptions to this ecocritical consensus comes from Dana Phillips who contends that "the success of our efforts to discover whatever we can about the ecological character of the natural world does not hinge on the right representation of nature" (xi).

15. This has become a common refrain in political ecology. See, for example, Bruno Latour's *Politics of Nature* ("nature is the chief obstacle that has always hampered the development of public discourse" [9]); Timothy Morton's *The Ecological Thought* ("Ecology can do without a concept of something, a thing of some kind, 'over yonder,' called Nature" [3]); and Ulrich Beck's *Ecological Politics in an Age of Risk* ("the ecological movement . . . reacts to and acts upon a blend of nature and society that remains uncomprehended, in the name of a nature no longer extant, which is at the same time supposed to serve as a model for the reorganization of an 'ecological society'" [7]).

16. Karvel is a parody of real-life artist Thomas Kinkade whose saccharine scenes of the American landscape are as wildly popular as they are aesthetically bereft.

17. This conclusion cleverly reverses the ending of Poe's text in which Pym and his partner Peters (both white) flee Tsalal on a boat with one black tribesman who dies as they sail toward the all-white world of the Tekelians.

18. See Timothy Morton's *Ecology without Nature* and *The Ecological Thought*, both of which describe nature as a "strange stranger" whose radical alterity undermines the distinction between self and other. These strangers "wander into and out of the world, constituting it as its boundaries, but also undermining its coherence" (*Ecology* 81). This strikes me as an apt description of the Tekelian ice monsters.

19. This is in line with the way Latour, Morton, and Beck all think about science. Latour distinguishes between Science, the domain of purportedly objective facts, and the sciences, which "constitute the common world and take responsibility for maintaining the plurality of external realities" (*Politics* 249). Morton premises his *Ecological Thought* on the notion that "the more we know, the less certain and the more ambiguous things become, both on a micro and on a macro level (14). And given the proliferation of ecological risks that exceed the institutions and technologies that have produced them, Beck contends that science can only complicate uncertainty. (See, in particular, his *Ecological Enlightenment*.)

20. The dissolution of the Treaty and a few nifty gadgets are the only things that make Robinson's novel science fiction. This is in keeping with much of his work, set in the very near future, that imagines plausible scenarios that have nevertheless not yet come to pass.

21. Latour notes, "An assembly will be all the better to the extent that it succeeds in detecting, for each proposition that is a candidate for existence, the most competent jury to judge it that can satisfy the requirement of relevance" (*Politics* 169).

22. All that I have summarized here can be found in the third chapter, "A New Separation of Powers," in *Politics of Nature*.

23. Robinson makes this point explicitly when one of the scientists' assistants notes, for example, that science will never lead to "guillotines . . . revolution . . . [or] strike[s]" (68). Similarly, Wade reports to his senator that his constituents want "a reform process leading to a desirable goal," not "revolution" (84).

24. This is perhaps most clearly evident in a scene from *Forty Signs of Rain*, the first novel in Robinson's "science in the capital" trilogy. In the fourth chapter, Robinson devotes nearly fifteen pages to detailing the step-by-step peer review process for grant submissions to the NSF. It's painful, but that's precisely the point.

25. For an expanded take on what this looks like, see the discussion of circulating reference in the introduction.

26. See Martha Nussbaum's *Poetic Justice* for a canonical, literature-is-good-for-you argument.

27. Crucially, the nonidentical is not a deconstructive aporia. This is not irony as constitutive absence—e.g., de Man's sense of irony as "permanent parabasis" (179)—but is instead a mode of approaching what's already there that has nevertheless not yet been included. It's the way Erasmus hopes to approach the Inuit.

28. For an expanded treatment of this idea, see McCarthy's description of what literature does and how it works in *Transmission and the Individual Remix*, a clever rewriting of T. S. Eliot's "Tradition and the Individual Talent."

29. The same thing happens in J. G. Ballard's *Crash*, a novel that McCarthy describes as "the truest novel of recent modernity" (*Believer* para. 22). In the novel, Vaughn, the protagonist, tries

to die in a head-on collision with Elizabeth Taylor at the precise moment of orgasm. He spends months planning it, down to the last, minutest detail (working out at what time she'll be passing such and such a spot, the approach angle his car must take towards hers, and so on). But, disastrously, he gets it wrong and misses her car by inches; subsequently, while Taylor stands alone, frozen in ambulance light, touching her gloved hand to her throat, he drowns in his own blood. Vaughn, who has been in thousands of car crashes, has met with his first accident. (para. 23)

Describing this as "the überaccident that fails to take place, that occurs precisely because it doesn't happen" (para. 23), McCarthy acknowledges that this is what he and members of The International Necronautical Society are "trying to feel our way toward: the breach, the sudden, epiphanic emergence of the genuinely unplanned, the departure from the script" (para. 24). We of course saw something remarkably similar in the catastrophes of Whitehead's *The Intuitionist*.

30. I borrow the idea of a "dark ecology" from Timothy Morton, who, insisting that he'd "rather be a zombie than a tree hugger," argues, "We should be finding ways to stick around with the sticky mess that we're in and that we are, making thinking dirtier, identifying with ugliness" (*Ecology* 188). He continues, here circling *After Critique* back around to its opening discussion of *Zone One*, "The task is not to bury the dead but to join them, to be bitten by the undead and become them" (201). In this formulation, nature, in all of its impenetrable otherness, is the dead, and as such, it is no longer "a world in which we can immerse ourselves" (204). But we should also not just keep our subjective distance from nature's object world over there. Instead, Morton advocates an approach that counter-acts such purified dualisms precisely by "hanging out in what feels like dualism"—that is, in what Latour might call hybridity. In such a state we are neither immersed in pure flow nor irrevocably distanced from the world out there. Instead, as in *Remainder*, we are distanced and different from the world, but not as subjects. And this is the role death plays. It annihilates the illusion of transcendent subjectivity and allows us to "jump down into the mud" rather than "trying to pull the world out of the mud." As Morton concludes, speaking like a card-carrying necronaut, "We choose and accept our own death, and the fact of mortality among species and ecosystems. This is the ultimate rationality: holding our mind open for the absolutely unknown that is to come. Evolution will not be televised. . . . We choose this poisoned ground. We will be equal to this senseless actuality" (205).

31. Not surprisingly, the culminating scene of McCarthy's *C.* occurs at an archaeological site in Egypt, and in *Pandora's Hope* Bruno Latour grounds his discussion of circulating reference in the carefully measured matrices of soil sampling.

32. A third possibility appears in the Necronaut's "Joint Statement on Inauthenticity," where the word "risidual" is defined as "a laughable doubling." That is, a risible residual.

33. Zadie Smith suggests something similar, favorably comparing *Remainder* to Joseph O'Neill's *Netherland*, in "Two Paths for the Novel."

Coda

1. Beyond the purview of these concluding thoughts, I'd briefly note that this marks an important pivot in Wallace's career. Specifically, it represents a move away from the ethical leaps of intersubjective faith that provide the moral scaffolding of *Infinite Jest* (where it's most conspicuously manifest in Alcoholics Anonymous) toward an ethics grounded on the organization of complex quantitative systems (represented in *The Pale King* by accounting). On the other hand, Burn ("Paradigm") and Clare offer compelling takes on the relative continuity between *Infinite Jest* and *The Pale King*.

2. See, for example, Konstantinou, who observes that Wallace's ideal literary rebel is a trusting believer who "risks accusations of credulity" ("No Bull" 93); Kelly, who avows that "true sincerity . . . is in fact made possible by the impossibility of its certain identification" (140); and Jenner, who makes much of Wallace's insistence that the truth of John McCain can only be found in our hearts (206).

3. Readers of Wallace's work will recognize the structure of Meredith Rand's complaint from countless other characters similarly paralyzed by overthinking.

4. As with most of the other novels treated in *After Critique*, this reluctance to judge pervades *The Pale King*, most notably in Chris Fogle's story about his Christian roommate's girlfriend's "salvation" narrative (214).

5. I also have in mind here Heather Love's notion of reading that is close without being deep. Love emphasizes ethnographic and sociological reading models, contending that "[t]hese fields have developed practices of close attention, but, because they rely on description rather than interpretation, they do not engage the metaphysical and humanist concerns of hermeneutics" (375). I would suggest that Wallace sees similar promise in accounting.

6. According to several notes included at the end of Wallace's unfinished text, Wallace intended this shift in the logic and operation of the Service to drive the novel's plot (546). In the novel's current form, the overhaul is a frequent topic of conversation hovering in the background of the novel, but it never really motivates the novel's dramatic action in any significant way.

7. In accord with these aspects of his narrative voice, Fogle counts words, a "talent" he has to suppress if he hopes to gain any meaning from them.

8. I will use David Wallace to distinguish the character from the author, whom I will call either David Foster Wallace or simply Wallace.

9. Again, beyond the purview of this conclusion, David Wallace's insistence on the absolute veracity of the text, even as a quick Google search will inform readers that David Foster Wallace never worked at the IRS, marks a significant shift in Wallace's decades-long preoccupation with the trusting relationship ideally forged between readers and authors. It also, it seems to me, poses a challenge to the connection Walter Benn Michaels makes between artistic intent and aesthetic form, a connection Michaels deploys as an antidote to what he sees as neoliberalism's "refusal of form" ("Neoliberal Aesthetics" para. 33). In short, the figure of David Wallace indicates that formal intentionality can't always be trusted.

10. See Boswell, who reads this trio of epiphanies as a William James–esque religious experience that deserves to be taken seriously.

11. This is the point Ellen Rooney misses in her takedown of surface reading. Assuming that meaning is something that texts contain, she incorrectly associates surface reading with mere description. She argues that surface reading advocates—e.g., Sharon Marcus and Steven Best—naively believe that they can "[report] what the text says in its own words" (115), that their job is merely to "[repeat] what the text confides about itself" (133). But there's nothing tautological about surface reading. As Wallace demonstrates, it's massively difficult, requiring readers to translate and transmit content without reducing it to either subjective or neoliberal ends. Or to put some of the blame on Marcus and Best, the name "surface reading" doesn't adequately capture what reading exomodern literature requires because that phrase doesn't fully speak to the many non-representational ways contemporary fiction goes about producing meaning and value.

{ BIBLIOGRAPHY }

Adams, Rachel. "The Ends of America, the Ends of Postmodernism." *Twentieth Century Literature* 53.3 (Fall 2007): 248–272.

Ahmed, Sara. "'Liberal Multiculturalism is the Hegemony—Its an Empirical Fact'—A response to Slavoj Žižek." *darkmatter*. February 18, 2008. http://www.darkmatter101.org/site/2008/02/19/%E2%80%98liberal-multiculturalism-is-the-hegemony-%E2%80%93-its-an-empirical-fact%E2%80%99-a-response-to-slavoj-zizek/.

———. "The Nonperformativity of Antiracism." *Meridians: feminism, race, transnationalism* 7.1 (2006): 104–126.

Amin, Ash. "Urban Planning in an Uncertain World." In *The New Blackwell Companion to the City*, edited by Gary Bridge and Sophie Watson, 643–55. Oxford: Wiley-Blackwell, 2011.

Amin, Ash, and Nigel Thrift. *Arts of the Political: New Openings for the Left*. Durham: Duke University Press, 2013.

Anthonissen, Christine, and Anne Blommaert, eds. *Discourse and Human Rights Violations*. Philadelphia: John Benjamins Publishing, 2007.

Appleyard, Bryan. "Bryan Appleyard's Full Account of His Interview with Ishmael Beah." *Times Online*. February 3, 2008. http://www.bryanappleyard.com/article.php?article_id=36.

Badiou, Alain. *Deleuze: The Clamor of Being*. Translated by Louise Burchill. Minneapolis: University of Minnesota Press, 1999.

Balfour, Ian, and Eduardo Cadava. "The Claims of Human Rights: An Introduction." *South Atlantic Quarterly* 103.2/3 (Spring/Summer 2004): 277–296.

Barnett, Clive. "Bad Foucault." *Pop Theory*. December 15, 2014. https://clivebarnett.wordpress.com/2014/12/15/bad-foucault/.

———. "The Consolations of 'Neoliberalism.'" *Geoforum* 36 (2005): 7–12.

———. "Publics and Markets: What's Wrong with Neoliberalism?" In *The SAGE Handbook of Social Geographies*, edited by Susan Smith et al., 269–296. London: SAGE, 2010.

Barrett, Andrea. *The Voyage of the Narwhal*. New York: W.W. Norton & Co., 1998.

Barros, D. Benjamin. "Nothing 'Errant' About It: The *Berman* and *Midkiff* Conference Notes and How the Supreme Court Got to *Kelo* with Its Eyes Wide Open." In *Private Property, Community Development, and Eminent Domain*, edited by Robin Paul Malloy, 57–74. Hampshire: Ashgate, 2007.

Baudrillard, Jean. *Simulation and Simulacra*. Translated by Sheila Glaser. Ann Arbor: University of Michigan Press, 1995.

Baxi, Upendra. *The Future of Human Rights*. 2nd ed. Oxford: Oxford University Press, 2006.

———. *Human Rights in a Posthuman World: Critical Essays*. Oxford: Oxford University Press, 2007.

Beah, Ishmael. *A Long Way Gone: Memoirs of a Boy Soldier*. New York: Farrar, Straus and Giroux, 2007.

Beck, Ulrich. *Ecological Enlightenment: Essays on the Politics of the Risk Society*. Translated by Mark Ritter. Atlantic Highlands, NJ: Humanities Press, 1995.

———. *Ecological Politics in an Age of Risk*. Translated by Amos Weisz. Cambridge: Polity Press, 1995.

Bénézet, Delphine. "Beyond Blank Fiction: Palimpsestic Flânerie and Converging Imaginaries in Karen Tei Yamashita's *Tropic of Orange*." In *The Idea of the City: Early-Modern, Modern and Post-Modern Locations and Communities*, edited by Joan Fitzpatrick, 169–179. Newcastle upon Tyne: Cambridge Scholars Publishing, 2009.

Bennett, Jane. "Systems and Things: A Response to Graham Harman and Timothy Morton." *New Literary History* 43 (2012): 225–233.

———. *Vibrant Matter: A Political Ecology of Things*. Durham: Duke University Press, 2010.

Bergson, Henri. *Duration and Simultaneity: Bergson and the Einsteinian Universe*. Translated by Leon Jacobson and Mark Lewis. Manchester: Clinamen, 1999.

Berlant, Lauren. "Intuitionists: History and the Affective Event." *American Literary History* 20 (Winter 2008): 845–860.

Bérubé, Michael. "Race and Modernity in Colson Whitehead's *The Intuitionist*." In *The Holodeck in the Garden: Science and Technology in Contemporary American Fiction*, edited by Peter Freese and Charles Harris, 163–78. Champaign, IL: Dalkey Archive Press, 2004.

Blomley, Nicholas. "Legal Geographies—*Kelo*, Contradiction, and Capitalism." *Urban Geography* 28 (2007): 198–205.

———. *Unsettling the City: Urban Land and the Politics of Property*. New York: Routledge, 2004.

Blühdorn, Ingolfur. *Post-Ecologist Politics: Social Theory and the Abdication of the Ecologist Paradigm*. London: Routledge, 2000.

Bonilla-Silva, Eduardo. *Racism without Racists*. 3rd ed. New York: Rowman & Littlefield Publishers, Inc., 2010.

Boswell, Marshall. "Trickle-Down Citizenship: Taxes and Civic Responsibility in David Foster Wallace's *The Pale King*." *Studies in the Novel* 44.4 (Winter 2012): 464–479.

Bové Paul. "Rights Discourse in the Age of U.S./China Trade." *New Literary History* 33 (Winter 2002): 171–187.

Brenner, Neil, David Madden, and David Wachsmuth. "Assemblages, Actor-Networks, and the Challenges of Critical Urban Theory." In *Cities for People, Not for Profit: Critical Urban Theory and the Right to the City*, edited by Neil Brenner, Peter Marcuse, and Margit Mayer, 117–137. London: Routledge, 2012.

Brenner, Neil, and Nik Theodore. "Neoliberalism and the Regulation of 'Environment.'" In *Neoliberal Environments: False Promises and Unnatural Consequences*, edited by Nik Heynen, James McCarthy, Scott Prudham, and Paul Robbins, 153–159. London: Routledge, 2007.

Brown, Bill. *A Sense of Things*. Chicago: University of Chicago Press, 2003.

Brown, Wendy. "Neo-liberalism and the End of Liberal Democracy." *Theory and Event* 7.1 (2003).

———. "Suffering the Paradoxes of Rights." In *Left Legalism/Left Critique*, edited by Wendy Brown and Janet Halley, 420–434. Durham: Duke University Press, 2002.

————. *Undoing the Demos: Neoliberalism's Stealth Revolution.* New York: Zone Books, 2015.

Buell, Lawrence. *The Environmental Imagination: Thoreau, Nature Writing, and the Formation of American Culture.* Cambridge: Harvard University Press, 1995.

Burn, Stephen. "'A Paradigm for the Life of Consciousness': Closing Time in *The Pale King.*" *Studies in the Novel* 44.4 (Winter 2012): 371–388.

————. *Jonathan Franzen at the End of Postmodernism.* London: Continuum, 2011.

Butler, Judith. *Precarious Life: The Powers of Mourning and Violence.* New York: Verso, 2004.

Calfee, Corinne. "*Kelo v. City of New London*: The More Things Stay the Same, the More They Change." *Ecology Law Quarterly* 33 (2006): 545–581.

Chakrabarty, Dipesh. "The Climate of History: Four Theses." *Critical Inquiry* 35 (2009): 197–222.

Chase, Jacquelyn, ed. *The Spaces of Neoliberalism: Land, Place and Family in Latin America.* Bloomfield, CT: Kumarian Press, 2002.

Cheah, Pheng. *Inhuman Conditions: On Cosmopolitanism and Human Rights.* Cambridge: Harvard University Press, 2006.

Cherniavsky, Eva. "Neocitizenship and Critique." *Social Text* 27.1 (Summer 2009): 1–23.

Chomsky, Noam. *Profit Over People: Neoliberalism and Global Order.* New York: Seven Stories Press, 1999.

Chow, Rey. *Ethics After Idealism: Theory—Culture—Ethnicity—Reading.* Bloomington: Indiana University Press, 1998.

Clare, Ralph. "The Politics of Boredom and the Boredom of Politics in David Foster Wallace's *The Pale King.*" *Studies in the Novel* 44.4 (Winter 2012): 428–446.

Clune, Michael. *American Literature and the Free Market, 1945-2000.* Cambridge: Cambridge University Press, 2010.

————. "What Was Neoliberalism?" *The Los Angeles Review of Books.* February 26, 2013. http://lareviewofbooks.org/review/what-was-neoliberalism#.

Cochran, Carroll. *The Color of Freedom: Race and Contemporary American Liberalism.* Albany: SUNY Press, 1999.

Cohen, Samuel. *After the End of History: American Fiction in the 1990s.* Iowa City: University of Iowa Press, 2009.

Collier, Stephen. "Topologies of Power: Foucault's Analysis of Political Government beyond 'Governmentality.'" *Theory, Culture & Society* 26.6 (2009): 78–108.

Cooney, Kevin. "Metafictional Geographies: Los Angeles in Karen Tei Yamashita's *Tropic of Orange* and Salvador Plascencia's *People of Paper.*" In *On and Off the Page: Mapping Place in Text and Culture,* edited by M. B. Hackler, 189–218. Newcastle Upon Tyne: Cambridge Scholars Publishing, 2009.

Craig, David, and Doug Porter. *Development Beyond Neoliberalism? Governance, Poverty Reduction and Political Economy.* London: Routledge, 2006.

Cubilié, Anne. *Women Witnessing Terror: Testimony and the Cultural Politics of Human Rights.* New York: Fordham University Press, 2005.

Danto, Arthur. *The Transfiguration of the Commonplace.* Cambridge: Harvard University Press, 1983.

Dávila, Arlene. *Barrio Dreams: Puerto Ricans, Latinos, and the Neoliberal City.* Berkeley: University of California Press, 2004.

Dawes, James. "Human Rights in Literary Studies." *Human Rights Quarterly* 31 (2009): 394–409.

——. *That the World May Know: Bearing Witness to Atrocity*. Cambridge: Harvard University Press, 2007.

Dear, Michael, and Allen Scott. "Towards a Framework for Analysis." In *Urbanization and Urban Planning in Capitalist Society*, edited by Michael Dear and Allen J. Scott, 3–16. London: Methuen & Co., 1981.

DeChaine, D. Robert. *Global Humanitarianism: NGOs and the Crafting of Community*. Lanham: Lexington Books, 2005.

Deleuze, Gilles. *Bergsonism*. Translated by Hugh Tomlinson and Barbara Habberjam. New York: Zone Books, 1988.

De Man, Paul. *Aesthetic Ideology*. Minneapolis: University of Minnesota Press, 1996.

Dimock, Wai Chee. *Through Other Continents: American Literature Across Deep Time*. Princeton: Princeton University Press, 2006.

Doherty, Brian. "Concerned Leftists Rediscover Michel Foucault Might Not Have Been as Anti-Market as They'd Like." *Reason*. December 10, 2014. http://reason.com/blog/2014/12/10/concerned-leftists-rediscover-michel-fou.

Douzinas, Costas. *The End of Human Rights: Critical Legal Thought at the Turn of the Century*. Portland: Hart Publishing, 2000.

Drezner, Daniel. "Why Michel Foucault Is the Libertarian's Best Friend." *The Washington Post*. December 11, 2014. http://www.washingtonpost.com/posteverything/wp/2014/12/11/why-michel-foucault-is-the-libertarians-best-friend/.

Dubey, Madhu. "Post-Postmodern Realism?" *Twentieth Century Literature* 57 (2011): 364–371.

——. *Signs and Cities: Black Literary Postmodernism*. Chicago: The University of Chicago Press, 2003.

Duggan, Lisa. *The Twilight of Equality? Neoliberalism, Cultural Politics, and the Attack on Democracy*. Boston: Beacon Press, 2003.

Elliott, Jane. "The Return of the Referent in Recent North American Fiction: Neoliberalism and Narratives of Extreme Oppression." *Novel: A Forum on Fiction* 42 (2009): 349–354.

Eng, David. "The End(s) of Race." *PMLA* 123 (October 2008): 1479–1493.

Everett, Percival. *Erasure*. New York: Hyperion, 2001.

——. *Glyph*. London: Faber and Faber, 2004.

——. *I Am Not Sidney Poitier*. Minneapolis: Graywolf Press, 2009.

Farías, Ignacio, and Thomas Bender, eds. *Urban Assemblages: How Actor-Network Theory Changes Urban Studies*. London: Routledge, 2010.

Faulk, Karen. *In the Wake of Neoliberalism: Citizenship and Human Rights in Argentina*. Stanford: Stanford University Press, 2013.

Fax, Joanna. "Vulnerability as Hegemony: Revisiting Gramsci in the Age of Neoliberalism and Tea Party Politics." *Culture, Theory and Critique* 53.3 (2012): 323–337.

Feher, Michel. "Self-Appreciation; or, The Aspirations of Human Capital." *Public Culture* 21.1 (2009): 21–41.

Felski, Rita. "Context Stinks." *New Literary History* 42 (2011): 573–591.

Ferguson, James. "The Uses of Neoliberalism." *Antipode* 41 (2009): 166–184.

Fisher, Mark. *Capitalist Realism: Is There No Alternative?* Hants: Zero Books, 2009.

Foster, John Bellamy. *Ecology Against Capitalism*. New York: Monthly Review Press, 2002.

Foucault, Michel. *The Birth of Biopolitics*. New York: Palgrave, 2010.

————. *Dits et écrits IV*. Paris: Gallimard, 1994.

————. *The Use of Pleasure*. Vol. 2 of *The History of Sexuality*. Translated by Robert Hurley. New York: Vintage, 1990.

Franzen, Jonathan. "Mr. Difficult." *New Yorker*. September 10, 2002. 100–11.

————. "Perchance to Dream: In the Age of Images, a Reason to Write Novels." *Harper's*. April 1996. 35–54.

Freitag, Sibylle. *The Return of the Real in the Works of Jonathan Franzen*. Essen: Die Blaue Eule, 2009.

Garrard, Greg. "How Queer Is Green." *Configurations* 18 (2010): 73–96.

Gibson, William. *Virtual Light*. New York: Bantam Books, 1994.

Giles, Paul. "Sentimental Posthumanism: David Foster Wallace." *Twentieth Century Literature* 53.3 (Fall 2007): 327–344.

Gillespie, Andra, ed. *Whose Black Politics? Cases in Post-Racial Back Leadership*. New York: Routledge, 2010.

Gilroy, Paul. ". . . We Got to Get Over Before We Go Under . . . Fragments for a History of Black Vernacular Neoliberalism." *new formations* 80–81 (2013): 23–38.

Ginsburg, Mark. "Public private partnerships, neoliberal globalization and democratization." In *Public Private Partnerships in Education: New Actors and Modes of Governance in a Globalizing World*, edited by Susan Robertson, Karen Mundy, Antoni Verger, and Francine Menashy, 63–78. Cheltenham, UK: Edward Elgar, 2012.

Gladstone, Jason, and Daniel Worden. "Introduction: Postmodernism, Then." *Twentieth Century Literature* 57 (2011): 291–308.

Glaude, Eddie. *In a Shade of Blue: Pragmatism and the Politics of Black America*. Chicago: University of Chicago Press, 2007.

Goldberg, David Theo. *Racial State*. Malden, MA: Wiley-Blackwell, 2001.

————. *The Threat of Race: Reflections on Racial Neoliberalism*. Malden, MA: Wiley-Blackwell, 2009.

Goldberg, Elizabeth. *Beyond Terror: Gender, Narrative, Human Rights*. New Brunswick: Rutgers University Press, 2007.

Goldberg, Elizabeth, and Alexandra Moore, eds. *Theoretical Perspectives on Human Rights and Literature*. New York: Routledge, 2012.

Gopnik, Adam. "The Pieties of Perspiration." *The Moth*. May 14, 2014. http://themoth.org/posts/stories/the-pieties-of-perspiration.

Gostin, Larry. "Property Rights and the Common Good." *Hastings Center Report* 36.5 (Sept.–Oct. 2006): 10–11.

Green, Jeremy. *Late Postmodernism: American Fiction at the Millennium*. New York: Palgrave, 2005.

Greimas, Algirdas Julien. *On Meaning: Selected Writings in Semiotic Theory*. Translated by Paul J. Perron and Frank H. Collins. Minneapolis: University of Minnesota Press, 1987.

Grewal, Inderpal. *Transnational America: Feminisms, Diasporas, Neoliberalisms*. Durham: Duke University Press, 2005.

Grey, Thomas C. "The Disintegration of Property." In *Property*, edited by J. Roland Pennock and John W. Chapman, 69–85. New York: NYU Press, 1980.

Grosz, Elizabeth. *Becoming Undone: Darwinian Reflections on Life, Politics, and Art*. Durham: Duke University Press, 2011.

————. *Nick of Time: Politics, Evolution, and the Untimely*. Durham: Duke University Press, 2005.

Hackworth, Jason. *The Neoliberal City: Governance, Ideology, and Development in American Urbanism*. Ithaca: Cornell University Press, 2007.

Harman, Graham. *Prince of Networks: Bruno Latour and Metaphysics*. Melbourne: re. press, 2009.

———. "The Well-Wrought Broken Hammer: Object Oriented Literary Criticism." *New Literary History* 43 (2012): 183–203.

Hart, Matthew, Aaron Jaffe, and Jonathan Eburne. "An Interview with Tom McCarthy." *Contemporary Literature* 54.4 (Winter 2013): 656–682.

Hartmann, Thom. *Unequal Protection: The Rise of Corporate Dominance and the Theft of Human Rights*. New York: St. Martin's Press, 2002.

Harvey, David. *A Brief History of Neoliberalism*. Oxford: Oxford University Press, 2005.

———. "Introduction." *Sociological Perspectives* 33.1 (Spring 1990): 1–10.

———. *Rebel Cities: From the Right to the City to the Urban Revolution*. London: Verso, 2012.

———. "What's Green and Makes the Environment Go Round?" In *The Cultures of Globalization*, edited by Fredric Jameson and Masao Miyoshi, 327–355. Durham: Duke University Press, 1998.

Hauser, Johannes. "Structuring the Apokalypse: Chaos and Order in Karen Tei Yamashita's *Tropic of Orange*." *Philologie im Netz* 37 (2006): 1–32.

Hayner, Priscilla B. *Unspeakable Truths: Confronting State Terror and Atrocity*. New York: Routledge, 2001.

Heise, Ursula. "Postmodern Novels." In *The Cambridge History of the American Novel*, edited by Leonard Cassuto, 964–985. Cambridge: Cambridge University Press, 2011.

Heller, Agnes. "The Contingent Person and the Existential Choice." In *Hermeneutics and Critical Theory in Ethics and Politics*, edited by Michael Kelly, 53–69. Cambridge: The MIT Press, 1990.

Hesford, Wendy. *Spectacular Rhetorics: Human Rights Visions, Recognitions, Feminisms*. Durham: Duke University Press, 2011.

Heynen, Nik, James McCarthy, Scott Prudham, and Paul Robbins, eds. *Neoliberal Environments: False Promises and Unnatural Consequences*. London: Routledge, 2007.

Hirsch, Arnold R., and Raymond A. Mohl, eds. *Urban Policy in Twentieth-Century America*. New Brunswick: Rutgers University Press, 1993.

Hoberek, Andrew. "Introduction: After Postmodernism." *Twentieth Century Literature* 53 (2007): 233–247.

Hodge, G., and C. Greve. "Public-Private Partnerships: An International Review." *Public Administration Review* 67.3 (2007): 545–558.

Hogan, Ron. "Australian Newspaper Questions Ishmael Beah's Memory." January 21, 2008. <http://www.adweek.com/galleycat/australian-newspaper-questions-ishmael-beahs-memory/7403>.

Holland, Mary. *Succeeding Postmodernism: Language and Humanism in Contemporary American Literature*. London: Bloomsbury, 2013.

Hsu, Ruth Y. "The Cartography of Justice and Truthful Refractions Found in Karen Tei Yamashita's *Tropic of Orange*." In *Transnational Asian American Literature: Sites and Transits*, edited by Shirley Geok-Lin Lim, John Blair Gamber, Stephen Hong Sohn, and Gina Valentino, 75–99. Philadelphia: Temple UP, 2006.

Huehls, Mitchum. "Ostension, Simile, Catachresis: Misusing Helena Viramontes's *Under the Feet of Jesus* to Rethink the Globalization-Environmentalism Relation." *Discourse* 29 (2007): 346–366.

———. *Qualified Hope: A Postmodern Politics of Time.* Columbus: The Ohio State University Press, 2009.

Hungerford, Amy. "On the Period Formerly Known as Contemporary." *American Literary History* 20 (2008): 410–419.

Hunt, Lynn. *Inventing Human Rights: A History.* New York: W.W. Norton & Company, 2007.

Ignatieff, Michael. *Human Rights as Politics and Idolatry.* Princeton: Princeton University Press, 2003.

Inscoe, John. "Race and Remembrance in West Virginia: John Henry for a Post-Modern Age." *Journal of Appalachian Studies.* 10.1–2 (2004): 85–94.

Institute for Justice. "Homeowners Lose Eminent Domain Case." *Institute for Justice.* June 23, 2005. http://www.ij.org/new-london-connecticut-release-6-23-2005.

Irr, Caren. *Pink Pirates: Contemporary American Women Writers and Copyright.* Iowa City: University of Iowa Press, 2010.

———. "Postmodernism in Reverse: American National Allegories and the 21st-Century Political Novel." *Twentieth Century Literature* 57 (2011): 516–538.

———. *Toward the Geopolitical Novel: U.S. Fiction in the Twenty-First Century.* New York: Columbia University Press, 2013.

———. "Toward the World Novel: Genre Shifts in Twenty-First Century Expatriate Fiction." *American Literary History* 23.3 (Fall 2011): 660–679.

Ishiwata, Eric. "'We Are Seeing People We didn't Know Exist': Katrina and the Neoliberal Erasure of Race." In *The Neoliberal Deluge: Hurricane Katrina, Late Capitalism, and the Remaking of New Orleans*, edited by Cedric Johnson, 32–59. Minneapolis: University of Minnesota Press, 2011.

Iweala, Uzodinma. *Beasts of No Nation.* New York: Harper Collins, 2005.

Jameson, Fredric. *Valences of the Dialectic.* New York: Verso, 2009.

Jenner, Paul. "Don't Compare, Identify: David Foster Wallace on John McCain." In *Consider David Foster Wallace: Critical Essays*, edited by David Hering, 199–208. Los Angeles/Austin: Slideshow Media Group Press, 2010.

Jensen, Tim, and Wendy Hesford. "Staging the Beijing Olympics: Intersecting Human Rights and Economic Development Narratives." In *The Megarhetorics of Global Development*, edited by Rebecca Dingo and J. Blake Scott, 121–146. Pittsburgh: University of Pittsburgh Press, 2012.

Johnson, Mat. *Pym.* New York: Spiegel & Grau, 2010.

Jones, Daniel Stedman. *Masters of the Universe: Hayek, Friedman, and the Birth of Neoliberal Politics.* Princeton: Princeton University Press, 2012.

Kelly, Adam. "David Foster Wallace and the New Sincerity in American Fiction." In *Consider David Foster Wallace: Critical Essays*, edited by David Hering, 131–146. Los Angeles/Austin: Slideshow Media Group Press, 2010.

Kerridge, Richard, and Neil Sammells, eds. *Writing the Environment: Ecocriticism and Literature.* New York: Zed Books, 1998.

Kevane, Bridget. *Profane & Sacred: Latino/a American Writers Reveal the Interplay of the Secular and the Religious.* Lanham, MD: Rowman & Littlefield, 2008.

Keynes, John Maynard. "The End of *Laissez Faire*." *Panarchy*. Accessed April 3, 2013. http://www.panarchy.org/keynes/laissezfaire.1926.html.

King, Richard H. *Civil Rights and the Idea of Freedom*. Athens: University of Georgia Press, 1996.

Kohn, Margaret. *Brave New Neighborhoods: The Privatization of Public Space*. New York: Routledge, 2004.

Konstantinou, Lee. "Anti-Comprehension Pills." *Los Angeles Review of Books*. March 28, 2012. http://lareviewofbooks.org/article.php?id=433&fulltext=1.

———. "No Bull: David Foster Wallace and Postironic Belief." In *The Legacy of David Foster Wallace*, edited by Samuel Cohen and Lee Konstantinou, 83–112. Iowa City: University of Iowa Press, 2012.

Laclau, Ernesto. *Emancipation(s)*. London: Verso, 1996.

Larner, Wendy. "Neo-liberalism: Policy, Ideology, Governmentality." *Studies in Political Economy* 63 (Autumn 2000): 5–25.

Lash, Scott. *Another Modernity, a Different Rationality*. Oxford: Blackwell Publishers, 1999.

Latour, Bruno. "An Attempt at a 'Compositionist Manifesto.'" *New Literary History* 41 (2010): 471–490.

———. "From Realpolitik to Dingpolitik or How to Make Things Public." In *Making Things Public: Atmospheres of Democracy*, edited by Bruno Latour and Peter Weibel, 14–41. Cambridge: MIT Press, 2005.

———. *Irreductions*. In *The Pasteurization of France*, translated by Alan Sheridan and John Law, 153–236. Cambridge: Harvard University Press, 1988.

———. *Pandora's Hope: Essays on the Reality of Science Studies*. Cambridge: Harvard University Press, 1999.

———. *Politics of Nature: How to Bring the Sciences into Democracy*. Translated by Catherine Porter. Cambridge: Harvard University Press, 2004.

———. *We Have Never Been Modern*. Translated by Catherine Porter. Cambridge: Harvard University Press, 1993.

———. "Why Has Critique Run Out of Steam?" *Critical Inquiry* 30 (Winter 2004): 225–248.

Lee, Sue-Im. "'We Are Not the World': Global Village, Universalism, and Karen Tei Yamashita's *Tropic of Orange*." *Modern Fiction Studies* 53 (2007): 501–527.

Lefebvre, Henri. *The Production of Space*. Translated by Donald Nicholson-Smith. Oxford: Blackwell, 1991.

Leitner, Helga, Jamie Peck, and Eric S. Sheppard. "Squaring Up to Neoliberalism." In *Contesting Neoliberalism: Urban Frontiers*, edited by Helga Leitner, Jamie Peck, and Eric S. Sheppard, 311–327. New York: The Guilford Press, 2007.

Lemm, Vanessa, and Miguel Vatter, eds. *The Government of Life: Foucault, Biopolitics, and Neoliberalism*. New York: Fordham University Press, 2014.

Lentin, Alana, and Gavan Titley. *The Crises of Multiculturalism: Racism in a Neoliberal Age*. London: Zed Books, 2011.

Lesjak, Carolyn. "Reading Dialectically." *Criticism* 55.2 (Spring 2013): 233–277.

Lipman, Pauline. *The New Political Economy of Urban Education: Neoliberalism, Race, and the Right to the City*. New York: Routledge, 2011.

Locke, John. *The Second Treatise on Civil Government*. New York: Prometheus Books, 1986.

Love, Heather. "Close but Not Deep: Literary Ethics and the Descriptive Turn." *New Literary History* 41 (2010): 371–391.

Lovins, L. Hunter, and Boyd Cohen. *Climate Capitalism: Capitalism in the Age of Climate Change*. New York: Hill & Wang, 2011.

Macedo, Donaldo, and Panayota Gounari. "Globalization and the Unleashing of New Racism: An Introduction." In *The Globalization of Racism*, edited by Donaldo Macedo and Panayota Gounari, 3–35. Boulder: Paradigm Publishers, 2006.

Machan, Tibor. "Betrayal at the Supreme Court." *The Independent Institute*. June 24, 2005. http://www.independent.org/newsroom/article.asp?id=1525.

———. *The Right to Private Property*. Stanford: Hoover Institution Press, 2002.

Mansbach, Adam. *Angry Black White Boy: or, The Miscegenation of Macon Detornay*. New York: Three Rivers Press, 2005.

———. "On Lit Hop." *Adam Mansbach*. Accessed April 8, 2013. http://www.adammansbach.com/other/onlithop.html.

Mansfield, Nick. "Human Rights as Violence and Enigma: Can Literature Really Be of Any Help with the Politics of Human Rights?" In *Theoretical Perspectives on Human Rights and Literature*, edited by Elizabeth Goldberg and Alexandra Moore, 201–214. New York: Routledge, 2012.

Marcus, Ben. "Why Experimental Fiction Threatens to Destroy Publishing, Jonathan Franzen, and Life as We Know It: A Correction." *Harper's*. October 2005. 39–52.

Marx, Karl. "On the Jewish Question." In *The Marx-Engels Reader*. 2nd ed. Edited by Robert Tucker, 26–52. New York: W.W. Norton, 1978.

Massey, Doreen. *Space, Place, and Gender*. Minneapolis: University of Minnesota Press, 1994.

Mayer, Margit. "Contesting the Neoliberalization of Urban Governance." In *Contesting Neoliberalism: Urban Frontiers*, edited by Helga Leitner, Jamie Peck, and Eric S. Sheppard, 90–115. New York: The Guilford Press, 2007.

McCann, Eugene, and Kevin Ward, eds. *Mobile Urbanism: Cities and Policymaking in the Global Age*. Minneapolis: University of Minnesota Press, 2011.

McCarthy, Tom. *C*. New York: Vintage, 2011.

———. *Remainder*. New York: Vintage, 2005.

———. *Transmission and the Individual Remix: How Literature Works*. New York: Vintage, 2012.

McCarthy, Tom, and Simon Critchley. "Declaration on the Notion of 'The Future.'" *The Believer*. November/December 2010. http://www.believermag.com/issues/201011/?read=article_ necronautical.

———. "INS Founding Manifesto." *The Times* [London]. December 14, 1999.

———. "Joint Statement on Inauthenticity." *INS Bulletin*. January 23, 2013. http://necronauts.net/declarations/ins_inauthenticity_new_york/inauthenticity_precis.html.

———. *The Mattering of Matter: Documents from the Archive of the International Necronautical Society*. Berlin: Sternberg Press, 2013.

McClennen, Sophia. "The Humanities, Human Rights, and the Comparative Imagination." *Comparative Literature and Culture* 9.1 (2007): 3–19.

McClennen, Sophia, and Joseph Slaughter. "Introducing Human Rights and Literary Forms; or, The Vehicles and Vocabularies of Human Rights." *Comparative Literature Studies* 46.1 (2009): 1–19.

McGeehan, Patrick. "Pfizer to Leave City That Won Land-Use Case." *New York Times*. November, 13 2009. http://www.nytimes.com/2009/11/13/nyregion/13pfizer.html?_r=0.

McGurl, Mark. "The New Cultural Geology." *Twentieth Century Literature* 57 (2011): 380–390.

———. "The Posthuman Comedy." *Critical Inquiry* 38 (2012): 533–553.

———. *The Program Era: Postwar Fiction and the Rise of Creative Writing.* Cambridge: Harvard University Press, 2009.

McLaughlin, Robert. "Post-Postmodern Discontent." *Symploke* 12.1–2 (2004): 53–68.

Medovoi, Leerom. " 'Terminal Crisis?' From the Worlding of American Literature to World-System Literature." *American Literary History* 23 (2011): 643–659.

Melamed, Jodi. *Represent and Destroy: Rationalizing Violence in the New Racial Capitalism.* Minneapolis: University of Minnesota Press, 2011.

Merleau-Ponty, Maurice. *Adventures of the Dialectic.* Translated by Joseph Bien. Evanston: Northwestern University Press, 1973.

Merriam, Dwight, and Mary Ross, eds. *Eminent Domain Use and Abuse: Kelo in Context.* Chicago: American Bar Association, 2006.

Michaels, Walter Benn. "The Beauty of a Social Problem (e.g., Unemployment)." *Twentieth Century Literature* 57 (2011): 309–327.

———. Interview with Yasmin Nair. March 2007. http://www.yasminnair.net/content/interview-walter-benn-michaels-celebrating-all-stripes-rainbow-enough-march-2007.

———. "Model Minorities and the Minority Model—The Neoliberal Novel." In *The Cambridge History of the American Novel,* edited by Leonard Cassuto, 1016–1030. Cambridge: Cambridge University Press, 2011.

———. "Neoliberal Aesthetics: Fried, Ranciére, and the Form of the Photograph." *Nonsite* 1 (Spring 2011). http://nonsite.org/issues/issue-1/neoliberal-aesthetics-fried-ranciere-and-the-form-of-the-photograph.

———. "The Neoliberal Imagination." *n+1.* Fall 2005. https://nplusonemag.com/issue-3/essays/the-neoliberal-imagination/.

———. "Plots Against America: Neoliberalism and Antiracism." *American Literary History* 18 (2006): 288–302.

———. *The Shape of the Signifier: 1967 to the End of History.* Princeton: Princeton University Press, 2004.

———. *The Trouble with Diversity: How We Learned to Love Identity and Ignore Equality.* New York: Metropolitan Books, 2006.

Mihaly, Marc B. "Public-Private Redevelopment Partnerships and the Supreme Court: Kelo v. City of New London." *The Supreme Court and Takings: Four Essays. Vermont Journal of Environmental Law* 22 (2006): 41–61.

Mills, Charles. *The Racial Contract.* Ithaca: Cornell UP, 1997.

———. "Racial Liberalism." *PMLA* 123 (October 2008): 1380–1397.

Miraftab, Faranak. "Public-Private Partnerships: The Trojan Horse of Neoliberal Development?" *Journal of Planning Education and Research* 24 (2004): 89–101.

Mitchell, Don. *The Right to the City: Social Justice and the Fight for Public Space.* New York: The Guilford Press, 2003.

Molotch, Harvey. "Objects and the City." In *The New Blackwell Companion to the City,* edited by Gary Bridge and Sophie Watson, 66–78. Oxford: Wiley-Blackwell, 2011.

Moretti, Franco. *Graphs, Maps, Trees: Abstract Models for Literary History.* New York: Verso, 2007.

Morton, Timothy. *The Ecological Thought.* Cambridge: Harvard University Press, 2010.

———. *Ecology Without Nature: Rethinking Environmental Aesthetics*. Cambridge: Harvard University Press, 2007.

———. "An Object-Oriented Defense of Poetry." *New Literary History* 43 (2012): 205–224.

Mukherjee, Bharati. "Immigrant Writing: Changing the Contours of a National Literature." *American Literary History* 23 (2011): 680–696.

Mullins, Greg. "Paradoxes of Neoliberalism and Human Rights." In *Theoretical Perspectives on Human Rights and Literature*, edited by Elizabeth Goldberg and Alexandra Moore, 120–132. New York: Routledge, 2012.

Murphy, Liam, and Thomas Nagel. *The Myth of Ownership: Taxes and Justice*. Oxford: Oxford University Press, 2004.

Murphy, Timothy. "To Have Done with Postmodernism." *Symploke* 12.1–2 (2004): 20–34.

Nadler, Janice, Shari Diamond, and Matthew Patton. "Government Takings of Private Property: *Kelo* and the Perfect Storm." In *Public Opinion and Constitutional Controversy*, edited by Nathaniel Persily, Jack Citrin, and Patrick Egan, 287–310. Oxford: Oxford University Press, 2008.

Nealon, Jeffrey. *Post-Postmodernism; or, The Cultural Logic of Just-in-Time Capitalism*. Stanford: Stanford University Press, 2012.

Newell, Peter, and Matthew Paterson. *Climate Capitalism: Global Warming and the Transformation of the Global Economy*. Cambridge: Cambridge University Press, 2010.

Nixon, Rob. *Slow Violence and the Environmentalism of the Poor*. Cambridge: Harvard University Press, 2011.

Nussbaum, Martha. *Poetic Justice: The Literary Imagination and Public Life*. Boston: Beacon Press, 1995.

Omi, Michael, and Howard Winant. "Once More, with Feeling: Reflections on Racial Formation." *PMLA* 123 (October 2008): 1565–1572.

Ong, Aihwa. "Mutations in Citizenship." *Theory Culture Society* 23.2–3 (2006): 499–531.

Patton, Paul. "Foucault and Normative Political Philosophy." In *Foucault and Philosophy*, edited by Timothy O'Leary and Christopher Falzon, 204–221. West Sussex: Blackwell, 2010.

Peck, Jamie. *Constructions of Neoliberal Reason*. Oxford: Oxford University Press, 2010.

Peck, Jamie, Nik Theodore, and Neil Brenner. "Neoliberal Urbanism: Models, Moments, Mutations." *SAIS Review* 29.1 (Winter-Spring 2009): 49–66.

———. "Postneoliberalism and Its Malcontents." *Antipode* 41.S1 (2009): 94–116.

Peck, Jamie, and Adam Tickell. "Neoliberalizing Space." *Antipode* 34.3 (2002): 380–404.

Peet, Richard, Paul Robbins, and Michael Watts. *Global Political Ecology*. New York: Routledge, 2011.

Phillips, Dana. *The Truth of Ecology: Nature, Culture, and Literature in America*. Oxford: Oxford University Press, 2003.

Polanyi, Karl. *The Great Transformation: The Political and Economic Origins of Our Time*. Boston: Beacon Press, 1944.

Prasad, Monica. *The Politics of Free Markets: The Rise of Neoliberal Economic Policies in Britain, France, Germany, & the United States*. Chicago: University of Chicago Press, 2006.

Proudhon, Pierre-Joseph. *What Is Property?* Charleston: Nabu Press, 2010.

Rambsy, Howard. "The Rise of Colson Whitehead: Hi-Tech Narratives and Literary Ascent." In *New Essays on the African American Novel*, edited by Lovalerie King and Linda F. Selzer, 221–240. New York: Palgrave, 2008.

Ramsey, William. "An End of Southern History: The Down-Home Quests of Toni Morrison and Colson Whitehead." *African American Review* 41 (Winter 2007): 769–785.

Reed, Adolph, Jr. "The 'Color Line' Then and Now: *The Souls of Black Folk* and the Changing Context of Black American Politics." In *Renewing Black Intellectual History*, edited by Kenneth Warren and Adolph Reed Jr., 252–303. Boulder: Paradigm Publishers, 2009.

———. "*Django Unchained*, or, *The Help*: How 'Cultural Politics' Is Worse Than No Politics at All, and Why." *Nonsite* 9 (February 2013): http://nonsite.org/feature/django-unchained-or-the-help-how-cultural-politics-is-worse-than-no-politics-at-all-and-why.

Reed, Adolph, Jr., and Kenneth Warren, eds. *Renewing Black Intellectual History*. Boulder: Paradigm Publishers, 2009.

Robbins, Bruce. "Temporizing: Time and Politics in the Humanities and Human Rights." *boundary 2* 32.1 (2005): 191–208.

———. "The Worlding of the American Novel." In *The Cambridge History of the American Novel*, edited by Leonard Cassuto, 1096–1106. Cambridge: Cambridge University Press, 2011.

Robinson, Kim Stanley. *Antarctica*. New York: Bantam Books, 1998.

———. *Forty Signs of Rain*. New York: Random House, 2004.

Rody, Caroline. *The Interethnic Imagination: Roots and Passages in Contemporary Asian American Fiction*. Oxford: Oxford University Press, 2009.

Rooney, Ellen. "Live Free or Describe: The Reading Effect and the Persistence of Form." *differences* 21.3 (2010): 112–139.

Rose, Carol. *Property and Persuasion: Essays on the History, Theory, and Rhetoric of Ownership*. Boulder: Westview Press, 1994.

Roweis, Shoukry T., and Allen J. Scott. "The Urban Land Question." In *Urbanization and Urban Planning in Capitalist Society*, edited by Michael Dear and Allen J. Scott, 123–157. London: Methuen & Co., 1981.

Russell, Alison. "Recalibrating the Past: Colson Whitehead's *The Intuitionist*." *Critique* 49 (2007): 46–60.

Saldívar, Ramón. "Historical Fantasy, Speculative Realism, and Postrace Aesthetics in Contemporary American Fiction." *American Literary History* 23.3 (Fall 2011): 574–599.

———. "The Second Elevation of the Novel: Race, Form, and the Postrace Aesthetic in Contemporary Narrative." *Narrative* 21 (January 2013): 1–18.

———. "Speculative Realism and the Postrace Aesthetic in Contemporary American Fiction." In *A Companion to American Literary Studies*, edited by Caroline Levander and Robert Levine, 517–531. Chichester: Wiley-Blackwell, 2011.

San Francisco Chronicle. "After the Homes Are Gone." November 28, 2009. http://www.sfgate.com/opinion/editorials/article/After-the-homes-are-gone-3209347.php.

Schaffer, Kay, and Sidonie Smith. *Human Rights and Narrated Lives: The Ethics of Recognition*. New York: Palgrave, 2004.

Schechner, Richard. *Performance Studies: An Introduction*. 2nd ed. New York: Routledge, 2006.

Sheppard, Noel. "Oprah: Racists Have to Die for Racism to End." *Newsbusters*. November 15, 2013. http://newsbusters.org/blogs/noel-sheppard/2013/11/15/oprah-racists-have-die-racism-end.

Shih, Shu-Mei. "Comparative Racialization: An Introduction." *PMLA* 123 (October 2008): 1347–1362.

Shiva, Vandana. "Recovering the Real Meaning of Sustainability." In *The Environment in Question: Ethics and Global Issues*, edited by David Cooper and Joy Palmer, 187–93. New York: Routledge, 1992.

Shrader-Frechette, Kristin. "Locke and the Limits on Land Ownership." *Journal of the History of Ideas* 54.2 (1993): 201–219.

Silver, Nate. *The Signal and the Noise: Why So Many Predictions Fail—But Some Don't.* New York: Penguin, 2012.

Singh, Nikhil. *Black Is a Country: Race and the Unfinished Struggle for Democracy.* Cambridge: Harvard University Press, 2004.

Slaughter, Joseph. "Enabling Fictions and Novel Subjects: The *Bildungsroman* and International Human Rights Law," *PMLA* 121 (October 2006): 1405–1423.

———. "Foreword: Rights on Paper." In *Theoretical Perspectives on Human Rights and Literature*, edited by Elizabeth Goldberg and Alexandra Moore, xi–xiv. New York: Routledge, 2012.

———. *Human Rights Inc.: The World Novel, Narrative Form, and International Law.* New York; Fordham University Press, 2007.

Smith, Neil, and Cindi Katz. "Grounding Metaphor: Towards a Spatialized Politics." In *Place and the Politics of Identity*, edited by Michael Keith and Steven Pile, 66–81. London: Routledge, 1993.

Smith, Rachel Greenwald. "Ecology Beyond Ecology: Life After the Accident in Octavia Butler's *Xenogenesis* Trilogy." *Modern Fiction Studies* 55.3 (Fall 2009): 545–565.

———. "Six Propositions on Compromise Aesthetics." *The Account Magazine.* Fall 2014. http://theaccountmagazine.com/?article–six-propositions-on-compromise-aesthetics.

Smith, Zadie. "Two Paths for the Novel." *The New York Review of Books.* November 20, 2008.

Song, Min Hyoung. "Becoming Planetary." *American Literary History* 23 (2011): 555–573.

Spivak, Gayatri. *Outside in the Teaching Machine.* New York: Routledge, 1993.

———. "Practical Politics of the Open End." *The Post-Colonial Critic: Interviews, Strategies, Dialogues.* Edited by Sarah Harasym. New York and London: Routledge, 1990.

———. "Use and Abuse of Human Rights." *boundary 2* 32:1 (2005): 131–189.

Stanton, Domna. "Top Down, Bottom Up, Horizontally: Resignifying the Universal in Human Rights Discourse." In *Theoretical Perspectives on Human Rights and Literature*, edited by Elizabeth Goldberg and Alexandra Moore, 65–86. New York: Routledge, 2012.

Stark, Andrew. *Drawing the Line: Public and Private in America.* Washington D.C.: Brookings Institution Press, 2010.

Steiner, Wendy. "Postmodern Fictions, 1970–1990." In *The Cambridge History of American Literature*, Vol. vii., edited by Sacvan Bercovitch, 425–538. New York: Cambridge University Press, 1999.

Steinmetz-Jenkins, Daniel, and Alexander Arnold. "Searching for Foucault in an Age of Inequality." *Los Angeles Review of Books.* March 18, 2015. http://lareviewofbooks.org/review/searching-foucault-age-inequality.

Stevens, John. "Majority Opinion." *Kelo v. City of New London.* No. 04-108. Supreme Court of the United States. June 23, 2005.

Stewart, Anthony. "Uncategorizable Is Still a Category: An Interview with Percival Everett." *Canadian Review of American Studies* 37.3 (2007): 293–324.

Thomas, Clarence. "Justice Thomas Concurring." *Parents v. Seattle School District* and *Crystal Meredith v. Jefferson County.* Nos. 05-908 and 05-915. Supreme Court of the United States. June 28, 2007.

———. "Justice Thomas Dissenting." *Kelo v. City of New London.* No. 04-108. Supreme Court of the United States. June 23, 2005.

Timmer, Nicoline. *Do You Feel It Too? The Post-Postmodern Syndrome in American Fiction at the Turn of the Millennium.* Amsterdam: Rodopi, 2010.

Toth, Josh. *The Passing of Postmodernism: A Spectroanalysis of the Contemporary.* Albany: SUNY Press, 2010.

Toth, Josh, and Neil Brooks. *Attending the Wake of Postmodernism.* Amsterdam: Rodopi, 2007.

Tucker, Jeffrey Allen. "'Verticality Is Such a Risky Enterprise': The Literary and Paraliterary Antecedents of Colson Whitehead's *The Intuitionist.*" *Novel: A Forum on Fiction* 43.1 (2010): 148–156.

Underkuffler, Laura S. *The Idea of Property: Its Meaning and Power.* Oxford: Oxford University Press, 2003.

Viramontes, Helena. Interview by Michael Silverblatt. *Bookworm.* KCRW, Santa Monica. August 16, 2008. Radio.

———. *Their Dogs Came with Them.* New York: Atria Books, 2007.

———. *Under the Feet of Jesus.* New York: Plume Books, 1996.

Wallace, David Foster. *The Pale King.* New York: Little, Brown and Company, 2011.

Warren, Kenneth. *What Was African American Literature?* Cambridge: Harvard University Press, 2011.

West, Cornel. *Keeping Faith: Philosophy and Race in America.* New York: Routledge, 1993.

Whitehead, Colson. *Apex Hides the Hurt.* New York: Doubleday, 2006.

———. *The Intuitionist.* New York: Anchor Books, 1999.

———. *John Henry Days.* New York: Doubleday, 2001.

———. *Sag Harbor.* New York: Doubleday, 2009.

———. *Zone One.* New York: Anchor, 2012.

Winant, Howard. *The New Politics of Race: Globalism, Difference, Justice.* Minneapolis: University of Minnesota Press, 2004.

———. "Racism Today: Continuity and Change in the Post-Civil Rights Era." *Ethnic and Racial Studies* 21.4 (1998): 755–766.

Winnubst, Shannon. "The Queer Thing About Neoliberal Pleasure." *Foucault Studies* 14 (2012): 79–97.

Wittgenstein, Ludwig. *Philosophical Investigations.* Translated by G. E. M. Anscombe. New York: Macmillan Publishing Co., Inc., 1958.

Wolfe, Alan. "Public and Private in Theory and Practice: Some Implications of an Uncertain Boundary." In *Public and Private in Thought and Practice: Perspectives on a Grand Dichotomy.* Chicago: The University of Chicago Press, 1997.

Yamashita, Karen. *Tropic of Orange.* Minneapolis: Coffee House Press, 1997.

Zamora, Daniel. "Can We Criticize Foucault?" *Jacobin.* December 10, 2014. https://www.jacobinmag.com/2014/12/foucault-interview/.

———. "Foucault's Responsibility." *Jacobin.* December 15, 2014. https://www.jacobinmag.com/2014/12/michel-foucault-responsibility-socialist/.

{ INDEX }